WASHINGTON AND ROME

WASHINGTON AND ROME
Catholicism in American Culture

Michael Zöller

Translated by Steven Rendall and Albert Wimmer

University of Notre Dame Press

Notre Dame, Indiana

Copyright 1999 by
University of Notre Dame Press
Notre Dame, IN 46556
All Rights Reserved
Manufactured in the United States of America

Library of Congress Cataloging-in-Publication Data

Zöller, Michael.
[Washington und Rom. English]
Washington and Rome : Catholicism in American culture /
Michael Zöller ; translated by Steven Rendall and Albert Wimmer.
p.   cm.
Includes bibliographical references and index.
ISBN 0–268–01952–5 (cl : alk.paper). — ISBN 0–268–01953–3
(pa : alk. paper)
1. Catholic Church—United States—History. 2. United States—
Church history.
BX1406.2.Z6513   1998
282′.73—dc21   98-3011
                                                                    CIP

∞The paper used in this publication meets the minimum
requirements of the American National Standard for
Information Sciences—Permanence of Paper for Printed
Library Materials, ANSI Z39.48-1984.

CONTENTS

TABLES

PREFACE

Catholicism in the United States:
A Cultural Improbability

Consider, for instance, the American Catholics . . . This faith is . . . ancient, metaphysical, poetic, elaborate, ascetic, autocratic, and intolerant. It confronts the boastful natural man, such as the American is, with a thousand denials and menaces. Everything in American life is at the antipodes to such a system. Yet the American Catholic is entirely at peace. His tone in everything, even in religion, is cheerfully American.

George Santayana
Character and Opinion in the United States

For the past five hundred years, America has engaged the European imagination far more than any other part of the world, and even in this century a historian has referred to the discovery of America as the most important event since the spread of Christianity (Arciniegas 1975, 5). Over the past hundred years in particular, there has been a flood of books in which Europeans have sought to make sense of the New World. In them America or the New World have become synonyms of the United States, and I shall use these terms in the same way.

Depending on their point of view, European travelers in America found what they feared or hoped for their own countries. In any case, they felt that looking at America was like looking at their own future, and that made this literature more interesting than reports on travels in other, even more exotic parts of the world. Authors and readers unknowingly confirmed the theories of social scientists who foresaw only a single road for modern societies of the Western type, along which some would proceed more swiftly because burdened with less baggage, but which all of them would sooner or later follow to its end. America was thus seen as being in the vanguard of a continuing European history.

American intellectuals resisted this view, emphasizing the special or exceptional nature of America. These "exceptionalists," as they were called, pointed out that in the eighteenth century there had been two revolutions in the West that produced quite different results. Seen in this way America was not the precursor of modernity, but rather an exception or model of a different kind of modernity, and in any case a ground for hoping that alternatives to European development were conceivable.

America's religious culture seems to offer an example of this special American road and also to counter the expectation that with the progress of modernization and the concomitant loosening of social ties, religion might disappear altogether. Recently, even authors who earlier described America as a "secular city" have again begun to quote Tocqueville's prediction that religion would not merely survive but flourish in America.

A different version of the secularization thesis is presented by authors who criticize a religion that is individualized and hence no longer publicly present; they also appeal to Tocqueville, although they turn his argument on its head. Tocqueville had explicitly limited to the political realm his fear that democracy might lead to privatism and thus to a withdrawal from the public sphere, because he considered the individualizing of religion to be the precondition of its gaining cultural and political significance—though the latter seemed to him conceivable only as an indirect effect. Religion takes a detour through the consciences of individuals, and its influence increases in the degree that it "rules people's hearts." Individualism has put an unmistakable mark on America's religious culture, and one may therefore ask whether it has actually weakened American political and religious institutions or—on the contrary—strengthened them. Either way, Western Europe's religious history is behind it and the most it can hope for is to participate in America's. At first, the development of religious history in America paralleled that in England, but toward the end of the eighteenth century a new, specifically American form emerged, and in the process the most diverse schools of thought agreed in asserting the individual's right not only to freely determine his own religious affiliation but also to judge his own religious competence. All religious movements, including those that resisted the weakening of

the power of congregations and their institutions, thus ultimately contributed to this individualization.

My interest in this crucial issue first arose when I realized that most
cultural and political upheavals in America began with a religious prelude, so that the history and sociology of religion could serve as a key
to political culture. I was able to test my ideas on my American colleagues through a series of "brown bag lectures," and then formulated
them in some articles that resulted in very fruitful contacts, and sometimes in friendships, with colleagues at Chicago and Stanford. I also
made friends while I was a visiting professor at Notre Dame, but above
all it was there that I encountered a cultural improbability: American
Catholicism.

America's religious culture already astonishes European observers,
and the notion of an American Catholicism will strike them as a contradiction in terms. Whether it is described as a theological system or
as a cultural principle, Catholicism, with its combination of anthropo-
logical skepticism and certainty of grace, its historical consciousness
and its stress on the institutions that are to protect us against ourselves, seems in every way to embody a principle diametrically opposed to American culture. In fact, in the first hundred years of its
history American Catholicism was occupied with justifying itself to
Rome and to Washington and fighting internally over the weight to be
accorded each of these loyalties. In the process it developed abilities
that were never required in the so-called Catholic countries, where today they are sorely missed. In any case, I began to take an interest in
the tense relationship between Catholicism and America. The country
itself had long fascinated me, and my fascination was in no way diminished as I became better acquainted with its problems: it would be
naïve to overlook these problems, but it is also obvious that Europeans
would be delighted to have some of them.

In America the question is not whether Christianity will survive
but rather whether a democratized and individualized religion can
adopt the cultural principle of the church so that it can be more than
the Common Man writ large. And so over the past few years I have
made myself familiar with American religious history and American
Catholicism, and as I did these abstract questions were gradually absorbed into a historical picture. In doing my work I drew on a rich

literature, and in a brief annotated bibliography I mention the books to which I owe not merely information but insights.

Here, however, I would like to mention those who have helped me survive my adventure. They include people who were patient with me, such as my wife and colleagues, and also the institutions that have supported me: the Wissenschaftliche Kommission der Katholischen Sozialwissenschaftlichen Zentralstelle under the direction of my colleague Anton Rauscher, whose unfailing interest first gave me the courage to undertake this study; the Fritz-Thyssen-Stiftung, which made it possible for me to work at the Stanford University Library; the Gerda-Henkel-Stiftung, without which our Amerika-Forschungsstelle (American Research Center) would not deserve its name; the Hanns-Martin-Schleyer-Stiftung, where I presented some of the impressions gained on my American pilgrimage; and finally the State of Bavaria, which granted me a leave that I considered a privilege even though I was entitled to it.

1

EUROPEAN OUTPOSTS IN
COLONIAL AMERICA
1492–1789

THE HISTORY OF Christianity in America begins with the arrival of Christopher Columbus—even if this history is viewed from a promontory in New England—and the varying opinions regarding America and Western culture are reflected in the changing assessments of Columbus himself.

In 1892 the United States, proud of the progress it had made, staged a world's fair and called it "The World's Columbian Exposition." A hundred years later people were suggesting that Columbus Day be made a day of mourning (Royal 1992, vii). The whole content of a particularly successful book that appeared in connection with the 1992 anniversary celebrations was summed up in its title, *The Conquest of Paradise*: Columbus conquered a paradise and in so doing destroyed it, because he brought war, genocide, and environmental destruction to its original inhabitants, who until then had been living in peace with each other and with nature (Sale 1990).

The discovery and conquest of America is no doubt full of lights and shadows, a mixture of good and evil, as people in North America would say. As a moral reproach, however, the legend of a paradise destroyed makes little sense. This is clear as soon as one considers the alternative—which would amount to preferring that America had never been discovered. This myth is not merely absurd but also misleading, because it dehistoricizes those involved regardless of whether they are assigned the role of victimizer or that of victims. It attributes to the Spanish explorers, conquerors, colonizers, and missionaries the same motives and modes of behavior, and describes the indigenous inhabitants of the New World as if they had not already had, before the arrival of the Europeans, their own history full of violence and oppression. It is important to correct such simplistic notions, not to excuse one shameful act by means of another, but because only in this way will we be able to understand how Spanish colonization of the Caribbean and Central America could ultimately come to involve both protecting the Indians and exploiting them, why the Indians expected the Spaniards (and later the French, Dutch, or English) to protect them from other tribes, and finally why missionary efforts among some tribes were temporarily successful while others were entirely unsuccessful.

1. From Florida to Sonoma: The Spanish Belt

Columbus and the "Noble Savages"

The first "Indians" Columbus encountered, the Tainos, belonged to Arawak-speaking tribes. In a letter to Ferdinand and Isabella, he describes them as peaceful, friendly, and showing no sign of practicing idolatry. Hence he advises his royal employers to see to it that these natives are converted to Christianity. Columbus wrote all this some three weeks after his arrival, at a time when neither he nor his companions understood the language of the natives. Presumably not only first-hand observations but also preconceived notions were included in these first reports. Like his modern critics, Columbus seems initially to have seen what he expected to see, namely a peaceful paradise and people in an innocent state of nature. Later, the Tainos appeared in a less favorable light; in particular, it became clear that they did not live in undisturbed peace, but rather in constant fear of another native group whose language, Carib, gave its name to the whole region. The latter were especially warlike and otherwise unpleasant neighbors, who conducted raids to provide themselves with concubines and future victims of their cannibalism. These victims, particularly the boys, were said to be fattened like cattle (Royal 1992, 3).

However, Columbus did not encounter "noble savages" but only tribes organized in differing ways and with quite distinct customs, whose relations were characterized by violence and exploitation and were anything but idyllic. Again, this provides no justification for the violence and exploitation inflicted by the Spanish conquerors and the new feudal lords. But it does explain why in both the Caribbean and Central America the natives tended to see the white conquerors and their God as allies or protectors. The Christian God required no human sacrificial victims, but rather sacrificed himself for humans.

This became still clearer when the Spaniards came upon the highly organized empires of the Aztecs and Incas on the Central American highlands. These empires rested on the long-standing, organized oppression of tribes that were forced not merely to pay tribute but also to supply young men intended for human sacrifices. Therefore it is hardly surprising that the Spaniards who conquered the Aztec capital, Tenochtitlan, were supported by twenty thousand Indian soldiers. Even the least reflective Spanish soldier must have realized that the Spanish expeditionary force had been able to overthrow the Incan and Aztec empires in so short a time only with the help of Indian allies and unplanned epidemics, and the Spanish Crown's foreign policy was based on this realization.

Spanish Missionary Efforts: Between the Crown's Conception of Rule and the New Feudalism

In 1493 Pope Alexander VI had already divided up the New World and assigned the responsibility for Christianizing it to the kings of Spain and Portugal, whom he described as Catholic kings and princes. In the bull *Inter Caeteris,* he drew a line running west of the Azores and confirmed the Portuguese claim to the Azores and Cape Verde Islands along with any further discoveries west of the line, while the Caribbean and the American continent were allotted to Spain. The next year the two powers agreed to move the borderline a little further to the west so Portugal could also have an American colony, the future Brazil. All of Central and North America remained in the possession of the Spanish Crown, which took its Christianizing mission very seriously. The Spanish monarchs were concerned not only to establish trading companies and to exploit gold and silver mines, but also to integrate their overseas possessions fully and completely into their empire. The idea of cultural and religious pluralism was far in the future, and Ferdinand and Isabella proceeded on the modern assumption that religion could be used to justify a centralizing claim to power: the year in which America was discovered had begun with the conquest of Granada, that is, with the completion of the *Reconquista.* A foundational myth was created that produced a direct relationship between the rulers of the kingdom that emerged from the *Reconquista* and their subjects. This new concept of governing, which directly related the Christian monarch to his Christian subjects, was obviously supposed to be applied as far as possible to the New World. The goal was not only to convert Indians to Christianity but also to use their conversion to incorporate them into the Spanish Empire.

Thus Spanish policy regarding colonization and missionary work was marked by two opposite perspectives. The Crown pursued a centralizing and unifying plan, but the latter was conflicted with the interests of those who had gone to the New World to escape the poverty of La Mancha. These settlers expected, as a reward for facing the dangers of the New World, to be able to live there like lords, with others doing their work for them. The religious orders charged with missionary work among the Indians, particularly the Dominicans and Franciscans, operated between these perspectives. Their emphases differed in many respects. For instance, the Franciscans were more inclined to accept Indian traditions and to include Indian customs in their missionary work, whereas the Dominicans insisted that the pagan past be completely abandoned. They tended to distrust new converts, and hence did not encourage the development of an indigenous clergy.

Despite such differences in emphasis, the Dominicans and Franciscans both realized that their missionary labors could succeed only if Indians and Europeans remained separate, and this conflicted with the Crown's goal of integration. On the other hand, they supported this policy by advocating equality before the law for Indians.

In any case, the Indians were to be accustomed to living separately from the Europeans and to the regular alternation of work and Christian holidays. It was hard enough to convert the Indians to a Christian way of life, and this task was not much eased by the Indians' contacts with the Europeans in the colonies, who were not exactly the most virtuous sons of Spain. This conception of separate development included an effort to maintain the lower levels of the Indian aristocracy. The *caciques* received houses in the middle of carefully designed settlements, a concession to feudal organizational structures that the Crown would probably have been prepared to make regardless of its tactical significance for missionary work. A systematic conflict thus developed when for economic reasons European colonists moved into such settlements or became dependent on them. The lords of these

---

encomiendas then sought to develop, on the basis of their ownership of land, a feudalistic landed aristocracy, legal jurisdiction, and administration, and thereby to take over the functions of the lower-level Indian official nobility.

On these grounds, Horst Pietschmann has argued that the Crown considered it possible to colonize the Americas only in cooperation with the Indians, and not against them. Accordingly, there were countless exhortations to treat the Indians well, that is, to seek to convert them without using force, to see to it that they received fair compensation and to limit to a reasonable level the tributes demanded of them. Pietschmann draws attention to the administrative directives issued in 1501 by the first governor of La Española (Hispaniola, today Haiti) (Pietschmann 1992, 5), and the instructions Ferdinand gave Ponce de León, the discoverer and first governor of Florida (Gaustad 1932, 1: 63), are in the same vein. Such exhortations prove that there was no lack of reasons for complaint, but they also show that the Crown was serious about protecting the Indians, partly on pragmatic grounds, and partly because they were impressed by the Dominicans' view and found it in accord with their own notion of how to rule. This pragmatic strategy is expressed, for instance, in a 1512 decree in which we read: "you know that the whole wealth of this region depends on the Indians; if they are destroyed, the area will remain unsettled" (Pietschmann 1992, 5). The Spanish Crown nonetheless contributed to the further elaboration and strengthening of a legal conception incompatible not only with Spanish practice but also with that of other contemporary European and non-European empires—not to mention the relationships existing in pre-Hispanic America.

The individual is supposed to be independent of his place as a legal subject in a larger order, that is, he is supposed to have rights not solely or primarily as a Spaniard or as a Christian. James Muldoon has shown how in the course of the Middle Ages there gradually emerged the notion that non-Christians were also capable of developing respectable civil orders, and that they could therefore legitimately demand that their freedom and their property be respected (Muldoon 1972). In denouncing the exploitation of the Indians, the Dominicans Montesinos and Las Casas were able to draw support from these doctrines, as well as from their confrere Francisco de Vitoria, who in an analogous way applied traditional teachings concerning just war to the right of conquest. In 1511 Montesinos gave a Christmas sermon that is said to have made a significant contribution to the Burgos edicts issued the following year. In any event these edicts specified that the Indians were to be treated as subjects of the Crown. The Crown's policy henceforth corresponded to this view; it sought, for example, to encourage intermarriage between Spaniards and Indians. Ferdinand's successor Charles V gradually succeeded in deposing the upstart feudal lords in the New World and in strengthening the Crown's control by appointing viceroys. In 1537, the Crown's policy was confirmed in Pope Paul III's bull *Sublimis Deus*. In this bull, which also acknowledges the importance of Las Casas's work, the pope once again stresses that the Indians and other peoples yet to be discovered must not be deprived of their freedom and their possessions, whether or not they accept the Christian faith (Ellis 1967, 1: 63). The fact that the pope thought it necessary to reconfirm a proclamation issued twenty-five years earlier suggests what was really happening.

The missionary work of the Dominicans and Franciscans was thus closely connected with Spanish rule. The conceptions of missionary work and rule corresponded to each other insofar as the unity of the Empire and the equality of baptized and unbaptized subjects were interdependent. Hence the church's power reached only so far as the Crown's. Only where the central power succeeded in making the Indians adopt a sedentary mode of life and in ensuring the independence of their settlements was missionary work successful. Conversely, the missionaries' prospects of success diminished in proportion to their temporal and spatial distance from the Crown's power: Spanish rule disintegrated, but Spanish lords remained.

Even during the sixteenth century, at the high point of Spanish power, the farther missionaries moved across the North American continent, where they encountered mainly nomadic tribes, the less success they had. Only rarely were they able to establish Indian settlements around a mission station. First there was Florida, which Ponce de León had discovered on Easter Sunday (*Pascua florida*), 1513. The Spaniards initially thought that Florida was a large island, but when they realized their error, the peninsula became the starting point for expeditions such as that of Hernando de Soto, who explored southwestern North America, and that of Cabeza de Vaca, who traveled to Mexico by way of Texas.

In 1564, Florida gained still greater attention when Spain first encountered a European rival on American soil and Catholicism and Protestantism collided as a result of the French Huguenots' establishment of a fortified settlement in northeastern Florida, not far from the later city of Jacksonville. The Spanish viewed this settlement, known as Fort Carolina, as a threat to their shipping routes. The Spanish general Pedro Menéndez de Avilés was dispatched to avert this danger, and on the feast of St. Augustine, 1565, he landed at Cape Canaveral. They named the place after the saint, and then attacked the French fort, killing all its defenders. Menéndez became governor of Florida, and unlike his predecessor Ponce de León, who had received this title in recognition of his discovery, he actually acted as governor and therefore also sought to recruit missionaries.

In 1549, near present-day Tampa, Luis Cancer, a Dominican, went ashore and was slain by Indians as his ship's crew looked on. This put an end to missionary activities. Menéndez then turned to the Jesuits, who also sent a group of priests. Their ship went off course, and when in 1566 their superior, Fr. Pedro Martinez, took a small band of sailors ashore on San Juan to reconnoiter the island, he and his companions were killed by Indians. Four years later, eight more Jesuits met with the same fate when they set out from St. Augustine for Virginia, under the leadership of Juan Segura. They died near Jamestown, where the English colonization of Virginia was later to begin. In 1571, the mounting casualties and the failure of missionary efforts finally led the Jesuit General, Franciscus Borgia, to withdraw his men from Florida.

Menéndez then brought in the Franciscans, but their initial experience was scarcely more encouraging than that of the Jesuits. Toward the end of the sixteenth century, however, the Franciscans increased their efforts, establishing about forty mission stations along two routes, one going up the Atlantic coast through present-day Florida and Georgia and the other leading west toward the Gulf of Mexico. Once established, these missions again had to fight on two fronts. It was difficult to get the Indians to settle in one place and to abandon customs such as polygamy. Thus Fr. Pedro de Corpo's decision that the son of a chief could succeed his father only if he gave up his concubines led in 1597 to the so-called Guale uprising in several settlements along the coast of Georgia. Five of the six Franciscans working among the Guale were killed during the subsequent fighting. The fate of the sixth,

Fr. Francisco de Avila, illustrates the other enduring problem that confronted Spanish missionaries in Florida and elsewhere: the Indians kept him as a slave. After his release, however, he refused to testify against the Indians because he was afraid the leaders of the uprising would be executed.

Some governors attempted to nip Indian uprisings in the bud by making examples of those who were involved in them. In 1656, long after the Guale uprising, the Franciscans succeeded in having Diego de Rebolledo, who had responded to a riot by publicly executing eleven chiefs (Hennesey 1981, 13), removed from his post.

At first, the area west of Florida remained largely unexplored. Setting out from Mexico, Francisco Vasquez Coronado made from 1640 to 1642 his legendary trek through the regions on both sides of the Mississippi, but turned back because he had found neither gold nor cities of any kind. When he marched south again, he left behind in the region that is now Kansas three Franciscans who hoped to convert the Indians. One, Fr. Juan de Padilla, was promptly killed. No one knows what happened to the other two, Fr. Juan de la Cruz and Brother Luis de Ubeda.

Still further west, in present-day New Mexico, the situation developed in the same way it had earlier in Florida. Colonization began in 1595 under Governor Don Juan de Oñate. The Franciscan Juan de la Escalona's report to the viceroy in a letter concerning the way the governor's troops dealt with the Indians sounds familiar. Preaching the Gospel was nearly impossible, he wrote, because the soldiers would not allow the Indians to keep any part of their corn harvest and because any resistance to their plundering was suppressed by means of extreme atrocities (Gaustad 1982, 1: 71).

Nevertheless, one thing about New Mexico seemed promising: the Pueblo Indians were already sedentary and their village organization could be built upon. The Franciscans introduced cattle and in other ways made every effort to promote agriculture. By 1630 they had baptized over 50,000 Indians, and the region's economic growth could be measured by development of Santa Fe, the only Spanish outpost in the Southwest that was gradually taking on the appearance of a city. Yet this boom did not last very long. During the great Pueblo uprising of 1680 the Spaniards were driven out, all their missions were destroyed, and twenty-one Franciscans lost their lives.

The Spaniards slowly returned, and during the eighteenth century a clergy developed consisting of Spanish Franciscans and native-born priests of Indian descent whose way of life and sense of pastoral responsibility were duly noted by the bishop of Durango, who resided more than a thousand miles away. Until Mexico gained independence in 1821 and even beyond, this clergy kept the life of the church in a state of sleepy backwardness from which French priests revived it in the middle of the nineteenth century, after the United States annexed the region. I refer here particularly to Jean Bernard (later John B.) Lamy, a priest from central France, who after doing ten years' missionary work among the Huron Indians, was sent on the recommendation of his Canadian bishop to serve as Apostolic Vicar in New Mexico. By the time he died in Santa Fe after decades of service as archbishop, Lamy had managed to work miracles. The same could be said about Jean Marie Odin; as Apostolic Vicar of the Republic of Texas, he reorganized the church there, and in 1847 was ordained the first bishop of Galveston. We know considerably more about Lamy, because he was the model for the archbishop Jean Marie Latour in Willa Cather's novel *Death Comes to the Archbishop,* in which she made use of sources relating to the history of the church in the Southwest (Cather 1971).

The Spaniards did not colonize the Far West in the way they had colonized Florida until the activities of other European countries forced them to do so. Although Cabrillo had landed at the site of present-day San Diego and explored the coast of California, it was not until the Russians advanced south from Alaska that the Spaniards began to work their way north by establishing a series of military posts (*presidios*) and mission stations. The first of these was built on San Diego bay; they eventually extended into what is now Sonoma county, close to the southernmost outpost of the Russian fur trading company. Starting in 1768, twenty-one missions were built. Nine of them were founded by Junipero Serra, who at the age of 36 had left his position as professor at a seminary in Mallorca and for the next thirty-five years traveled indefatigably as a missionary before dying at Monterey's Mission San Carlos in 1784 (Ellis 1967, 1: 34).

The Franciscans developed these missions into large agricultural communes. It has been estimated that at the height of Franciscan missionary activity in California, some 40,000 baptized Indians, whom the Franciscans also ruled as their worldly lords, were employed in manual labor and agriculture. They were brought back by soldiers whenever they attempted to flee the settlements' monastic life, which was conducted in accord with the Rule of St. Benedict (Hennesey 1981, 20). When Mexico won independence in 1821 the system, which had been ruled with an iron hand, began to break down, and the whole of California entered into decline. Spanish priests who were unwilling to swear allegiance to the Mexican Republic left the country, and the secularization that took place in 1834 did not result in the Indians' receiving the land they had been promised, but instead put enormous tracts into the hands of Mexican politicians and their friends, the so-called *Californios*. When the diocese of Los Angeles was established in 1840 and the Jesuit Peter de Smet, later famous for his books about the Indians, began his missionary work among the Indians of Oregon, the church throughout the Spanish belt, which reached from Florida through Texas to New Mexico and all the way to the Pacific, found itself in the same, hardly advantageous condition.

As we have noted, the fate of the Spanish mission was inseparable from that of Spanish rule. It shared the Crown's far-reaching ambitions and its vision of the equality of all Christian subjects, and like the Crown it failed to impose this vision on either the Crown's adminis-trators and soldiers or the new feudal lords in the Americas. Thus the missionaries remained dependent on the protection of the soldiers who had preceded them and who repeatedly undid what the missionaries had achieved. In practice, little remained of the peculiarly Spanish con-ception of rule, because the colonial administration had overextended itself. Therefore the viceroys were no more capable of controlling gov-ernors and generals at the farthest reaches of the empire than were the bishops and priests. Moreover, of course, Spanish power was in decline. The example of Florida is particularly instructive in this respect: at the end of the Seven Years' War in 1763, it came under British rule, but twenty years later it reverted to Spain as a result of the American revolution, and finally became part of the United States in 1821. Gone were the days when Spain could insist on the line west of the Azores that Pope Alexander had drawn the year after Columbus's voyage to the New World, and Spain was no longer the only aspirant to the title of "Catholic power." Thus it is symbolically significant that it was the

French bishops who took it upon themselves to pick up the pieces left behind by the Spaniards in the American Southwest.

2. From Arcadia to Louisiana: The French Crescent

Between the collapse of the Spanish colonial church and the Americanization of the American church by the Irish, it was especially the French—as missionaries, organizers, and educators of future priests—who were responsible for the survival of the Catholic church in the New World. This part of the story I am telling here begins long before the time of bishops Lamy and Odin.

The French Mission amid European Rivalries and Traditional Indian Tribal Warfare

In 1534, after Giovanni da Verrazano, an Italian captain serving under the French, had explored the eastern seaboard of North America, Jacques Cartier pushed farther north to the mouth of the St. Lawrence River. From there the French moved along the waterways into the interior, reaching first the Great Lakes, and then descending the Mississippi as far as the region bordering on the Gulf of Mexico, which they named Louisiana. Their goal was to secure these transport routes for their trading activities, especially fur trading, and anyone who looks at eighteenth- and nineteenth-century portraits, and especially a well-known one of Jean-Jacques Rousseau, will see the importance of the latter trade. It has been estimated that in 1760, the year in which the French surrendered Montreal to the British and thirty years before any official census was taken, the population of the British colonies was between 1.5 and 2 million, and that of the French territories about 70,000 (Hertling 1954, 314). Although the French were more interested in crossing the country safely than in colonizing it, their settlements along the way from the St. Lawrence to the Mississippi delta were not mere outposts. Fortified landing areas soon developed into settlements; if you want to be a player in world politics, it is difficult to keep your trade activities inconspicuous. At least at the beginning and the end of the long French crescent, as well as around the Great Lakes, the French presence led to the establishment of important settlements. First, French Acadia was formed in the eastern part of modern-day

Canada. Setting out from Port Royal, Samuel de Champlain founded Quebec four years later. With Champlain also began the entanglement in enmities arising from Indian alliances that marked French colonial policy in America as well as French missionary efforts. Champlain allied himself with the Ottawas, a confederation of different tribes under the leadership of the Hurons. The latter remained faithful French allies to the end, and even after the French surrender Chief Pontiac tried, with the help of a few other Ottawa tribes, to continue the war against the British.

Any friend of the Hurons and their allies soon found he had enemies as well. In Champlain's case it was the Iroquois, a confederation of tribes headed by the Mohawks. Before the French arrived, the Ottawas had driven the Iroquois out of the area near the St. Lawrence River, and they now controlled an area reaching from the northern part of present-day New York to Lake Erie. Whereas the French wanted to keep the Iroquois confined to this area, far away from their trading activities, the Iroquois were backed by the Dutch, who had established themselves along the Hudson as early as the beginning of the seventeenth century by founding Fort Orange (Albany) in 1609 and in 1618 Fort Amsterdam on Manhattan Island. The Iroquois's friendship was later extended to the new masters of the Hudson Valley. Hence the Dutch as well as the English were seen as enemies of the enemy's friends.

Thus the long-standing feuds among Indians were bound up with the rivalries among European powers in a way that limited not only the scope of French colonial policy but also the activities of French missionaries, who succeeded almost exclusively among Indian allies of the French. Failure and usually martyrdom as well were certain if the French priests sought to convert the Mohawks and their allies, or if they fell into the latter's hands on their way to the Hurons. On the other hand, missionary successes not only increased the Indians' hostility, since the Mohawks hated Christian Hurons even more, but also added a religious dimension to conflicts among European powers on American soil. An extreme example is the fate met with by the Jesuit priest Sebastien Rall during the War of the Spanish Succession, known among the English as Queen Anne's War (1701–1713). In eighteenth-century wars the European belligerents paid their Indian allies a bounty for scalps. The Abenaki Indians, whose territory lay north of Massachusetts in present-day Maine, were not only allied with the French but under the influence of Père Rall had adopted the Catholic faith. Thus when in 1704 the Abenakis attacked the village of Deerfield in Massachusetts and killed all its inhabitants, the event was seen as more than just another Indian raid. A Protestant missionary was sent out from Boston, but to no avail; the Abenakis had clear notions of friend and foe, and trusted only the true "black robes." So the Massachusetts colonial authorities offered a reward of $200 for the capture of Père Rall. But it was only twenty years later, after the Deerfield massacre, that a mixed force of so-called New England militia and Mohawks raided Père Rall's mission station in Abenaki territory, killed him, and took his scalp back to Boston. This often-told tale can be found in a book by the Jesuit James Hennesey, who currently teaches history at Boston College (Hennesey 1981, 24).

From the beginning of the eighteenth century onward, missionaries had been involved, whether they wanted to be or not, in the secondary wars between England and France over the possession of Canada, a conflict that was fought out in northeastern America in stages until the French and Indian War brought it to an end in 1760 and it was finally settled by the Treaties of Paris in 1763. Acadia and the so-called Ohio Territory became British.

The fame and subsequent impact of French missionary activity remained, however, largely independent of the presence of the French king's power, and outlived it. One reason was that Indian missionary work carried on by French Jesuits and Dominican diocesan priests from Quebec reached far westward. Thus it was separated not only from the geographical center of the colonial war between the English and the French, but also from the aftereffects of the hostilities. Americans found it much easier to incorporate into American history the fact that one byproduct of the Jesuits' missionary activities on the Great Lakes was the opening-up of the region later occupied by Michigan, Wisconsin, Illinois, and Indiana, and that traces of them are found from St. Ignatius (between the lower and the upper peninsulas of Michigan) to St. Louis, than the activities and the fate of someone like Père Rall. Thus in the rotunda of the nation's Capitol building the state of Wisconsin is represented by a statue of Jacques Marquette, not because he was a Jesuit, but because he explored the Mississippi.

Like their achievements in geography and cartography, the Jesuits' missionary reports have won a place in American history. The *Rela-*

tiones, their regular reports, probably constitute the most important source for the early history of the Midwest. That is why seventy-three volumes of them have been published, along with a few other documents related to the subject (Thwaites 1896–1901; Moore 1985). This collection served as the basis for Brian Moore's novel *Black Robe*, which went through a number of reprintings and was made into a film. Moore dramatized these mainly very sober reports, not only erecting a monument to the self-sacrificing discipline and energy of the French Jesuit missionaries, but also showing the futility of their hardships.

In 1611, when the French had hardly moved beyond their beachheads along the Atlantic coast, Père Pierre Baird reported from Port Royal that the land was really no more than a forest, and that the Indians felt themselves bound to a single location neither by family relationships nor by their dwelling places. Starting in about 1620, the Jesuits extended their missionary activities into the enormous Huron territory around the Great Lakes. "No matter where you are going, you have to travel for weeks," wrote Père Jean de Brébeuf, who had spent two years studying the language and customs of the Hurons. His confreres should be prepared, he said, to be packed day after day into a canoe, without even enough room to move, and to be tormented by the sun during the day and by mosquitoes during the night (Ellis 1967, 1: 81). Like the other priests at the Great Lakes mission stations, Père Brébeuf endured this life for years until 1649, when the Iroquois, in a genocidal war against the Hurons, destroyed everything. Ten thousand Hurons died in this massacre, and it may be assumed that many of them were tortured in the cruelest ways. In 1649, in northern New York State, Brébeuf himself fell into the hands of the Mohawks (Gaustad 1982, 1: 77). Reports suggest how limited was the Jesuits' success among their model children. The Hurons were able to incorporate the much-admired "black robes" into their own system of friends and foes. In every other respect there was a clash between two incompatible cultures; the Hurons shared none of the presuppositions necessary for understanding the ethics taught by the Jesuits. The Jesuits' disapproval of the Indians' promiscuity and their lack of interest in similar activities seemed to the Hurons to result from some hidden magic. They obviously held the same view of the appearance of previously unknown diseases.

The Fame and Impact of the "Black Robes"

The Indian missionary efforts made by the Jesuits and other French religious orders and clerical communities continued after 1649, and their effects were felt even after the French colonial period. Thus in the years following 1763 some northeastern tribes earlier allied with the French—such as the Penobscots, who belonged to the Abenaki confederation—sought to come to an arrangement with the authorities in Massachusetts. Various other tribes took advantage of the opportunity to ask that priests be sent to them; in many cases, Protestant ministers were sent. The Indians responded by explaining that they wanted a Catholic priest or a French père, and were not willing to hear prayers from old England (Marty 1984, 105). As late as 1831 Indians near Montreal sent a delegation to the bishop of St. Louis, and their spokesman, a man called "old Ignatius," asked that a priest be sent to them (Hennesey 1981, 132). These episodes were in fact only a distant echo of the French Indian mission.

Nonetheless, the influence of French Catholicism endured long after the French colonial period and the Jesuits' missionary activities had ended. One reason for this was that the French, during the hundred years between the massacre of the Hurons and their own defeat, were compelled to literally fortify their outposts in the area west of the Atlantic colonies.

Especially in the first half of the eighteenth century, the French and English repeatedly clashed in America. Not only did they pursue on American soil wars that had begun in Europe but also fought, from 1754 to 1760, for control of northeastern America. Contrary to their original intentions, the French were forced to do more than fortify a few strongholds. Thus, by founding New Orleans in 1718, they emphasized their claim to the whole of the Mississippi valley and controlled a crescent reaching from the northeastern Atlantic coast to the Gulf of Mexico. The French character of the Mississippi delta was significantly increased when in 1755 the English began to drive Catholics out of Acadia, that is, the eastern part of Canada. Many Acadians settled in Louisiana and greatly influenced its later development. Others moved only as far as the area east of the Great Lakes, which was still under French control, and where in 1700 Antoine de la Mothe Cadillac had already established a base that later became the city of Detroit. The Detroit automobile industry has immortalized not only the name of the city's founder, but also that of a faithful French ally, Chief Pontiac. But not until 1754, during the colonial war, did the French begin to fortify the so-called Ohio Territory against the English moving in from the northeast by building Fort Duquesne on the Ohio, which later grew into the city of Pittsburgh. Soon afterward Canada and the Ohio Territory became British possessions, while Louisiana fell for the rest of the century under Spanish control. In 1800 Louisiana became French again, but in 1803 Napoleon sold it to the United States for fifteen million dollars. The Louisiana Purchase more than doubled the territory of the United States and provided room for the first wave of its western expansion.

The French heritage is reflected not only in French place names but also in a French-oriented form of Catholicism that established itself at both ends of the French crescent, in Louisiana and Quebec. As usual, ecclesiastical organization followed the transformation of political relations. Thus from 1658 on there was an Apostolic Vicar for New France, who in 1764 became bishop of Quebec when the diocese was established. French possessions in America remained under his jurisdiction until 1763. Thereafter both Spanish Louisiana and Florida fell under the jurisdiction of the bishop of Santiago de Cuba until a separate diocese of Louisiana was established, with its see in New Orleans.

There is still another important reason why French Catholicism outlasted the century and a half of New France's existence. America offered an alternative to the bishops, priests, and members of religious orders who were unwilling to come to terms with the new masters and the new conditions following the French Revolution. It was a matter of breathing new life into French structures before they collapsed. Depending on one's theological orientation, the New World even offered a choice between two distinct cultural environments, since the American Revolution had led to exchanges of intellectual elites. Loyalists, for whom life in America after the Revolution was not easy, went to Canada, and Canadian progressives moved to Massachusetts and New York. These emigrations helped homogenize the differing "climates of opinion" (Lipset 1983).

As for Canada, where twenty years before Catholics had been expelled, the Quebec Act passed by the English parliament in 1774 guaranteed Catholics free exercise of their religion and additional privileges in regions where they were in the majority, as they were in Quebec. Conservative French priests could therefore easily warm to the idea of offering their services to the bishop of Quebec. Modernists, on the other hand, found in the new American republic a revolutionary tradition that was not directed against religion and an interpretation of the constitution that encouraged the free development of competing religions. Moreover, a church was developing that obviously needed priests and professors of theology, and for this reason the Paris-based congregation of the Sulpicians was commissioned in 1791 to establish in Baltimore the first seminary. French bishops, diocesan priests, professors, and teaching nuns were soon assigned important roles as the church grew along with the republic's westward expansion, and while it developed its own Irish-American clergy. In 1827, John England, one of the first bishops from the latter group and an avid Americanizer, wrote in a letter to Rome that the French could never become Americans and did not know how to present Catholicism as a religion compatible with American principles (Cogley 1986, 33). This is an unfair but typical judgment that already contains in germ the conflict that was later to bedevil the American church.

Spanish missionary activity left behind a belt reaching from Florida to California, while the French crescent extended from eastern Canada to the Gulf of Mexico. These two chapters of American prehistory, at first isolated and separate, were soon overtaken by the history of the republic. For two centuries, their centers were both located in narrow strips along the coasts, for during the sixteenth century the Spanish extended their Caribbean and Central American colonies northward without encountering European rivals, and the westward expansion of the United States did not begin until 1803. At the beginning of the seventeenth century, however, European trading stations and settlements were established in quick succession. In 1604, the French began to construct their northernmost base, Port Royal in Acadia, and the British Virginia Company followed suit in 1607 by building Jamestown. Since from the outset plantations were the preferred mode of agriculture in Virginia, the Dutch, who had already been involved in the slave trade with Central America for a century, competing with the Portuguese and cooperating with African chiefs and Arabic caravans, began in 1610 to bring African slaves to Virginia.

In comparison, other Dutch enterprises in North America were short-lived and less profitable. Their bases on the Hudson (from 1609 and 1618) and on the Delaware (from 1655) were quickly absorbed into the surrounding British territories, and the Swedish colony on the Delaware underwent the same fate.

3. England under Different Conditions: The Atlantic Coast Colonies

In the course of the seventeenth and eighteenth centuries the European trading companies' American bases all became British colonies, and thus the religious history of these colonies is largely an extension of British history—under different conditions, to be sure, and on a more modest scale. In England, the Anglicans were strong and the various groups of dissenters, including Presbyterians, Congregationalists, Baptists, and Quakers, comparatively weak; in the colonies, the opposite was the case, and this tendency was increased by the immigration of German, Bohemian, Dutch, and Scandinavian Protestants. Even the Lutherans, who were well disposed toward the government, developed in America a free ecclesiastical structure closer to that of the Congregationalists than to that of the Anglicans.

The number of dissenters was generally small, firstly because on the whole they had a much more selective and restrictive conception of the church and its membership than did, say, Anglicans or Catholics. They did not see themselves as an inclusive church, but rather as an exclusive "community of saints," and admitted only those who met their standards by leading a corresponding way of life. Secondly, no religious community at that time counted many members. Theodore Caplow has summarized the available data in a table showing that in the eighteenth century few Americans belonged to a religious community, and that since then the number affiliated with a religion has steadily increased (Caplow 1983, 29).

The Pluralism of Religious Monopolies

With the exception of the Puritan experiment in New England, early colonial America hardly seemed a society determined by religion. Nor was any religious political goal discernible in English colonial policy. To be sure, there was no lack of relevant demands, but these apparently

Table 1
Affiliation with Religious Communities (1650–1978)

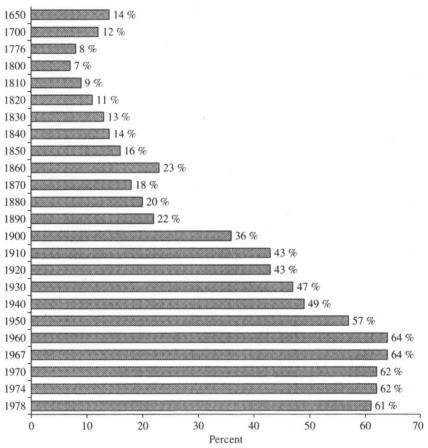

Source: Caplow 1983, 29.

had little effect. The writings and sermons of the Anglican priest Richard Hakluyt, who in Queen Elizabeth's time recruited people for England's missionary activities, are said to have impressed the queen as well as the Raleigh brothers. In his *Discourse of Western Planting*, which appeared in 1584, Hakluyt wrote that it was the duty of the Christian monarchs of England to ensure the propagation of the right faith in the Western Hemisphere. To this end they should establish one or two colonies so that missionaries could safely study the language and customs of the Indians, and then, after careful preparation, begin their conversion. Otherwise, Hakluyt suggested, they would risk suffering the same fate as the Spanish missionaries in Florida. In the meantime, he noted, even the Spanish had learned their lesson and founded three dioceses and two hundred religious institutions of all kinds. However, if the Spaniards, "in their superstition," had been able to achieve so much, "what may we hope for in our true and sincere religion?" (Gaustad 1982, 1: 54).

This text allows us to gauge the English climate of opinion, but Hakluyt's appeal did not result in any notable activities. The colonies he called for were founded years later, and when they were, England's religious conflicts were not immediately transferred to America. Along with the right to found colonies, which was granted to both individuals and companies, a pluralism of religions existing side by side was introduced in accord with the principle *cuius regio eius religio*. Thus official establishment of a given religion did not simply mean that it was in the majority: concrete political and legal privileges followed, ranging from the levying of church taxes to the reservation of public offices for those who belonged to that religion. In Virginia, for instance, where the Church of England was "established," a Quaker or Baptist could live undisturbed if he sought no office and was prepared to pay levies benefiting another church. The few Catholics and Jews sensed, however, that they were tolerated not because they had legal rights, but rather because they were the objects of a kind of apathetic good will. The situation of Catholics was always precarious whenever public opinion was dominated by one of the recurrent moods of anti-Catholic feeling. These were produced first of all by the repercussions of events in England, such as the revolution of 1688. However, an aggressive anxiety about foreigners also became increasingly evident. On one hand, growing immigration put the Protestant character of America in question, and on the other, the only thing the increasingly varied forms of American Protestantism had in common was often their opposition to and propaganda against Catholicism.

In the British colonies there was no monopoly with regard to religion, but religions still did not compete on an equal footing; rather, in each colony local monopolies of very different kinds emerged. "Catholic" Maryland offered a freedom of religion that was unknown in the other colonies, for even in Maryland the Catholics were in the minority and thus in a position that tended to make them tolerant. This nominally Catholic colony was soon drawn into the English Civil War, so that its exceptional situation did not last long.

At the other end of the spectrum stood the New England Puritans, who maintained their local monopoly with extreme persistence. They interpreted the royal charter as a license to carry out in their colony an experiment in political theology, and in doing so they set in motion an entirely different development, namely the elaboration of the American model of religion, understood in individualistic terms and pluralistically organized, which in the course of the eighteenth and nineteenth centuries transformed American Protestantism. This history can serve as an example showing that social relationships do not result from conscious planning, that is, they do not result from a will to create these precise relationships. They are produced by the unintended effects of acts with quite different intentions. Thus American culture cannot be understood as merely secularized Puritanism or popularized liberalism based on natural law. The essential contribution made indirectly to American culture by the Puritan experiment arose instead from its unsuccessful attempt to establish a government of saints, the reactions to this attempt, and the repeated counter-reactions they prompted. It is also important to be aware of the Pilgrims' ideas, not because the American realm of ideas was already implicit in them, as many people believe (Zöller 1992), but in order to understand why they led to results so different from what the pious immigrants had intended.

It is well known that New England was settled by immigrants whose reasons for leaving their English homeland were not economic. The founders of the Massachusetts Bay, Plymouth, New Haven, and Connecticut colonies were chiefly interested in the unhindered pursuit of their vision of the kind of life God wanted them to live. Like the Scottish Presbyterians, they followed the teachings of John Knox, who had fled to Geneva during the reign of Queen Mary. Just as the Church of England had done, Knox rejected the pope's authority, but he went even further, denying the authority of the bishops as well. He maintained that the necessary decisions should be made, with the guidance of the Bible, by the congregation itself or by elected church elders (presbyters). This form of church government was what most clearly distinguished dissenters, and gave them their name. They were called

Puritans because they were interested not only in congregational reform but also in ridding the church of everything unnecessary. According to Knox, the sacraments should be limited to "Baptism and the
holy supper of the Lord Jesus." Everything else was "idolatry" and a
human invention. Like all reformers, the English dissenters wanted
not to divide the church but to renew it. They even set particular store
by unity, since to them denominational pluralism was as alien a notion as the separation of church and state, which they saw as "two
twinnes." Thus the dissenters long debated whether it might be possible to introduce the desired reforms within the Church of England
(Marty 1984, 64).

The New World's attraction consisted in the hope of not having
to choose between church unity and dogmatic purity. In addition,
it seemed possible to construct there a community of God-fearing be-
lievers and law-abiding citizens in which religion and politics would be
at one.

Like most other prominent New England Puritans, John Winthrop,
the leader of the Pilgrims whose ship "Arabella" landed in 1630 near
the later site of Boston, was no theologian. He nevertheless saw himself
as the religious leader of this group of emigrants, and on the ship he
had already begun to deliver lectures and sermons, some of which were
afterward published. He repeatedly emphasized how important it was
that the community work together in order to achieve the goal of the
new colony. This goal was, he said, "to improve our lives, to do more
service to the Lord . . . that ourselves and posterity may be better preserved from the common corruptions of this evil world." Freedom
could therefore be conceived as permission to do what was good, just,
and honorable. Or as Nathaniel Ward put it, freedom of conscience
is nothing other than freedom from sin and error. Agreeing with St.
Augustine, whom they venerated, the Puritans considered the *libertas
errandi*, the freedom to err, a peril that could hardly be overestimated.
Anyone who argued for freedom in matters of religion, Ward maintained, was putting moral standards in question. Therefore he took
it upon himself, in the name of New England, to explain to the
world that those who adhered to various erroneous doctrines were free
to stay away or to abandon such doctrines, the sooner the better
(Winthrop and Ward, in Brown 1983, 18, 33).

Regardless of whether one prefers Nathaniel Ward's powerful,

Luther-like language or John Winthrop's much more sober style, the Pilgrims' ideas can hardly be seen as the source of the "American Creed," even if Gunnar Myrdal and many textbooks leave this impression (Myrdal 1975).

The Unplanned Democratizing of Religion

Puritan thinking begins by emphasizing original sin and stands, in opposition to individualism, against the idea that human beings can redeem and perfect themselves. However, a strict orthodoxy amounting to a very direct social control through the community rather than by a remote, institutionally organized church was not the only result. In addition, the community distinguished, in a completely non-egalitarian manner, between recognized members of proven religious and moral standing on one hand, and persons of doubtful reputation on the other.

The mostly unintended but momentous consequences of this system resulted from the dual relationship between law and religion that was so important to the founding fathers. This bond between church and state was unmistakably characteristic of New England and for the most radical among the orthodox, such as Roger Williams, it became a problem as great as the increasing number of immigrants who were not religiously motivated.

Whereas Roger Williams thought that the church's closeness to the state would lead it to degenerate into a "filthy dunghill and whorehouse" (Marty 1984, 78), others had to learn that both active and passive voting rights depended on membership in the community of saints. In addition to this practice of establishment, which was familiar from England, in 1637 not only these particular civil rights but all civil rights, including immigration, were made dependent on a person's having the right beliefs. A heavy price was paid for this linking of religious qualification and legal status, as religion was increasingly put to use for non-religious ends. Instead of the profane becoming religious, as had been hoped, religion was profaned.

Thus was laid the foundation for a political culture in which it was advisable to couch all kinds of interests in religious terminology. Moreover, since all legal grounds for an individual's existence as a citizen depended on his religious qualification—which itself became visible and effective only through affiliation with the community of saints—the elitist religious self-image of the community conflicted with the civil claims of those who were kept outside it.

Compromises began in 1662 with the "Halfway Covenant." This "meeting halfway" consisted in giving outsiders access to one of the two sacraments, namely baptism. Thus second-class citizens became second-class church members, who were not allowed to take communion and were granted no voting rights. This halfway solution satisfied neither old members who wanted to preserve the exclusive nature of the congregation, nor the new members, who wanted full recognition, and so the next step became all the more unavoidable. The famous preacher Solomon Stoddard took this step, and today his name remains associated with the confession he initiated. "Stoddardism" refers to the view that all baptized persons have the right to full church membership. As usual, the name was invented by opponents of this practice, but the name and the procedures associated with it prevailed until the end of the century.

However, this opening up, the admission of more and more members whose qualifications were no longer subjected to any particular requirements, provoked others to withdraw into more exclusive congregations. The basic pattern for the ever-increasing differentiation of American Protestantism's organizational structure, which determined its later history, becomes clear in this interplay between the liberalizing of the established religion and the protest reaction against this liberalization. As soon as individual religions are no longer granted official privilege, finances alone set limits to further diversification. Profound conflicts were therefore not to be fought out; on the contrary, they could be "resolved" by sects becoming independent, that is, by opposing minorities splitting off—and thus by the end of the nineteenth century there were more than three hundred Protestant denominations.

In any case, the Puritans provoked the very pluralism they wanted to avoid. But this is also true of later religious movements that ended up providing grist for the same mill, quite independently of their original goals. The increasingly individualistic and emotional forms of religiousness and the flexible ways in which they were organized mutually determined and reinforced each other. The controversial opening up of New England's Congregational churches ushered in a new style of evangelizing that confirmed the fears of its critics. Previously, each individual had to make credible his awakening, his personal conversion experience, because his admission to the congregation depended on his ability to do so. Now progressive ministers lacked proof. After filling the pews with unrepentant sinners, they had at least to follow up by doing everything they could to make the new members into new human beings.

Once again, Stoddard is supposed to have been the one who showed his fellow ministers the way, trying to arouse his congregation by giving emotional sermons. This style of preaching became dominant through the two revival movements of the eighteenth and nineteenth centuries, and especially through the "Great Awakening" that seized all the colonies between 1730 and 1760, but which contemporary reports suggest spread like an epidemic among the Dutch and German Calvinists of the mid-Atlantic seaboard and among their like-minded brethren in New England.

The general agreement regarding the consequences of this phenomenon justifies terming it an epidemic, although obviously it is harder to describe the specific virus and how it was transmitted. Since Perry Miller (Miller 1956) and Edwin Scott Gaustad (Gaustad 1957), it has been taken for granted that the revival movements (and especially the first "awakening," also known as the Great Awakening) had an effect on American culture that extended far beyond the domain of religious history. William G. McLoughlin raised more difficult and almost unanswerable questions that must at least be mentioned here. Whereas Gaustad discussed solely the Great Awakening in New England, and Miller included it in his description of the cultural and intellectual history of "The New England Mind," McLoughlin distinguished and described four American revival movements (Hudson 1981). His book led to debates in which all the problems associated with the concept of an "awakening" or revival movement emerged. These include less fundamental questions such as whether his distinction of four movements is convincing and whether connections with the corresponding developments in Europe are taken into account and correctly described.

The chief problem, however, has to do with the possibility of comparing the different American events and with the closely associated assumption that American religious and cultural history is cyclical. As we might expect, this interpretation is rejected by those who see the process of social modernization and secularization as continuous. In opposition to the latter view, Samuel P. Huntington (Huntington 1981, 67) clearly follows McLoughlin's lead in describing America's political history as a series of upheavals and calm periods in which religious revival movements precede major political changes and fore-shadow in religious terms the new conflicts that arise. Despite this rather vague formulation, two general observations may be made. First, in the Great Awakening a new religious style was established, which had in fact become discernible in earlier conflicts; second, this change resulted in a strengthening of the "new" churches that propagated this style. The young preacher Theodor Frelinghuysen, who in the 1720s was already enjoying great success among congregations of the Dutch Reformed Church in New Jersey and New York, may be counted among the precursors of this great revival movement. The movement is usually said to have reached its high point in the sermons delivered in several New England towns by Jonathan Edwards, a grandson of Solomon Stoddard's, beginning in 1734. Toward the end of the same decade the English preacher George Whitefield arrived on the scene. He became a model for many itinerant preachers, because he drew large crowds wherever he went. All three of these preachers, including the more intellectually oriented Edwards, employed a rousing, emotional style and appealed to an individual, enthusiastic religious-ness, and sometimes to pure sentimentality. Whitefield, who did not lack self-confidence, averred that many congregations were so dead because "dead men preach to them" (Marty 1984, 116).

Instead of doctrine, supervision of conduct, and communal discipline, these preachers emphasized the authenticity and spontaneity of subjective religious experience, which cannot be judged by another person. In this way not only did all American Protestants acquire the status of qualification and election, but also from the "Halfway Covenant" a new covenant was conceived, to which Jonathan Edwards even attributed a missionary obligation by associating Protestantism with America. If Christianity had originally been Europe's gift to the New World, in the interim the relationship between giver and recipient had been reversed. This was in accord with Divine Providence, Edwards claimed, for America had remained so long hidden precisely in order that it might serve as a base from which Protestantism could wage its battle against the great Christian heresy, Catholicism (Hennesey 1981,

39). The new religious style was thus directed toward the spiritual and emotional needs of the individual. At the same time, it presented itself as the self-assured expression of an independent American culture. Therefore it is not surprising that at first the response was significantly stronger in the North. The Church of England distrusted emotional evangelizing, and thereby contributed to the spread of Methodism, which under the leadership of the brothers John and Charles Wesley severed its ties with the Church of England.

As an "enthusiast," Whitefield was banned from many English parishes. Thus he was, so to speak, driven to work the American field, but even there the Church of England maintained its reserve. No invitations were forthcoming from the South, and moreover the audience that preachers found in the North was lacking. In contrast to the southern colonies, where hardly any independent social strata had developed alongside the plantation aristocracy, in the North a comparatively well-off and self-confident middle class had emerged over the past hundred years, both in the country and in the many small towns and cities. Their religious ideas had been developed in the course of the long debates concerning the Calvinistic principle of religious qualification, and they now gave this principle a democratic twist: religion serves the individual's control over his life, and when it is properly presented, it is available to everyone, provided only that it is organized in such a way that it becomes *responsive* to the fundamentally similar needs of human beings.

This religious understanding opened the way to a religious marketplace in which it was precisely the competition among Protestant denominations that was to make them as similar as the sermons of the Congregationalist Edwards and the Methodist Whitefield. Initially, this competition was limited. It was chiefly the Methodists and the Baptists who benefited from the popularity of the new style. As part of this renewal, the Methodists had separated from the English church, and seemed to represent it more powerfully than other groups. However, as early as 1638 the Baptists established themselves in Rhode Island, which was seen in both Boston and New Amsterdam as a place of refuge for sectarians of all kinds. The American version of the Baptist creed first emerged when Isaac Backus and his followers separated from the New England Congregationalists in 1750. In contrast to the Methodists, who were to some degree still Anglicans, the Baptists recognized neither bishops nor any other hierarchical structure above the congregations, and in this they remained true to their tradition, namely that of the Congregational Church. Thus they were able to respond quickly to local conditions and new developments. Backus himself became the forerunner of a new kind of preacher, the "circuit rider" who made the rounds on horseback from one farm to the next over a wide area and as a symbolic figure remained associated with the opening up of the West.

Until then, that is, until the western expansion began in earnest and the Methodists and the Baptists started to compete with each other, the latter could only take advantage of the openings left by the system of established local monopolies. In the South they could sometimes get around the Church of England, and two factors made this increasingly easy. First, the Anglican clergy, who were publicly financed and thus had little need to respond to popular demand, persisted in their rejection of enthusiastic modes of evangelizing, and thereby allowed a "market niche" to open up. Secondly, it became increasingly difficult for the Church of England to use its political power to maintain its monopoly, and after the Revolution began its monopoly existed only on paper. The principle of granting legal privilege to one religion in each state survived the Revolution, however, and in some states it remained in effect well into the nineteenth century.

As we have seen, it is doubtful whether in establishing its American colonies England had in mind religious goals or even the conversion of the Indians that Richard Hakluyt demanded. The royal charter that authorized the founding of a colony gave the settlers very extensive freedoms, and these generally remained in effect until either conflicts emerged within the colony itself and one of the parties sought support in London, or the consequences of the turmoil in seventeenth-century England made themselves felt in the colonies as well. Basically, however, the notion of a charter can be interpreted as a license, and thus in the Anglican colonies—Virginia, the as-yet undivided Carolina, New York from 1674 on, and finally Maryland as well from 1702 on—the situation was completely different from that in the New England colonies, where the Pilgrims pursued with extreme persistence their attempt to shape society, only to be overtaken by the unforeseen repercussions of their efforts.

The Church of England was legally established, but its monopoly was handled in a manner befitting this already rather diverse church. The Church of England had risen as the official church and was not prepared to pay its own expenses as an independent church. The Anglican church had never been a center of religious fervor and missionary efforts, and it was not inclined to view the New World as a providential opportunity for a new beginning and thus to devote all its energies to making this Christian experiment a success in the eyes of the world. From the point of view of the Anglican clergy, the New World was for the time being a not very attractive continuation of the Old World. Although as early as 1619 Virginia's parliament had decided to pay the Anglican clergy with public funds, the complaint that parishes were not being established quickly enough is found in report after report. The faithful were scattered over a wide area, and church construction progressed very tentatively, even though neighboring farmland that could help pay the church's expenses was also made available. It was difficult to recruit clergy, and despite repeated petitions no American diocese was established. Because of the way the church was organized, this hindered its development.

"Catholic" Maryland and Its Brief History

While the New England Puritans saw their monopoly as an obligation, the Church of England saw its own monopoly as a self-evident privilege. In "Catholic" Maryland, on the other hand, there was never any question of making Catholicism the official religion. Even if the Crown had been prepared to tolerate the development of such a colony, nothing much would have come of it, because in Maryland as well the Catholics were a minority that sought more to be tolerated than to dominate. On closer inspection, the founder of Maryland seems to have received a charter not because of his Catholicism, but in spite of it. George Calvert had served as a secretary of state under James I and enjoyed royal favor. When Calvert converted to Catholicism in 1625, he gave up his office, but was created Baronet of Baltimore in the Irish peerage. Lord Baltimore, who had already successfully taken part in overseas enterprises, asked James I's successor, Charles I, for permission to found an American colony. He was eventually granted a region for settlement and development, and named it after Charles I's French Catholic queen, Henrietta Maria. However, George Calvert died before the charter could be drawn up, and it was ultimately ceded to his son

Cecilius. In 1634, Cecilius admonished Catholics about to set sail for Baltimore to practice their religion as privately as they could and to avoid all ostentation (Marty 1984, 83).

After a few weeks' voyage in two ships, the "Ark" and the "Dove," 320 people arrived in America, even though the British port authorities recorded a lower number. Martin Marty, who mentions this, offers an illuminating explanation: the officials not only recorded information regarding passengers and cargo, but also demanded from English citizens emigrating to the colonies an oath of allegiance that included an explicit condemnation of the pope and the Catholic faith. Thus either the inspector involved had been bribed, or the Catholics disembarked only after he had completed his task (Hennesey 1981, 41).

Traveling along with the settlers on the ships were Leonard Calvert, the younger brother of the second Lord Baltimore, as the latter's representative in Maryland, and three Jesuits, Father Andrew White, Father John Althom, and Brother Thomas Gervase. In Maryland, as in Virginia, a plantation system developed that was devoted almost exclusively to growing tobacco. The planters had to pay taxes to the Calverts, and the latter shared power with them by establishing the Maryland General Assembly on the model of Virginia's. This legislative assembly declared in 1639 that in Maryland churches (in the plural) were to enjoy all rights and freedoms (Cogley 1986, 14).

However, this tolerance, which was based on prudent realism, could not long be maintained, because when the English civil war began the Calverts and their policies were involved in increasing difficulties. In the colony itself the Puritans' power grew as a result of immigration. Moreover, the Maryland Puritans were supported by Virginia, where the Puritan leader William Claiborne had also gained political control. In 1645, Claiborne personally led an invasion of Maryland. The Virginia militia under his command banished the Jesuits, confiscated the property of Catholics, and occupied Maryland for two years until Calvert assembled troops of his own and drove out the interlopers (Hennesey 1981, 42). In 1649, the reestablished Maryland Assembly passed the Act Concerning Religion, which became known as the Act of Religious Toleration. However, the latter name does not withstand scrutiny because its provisions clearly restore the situation that obtained before the Assembly's declaration of 1639. It was in fact a compromise struck between the Catholic minority and the Puritans, who had in the meantime become politicized. Regarding tolerance, the act stipulated that no one who confessed belief in Jesus Christ should be harassed on account of his religion. Following the example of laws passed the preceding year in England, blasphemy and heresy were made subject to severe penalties such as whipping or imprisonment. In 1658, a Quaker accused a Jewish physician of waiting for the Messiah, but the court refused to decide whether the accused had the right to practice his religion in Maryland, and the case was dismissed (Hertling 1954, 41). In any event, the so-called Act of Religious Toleration marked less a highpoint of religious freedom distinguishing Maryland from other colonies than the beginning of the end of a short-lived exception. The English civil war and especially the Glorious Revolution of 1688 provoked an initial wave of anti-Catholic propaganda, and as we have seen, in colonial America this was already the clearest and most easily popularized commonality of a Protestantism whose pluralism developed otherwise unhindered in the colonies.

For seventeenth-century Protestants and their heirs, Catholicism was simply a corruption of the Christian message. Among English Protestants, this judgment was based less on reform theology than on a still-vivid memory of Queen Mary's reign. Above all, the burning of three hundred Protestants in Smithfield after 1555 pointed to the common enemy that had martyred their forebears. Thus it was important to preserve the memory of the Protestant martyrs and to be on guard against the continuing machinations of the pope, the Jesuits, and the Catholic powers Spain and France. The memory was kept alive in particular by John Foxe's *Actes and monuments of these latter and perillous dayes*, commonly known as *The Book of Martyrs*. In New England, this book, which was first published in 1563 and went through several editions, appears to have been almost as ubiquitous as the Bible. The task of making credible the persistence of a Catholic menace was assumed by a plethora of later publications, especially in the nineteenth century.

In the second half of the seventeenth century, however, the repercussions of events in England sufficed to create in the Atlantic seaboard colonies anti-Catholic animosities that contrasted strangely with the number of Catholics involved. Even in Maryland and Pennsylvania, the two colonies with significant Catholic populations, the number of Catholics remained under ten percent in the seventeenth and eighteenth centuries. In 1790, the first United States census counted 35,000 Catholics in a total population of almost four million—less than one percent (Gaustad 1982, 1: 96, 148).

Nonetheless, the English dread of Catholic plots and the pope's machinations was transferred to the colonies along with English conceptions. Catholics were "recusants" or "popish recusants" who did not conform to the Church of England. Popish recusants were excluded from holding public offices in Virginia as early as 1641, and popish priests were not allowed to remain in the colony more than five days. In 1700, New York (which was not yet a British colony) passed a similar law whose tone and content reveal, after the Glorious Revolution, a distinct increase in severity. The notion of "popish priests" is still more pejorative than "popish recusants," since it refers to Jesuits and other "popish priests." These and other persons appointed by the pope, who showed themselves to be such through preaching, doctrine, or the performance of "romish ceremonies and rites," were to be called to account and sentenced to life in prison for disturbing public peace and security. If they escaped and were recaptured, they were to be put to death. Anyone who sheltered a Jesuit or any other "ecclesiastical person of the romish clergy" was subject to a fine of two hundred pounds, half of which went to the person who had informed the authorities of the offense (Ellis 1967, 1: 137).

After 1688, even the compromises contained in the so-called Act of Religious Toleration of 1649 could no longer be maintained. Anti-Catholic agitators in Virginia and Maryland founded the "Association in Arms for the Defense of the Protestant Religion and Assisting the Rights of King William and Queen Mary." That this was an "association in arms" was proven the following year, when it occupied Maryland. The king canceled the Calverts' charter, and the colony was granted the status of a royal province dependent directly on the king. In 1712, the Church of England was officially established in Maryland as well. For the Catholics in Maryland, who had already been banned from public life, the only remaining option was to practice their religion as discreetly as possible—for instance, by celebrating the Eucharist in private homes—and to concentrate their efforts on their business enterprises. Some of the latter were so successful that they provided an excuse for further persecution.

The distribution of the land under the Calverts had in fact laid the

foundations for the wealth and influence of many a family of plantation aristocrats, but this does not explain the rise of the Carroll family,
whose ancestors arrived in Maryland in 1688. The third-generation
Charles Carroll of Carrollton, as he proudly styled himself, was already considered the richest man in America and seen by his core-
ligionists and by government officials as the spokesman for Catholics
in Maryland. Whether or not he was as wealthy as people thought,
changes in the tax laws affected him more than others, and he is said
to have toyed with the idea of moving his family to Louisiana when
additional taxes made things still more difficult for Catholics. Like
Protestant dissenters, "popish recusants" had to pay taxes supporting
the Church of England, and a 1757 Maryland law doubling their tax
rates terrified them.

However, the Carrolls remained in Maryland, rather than joining
the exiled Acadians in Louisiana. For one thing, by selling their property they would have incurred heavy losses, and for another, things
were beginning to change. The development of a much more tolerant
climate did not result from a change in opinion so much as from a
shift in the constellation of interests involved. Up to that point England and France had competed for the northeastern part of America. Now, however, England and the American revolutionaries were
competing for the loyalties of Americans. Catholics in Quebec, Pennsylvania, and Maryland benefited from this change, and two fourth-
generation Carrolls became prominent figures. In the 1740s Charles
Carroll (the son of Charles Carroll of Carrollton) and his cousin John
Carroll were among the first pupils at Bohemia Manor, a Jesuit boarding school on Chesapeake Bay, and both were subsequently sent to
Europe in order to study at the Jesuit college of St. Omer in Flanders.
John stayed on in Europe, joined the Jesuit order, was ordained a priest,
and in 1773 returned to Maryland, after Pope Clement XIV, a Franciscan, dissolved the Jesuit order. Charles Carroll was already back in
Maryland in 1765 and replaced his father as head of the family business and as the unofficial spokesman for Catholics. Catholics were still
not allowed to hold public office, but Charles made a name for himself by expressing his opinions in newspapers such as the *Maryland
Gazette*. The regulations prohibiting Catholics from taking part in political activity were visibly threatened. In addition, alongside the official agencies patriotic revolutionary committees developed that gained

political influence in a gray zone that was unofficial but publicly effective.

In 1774 the first though short-lived Continental Congress met, and in the two subsequent years regulations regarding Catholics were dropped in the British colonies in which there were significant Catholic minorities. This began in the Canadian colonies acquired by the British in 1763, with the previously mentioned Quebec Act of 1774, and by 1776 Virginia, Pennsylvania, and Maryland were also ready to amend their laws. Virginia enacted a Bill of Rights proclaiming the principle of religious freedom. The Declaration of Rights passed a few months later in Pennsylvania made freedom of conscience the basis for its assertions that no one might be forced to contribute in any way to the maintenance of a church, and that no one who recognized the existence of God might be deprived of his civil rights because of his religion (Cogley 1986, 19).

Charles Carroll took advantage of the new arrangements. He participated in several political committees in Maryland and in 1776 was sent to the second Continental Congress, thus becoming one of the fifty-six signers of the Declaration of Independence. The denominational composition of the signers is worth examining, because it is the last reflection of the religious situation in colonial America, which was soon to change. According to John Cogley, of the signers of the Declaration of Independence twenty-nine—slightly more than half—were members of the Church of England. Twenty-three more—slightly less than half—were members of the various Congregationalist groups dominant in New England. The four remaining signers were a Baptist, a Quaker, Benjamin Franklin, who called himself a Deist, and the Catholic Charles Carroll (Hennesey 1981, 57, 64 ff.).

John Carroll, who had been living in Maryland since his return from Europe and had been active as a pastor there, was also drawn into revolutionary politics in 1776. This is an episode that clearly reveals how the Catholics could suddenly feel themselves courted and how difficult it was for the new American Republic taking its first steps in foreign policy to make its way between the principles of its own morality and the realities of power. The American revolutionaries hoped to persuade Canada to join them as the fourteenth rebellious province. Their prospects of success were already dim at the time of the first Continental Congress in 1774. On one hand, this Congress had criticized the English parliament's Quebec Act for making Catholicism the official religion of the "far-reaching land now called Canada"; this was considered "a serious threat to the Protestant religion, civil rights, and the freedoms of all Americans." On the other hand, the Continental Congress quickly sent a message to the residents of Quebec urging them to set aside trivial issues such as religious differences and make up their minds to be cordial friends of the American revolutionaries. They were not to allow their gratitude for the Quebec Act to stand in their way: religious freedom and freedom of conscience were after all gifts bestowed by God and not by the British parliament.

The opponents of the Revolution did not fail to note the contradictions among the various resolutions passed by the Continental Congress, and they also pointed out that most of its members were not exactly long-time supporters of religious freedom. Moreover, the next year American troops invaded Canada. Montreal surrendered, but Quebec withstood the siege, and about a year later, in the summer of 1776, the American troops withdrew.

Even before this retreat the second Continental Congress sent three of its members, Charles Carroll, Samuel Case, and Benjamin Franklin, on a diplomatic mission to Canada. Probably with the intention of showing Quebeckers that Catholics in the thirteen colonies had no problems with the Revolution, John Carroll was asked to accompany the group. But the whole undertaking proved to be as futile as might have been expected, and when Franklin became ill, Carroll made use of the opportunity to go back early with him.

When the Vatican soon thereafter sought to establish contact with the United States government in connection with the appointment of the first bishop in the new republic, it was Benjamin Franklin, the former United States ambassador in Paris, who was brought in for these consultations. He threw his full support behind Carroll, whose candidacy had been proposed by a council of priests.

2

SELF-ASSERTION IN
THE NEW WORLD
1789–1865

T𝗁ᴇ A𝗆ᴇʀɪᴄᴀɴ Rᴇᴠᴏʟᴜᴛɪᴏɴ could bridge religious contradictions only incompletely and thus only temporarily. But it did succeed in changing not only the outward appearance of religions but also their public function, both by leading to a new kind of politicization of religion and by altering the relative weight given the various religions in America. Many studies have shown that during the 1770s the Revolution was anticipated from the pulpit. In this, New England played a special role, because since the time of John Winthrop it had been common to deliver elaborate sermons and when possible to publish them. Written documents may offer a distorted image of actual conditions: just as the extensively documented missionary activity of the Jesuits is more easily accessible to us than that of other orders, we have numerous sermons that were given in New England churches, but we cannot compare them with Anglican sermons from Virginia.

1. Revolution and Religion

In his book *Rhetoric and History* Donald Weber examines sermons given by several New England ministers shortly before the Revolution. Like other authors, Weber is able to show that preachers in the 1770s contributed greatly to the popularization of John Locke's natural-law concept of freedom and the corresponding idea of the right to resist (Weber 1988).

A particularly well-known example of this kind of sermon is John Allen's *Oration on the Beauties of Liberty,* delivered in Boston's Second Baptist Church in 1772. Liberty, Allen maintained, was the "native right" of Americans, paid for with the blood of their forefathers. Attempting to subjugate Americans was as contrary to natural law as seeking to deprive the world of sunlight (Gaustad 1982, 1: 251).

The call for political independence and the rhetoric of liberty were particularly well received among Baptists, because these political demands seemed to them plausible extensions of their own battle for ecclesiastical independence. Isaac Backus had begun his resistance to the official Congregational Church by asking why it claimed for itself freedom from the Church of England but denied others a similar right to freedom. Therefore it is justifiable to emphasize the role of Baptists and of the republican preachers of revolutionary times, but the history of the Baptists also suggests that they had long adhered to such views. Just as the king would later become the epitome of repression and arbitrary rule, in the preceding decades, the possibility of an English bishop serving as an extension of the English Crown's power already seemed to symbolize a threat to both religious freedom and civil liberties.

Jonathan Mayhew can serve as an example. In the 1750s he was the best-known preacher and political commentator in Boston. He introduced into his sermons and treatises a right to resistance grounded in natural law, even though he did so much more circumspectly and academically than did John Allen. In 1750 he published a *Discourse Concerning Unlimited Submission and Non-Resistance to the Higher Powers* in which he stressed that God had granted rulers no authority to commit injustices, and therefore their orders were to be disobeyed insofar as they ran counter to reason and religion. Thus it is not surprising that Mayhew's writings were highly esteemed by John Adams and Thomas Jefferson. However, his fame rested chiefly on his long battle against the threat of a bishop being appointed in Boston. The fact that an Anglican came out from England and began building a house allegedly intended to serve as the bishop's residence was all Mayhew needed to launch his campaign. The so-called Episcopal Question no longer had anything to do with the Anglicans' pragmatic reflections on matters internal to the church. According to Gaustad, opposition to bishops became a mark of patriotism (Gaustad 1982, 1: 246), and conversely requesting that a bishop be appointed became for some people simply an opportunity to demonstrate their loyalty to the Crown. Nonetheless, before the Revolution neither the Anglicans nor the Methodists nor Rome appointed any more bishops.

Freedom of Choice and Competition:
The Religious Landscape after the Revolution

In the end, the Revolution substantially affected the relative strength of the various denominations. Those that had advocated independence emerged with increased power. This is especially true for the Baptists and the Congregational churches associated with them by religious history. Pacifist religious groups such as the Mennonites and Quakers were hard hit. However, the bitterest losses in membership and status struck the Anglicans, who had been on the "wrong side" of the conflict. The hysteria preceding and following the Revolution—discernible in the uproar over alleged plots such as the appointment of an Anglican bishop and in the treatment of actual or accused loyalists—was certainly not one of its finer moments. In a letter of October 1776 addressed to the Anglican *Society for the Propagation of the Gospel,* Charles Inglis of New York's Trinity Church wrote that patriots had adopted the motto "that those who were not for them, were against them." Self-appointed committees had arrested priests on charges of conspiracy, he reported; many had been dragged away from their lecterns or pulpits, while others had been forced to watch their houses being plundered on the pretext of searching them (Gaustad 1982, 1: 243–44).

The end of the Church of England in America was sealed when its American successor was founded. In May 1785, the Anglican clergy of Virginia gathered and constituted themselves as the Protestant Episcopal Church of the United States of America, thus stressing the latter's Protestant and American identity.

There remained the almost insoluble problem of how the new church was to be treated. Because of the legally privileged status of the Church of England the English legal tradition offered no concept for an entity intermediary between the established church on one hand and an association of individuals on the other. Constructs such as the juridical person or corporation were as yet unknown in English law. A makeshift solution was provided by a kind of incorporation comparable to entering names in an association's registry. In this way a legal capacity was created that could resolve, for instance, the question of the succession of church assets. In any case, the state of Virginia incorporated the new Episcopal Church and awarded it the assets of the Anglican church. Later controversies, particularly in the Catholic

Church, showed that it was not at all clear whether this kind of incorporation conferred legal status on individual congregations, the church as a whole, or certain individuals.

The dissenters took offense not only at incorporation as such but also at the resolution of property issues; Baptists insisted that a church was constituted by God's law and not by the state. At stake were the so called "glebe lands" or "glebes," that is, large tracts of land that former congregations had received in addition to the relatively small lots needed for the church, the vicarage, and the cemetery, and which they could farm themselves or lease out to pay the parish's expenses. To give up these properties that were part of the congregation's assets would be, Virginia's Presbyterians wrote, "too glaring a piece of injustice to pass unnoticed, or be suffered to continue in a free country" (Gaustad 1982, 1: 270 ff.).

Disestablishment

Such attempts to save what could still be saved did not prevent Anglicans, because of their weakened standing, from losing their status as the established church in Virginia in 1785. The first amendment to the United States Constitution, which forbade Congress to establish a religion, followed in 1791, and the individual states took their time implementing it. In New England disestablishment was obviously understood not as a logical consequence of religious liberty but as the punishment the Church of England deserved for having failed to demonstrate American patriotism. The Congregational Church remained the established church in Connecticut until 1818 and in Massachusetts until 1833. And even where freedom of choice and competition were recognized as the organizational principles of religion, there were still discriminatory laws that denied some of the competitors access to the marketplace. Moreover, there were laws forbidding Jews—implicitly, by granting all the relevant rights to Christians—and Catholics from holding public office. Such anti-popery regulations were still in effect in New Hampshire as late as 1877.

The Revolution produced a new kind of public realm and thereby shifted the country's spiritual center from New England to Virginia. From the beginnings of colonization to the onset of revolutionary unrest, intellectual debates took place in and around Boston. These debates focused on religion in the broadest sense, and were led by the Harvard-educated ministers of the established Congregational Church and their emphatically unacademic critics, the populist Baptist preachers.

Religion, Civic Religion, and the Republic:
The Constitutional Debate

Now, however, New England seemed to be a closed society in which the Puritans' established church clung to its possessions, but in which there was no discussion of religious issues. On the other hand, Virginia seemed to have awakened from lethargy and the center of the new Republic, geographically and otherwise, lay somewhere between Philadelphia and Virginia. From the convening of the first Continental Congress in 1774 to the adoption of the Bill of Rights in 1791, there was a long period of debate about the Constitution during which things appeared flexible and open to modification. In any event, the issue was always politics in the broadest sense of the word, and in contrast to the situation in New England, a historically and literarily cultivated, European-influenced elite stood ready to take over the arena that had just opened up. There were two reasons why this arena, the moral and political public sphere that the new elite now made its own stage, could be extended with particular ease in the center of the Republic.

First, there was neither an opposing cultural and political power nor an opposing elite, since the Anglican church and its clergy could no longer play this role. Secondly, the new political class's opportunities for action had expanded as a result of the increase in the number of institutions and their concentration in a single area. The same relatively limited group participated in the constitutional debates not only in Virginia, Maryland, and Pennsylvania, but also at the federal level: it held the offices in the new federal government as well as in the states and appointed the members of the legislatures.

New England had served for at least a century as America's religious and cultural laboratory, which led to unplanned and unwanted results. Now, during the upheavals of the 1770s and 1780s, Virginia emerged as the new spiritual and political center. Virginia's General Assembly formulated and decided in a preliminary way what the rest of the country would carry out in the decades to come. However, in its discussions intellectual controversies also emerged that could not be resolved by legislative decisions, and that would arise again and again. Thus the disestablishment of the Anglican church in Virginia in 1785 proceeded from a fundamental debate in which future debates about the relation between religion and politics and about the constitutional status of religion became discernible. Had the choice been only between establishment or disestablishment—that is, had it concerned only the question whether it was permissible to grant a specific religion legal privilege—then the discussion would have been over, because it was no longer possible to defend establishment in this sense. At most, there could have been a debate concerning the modalities of disestablishment, that is, differences of opinion about the way in which the succession was to be regulated, such as in fact occurred in reaction to the relatively generous treatment of the Episcopalians.

Things were not so simple, however, since those who were, in the Virginia Assembly's debates and later in history books, described all too summarily as the "opposition of disestablishment" (Marty 1984, 162) were not proponents of establishment in the sense previously defined; they did not want to grant any of the competing religions preference over others. Instead, they clung to the peculiar concept first introduced by eighteenth-century intellectuals in France and America as *religion civile* or "religion of the Republic." This concept repeatedly surfaced under different names such as "civic religion" until finally in the 1970s "civil religion," a literal translation of Rousseau's original expression *religion civile,* was generally adopted. These ideas were first proposed by people such as Jean-Jacques Rousseau and Benjamin Franklin, who were not exactly religious in the traditional sense but for that very reason all the more emphatic in stressing the public uses of religion; they were concerned with religion per se and with its contribution to the integration of society. As we have seen, the New England Puritans had conducted an experiment in political theology. Their goal, entirely in accord with Greek and Roman political theory, was to create the conditions for a good life that was pleasing to God. Politics was to serve religion, and access to the religious community was so restricted that an exclusive community could emerge. What counted was purity of doctrine, not a unified community. A century later, the precise opposite came to the fore. Civil religion was to provide the foundation for the social contract, that is, it was to guarantee the bond between civil society and the republic. Religion was to serve politics, and access to it was to be made as easy as possible. This inclusive concept clearly stressed unity rather than dogmatic consistency. Rousseau therefore propagated a "civic creed" whose dogmas were to be "simple, few in number, and comprehensible to all" (Rousseau 1947).

In his *Proposals Relating to the Education of Youth in Pennsilvania*, Franklin had written that a "public religion" would be useful. Such a public religion would not be in any way anti-Christian; on the contrary, it would be a way of demonstrating the superiority of Christianity. Like many other authors, Franklin did not make it clear whether he was thinking of a new, eclectic religion with its own creed and rites— like the Roman civic religion—that would, by making civic convictions sacred, rise over other religions, or only intended to emphasize the civic utility of all Christian religions, whose common denominator would become the content of the public religion. In the latter sense the cultural dominance of American Protestantism functioned as a civil religion throughout the nineteenth century. Only when this cultural establishment was challenged by the effects of massive immigration did the ideas of the 1770s and 1780s re-emerge; once again it was a question of social integration and religion's contribution to it.

The discussions in Virginia's General Assembly in 1785 and 1786, in which Jefferson's and Madison's ideas ultimately prevailed, began in 1779 with Patrick Henry's bill seeking to connect the necessity of disestablishment with the desire for a civil religion. Henry wanted to write it into law that the Christian religion was for all time "the established religion of this commonwealth." However, each individual was to freely decide to which church his own taxes would be given. In other words, Henry wanted to establish all Christian churches, so that taxes paid by each individual would go to support a church of his own choice rather than a single official church.

In opposition to Henry's plan, James Madison wrote a detailed "Memorial and Remonstrance against Religious Assessments" in which he argued that religion must remain a matter of individual conviction and personal conscience. If a public authority were entitled to establish Christian religion to the exclusion of all others, he said, then it could also establish a particular Christian denomination to the exclusion of all others. Henry's bill must be rejected, he concluded, because either it assumed that secular officials were competent to judge religious truths or saw "Religion as an engine of Civil policy." The first possibility Madison considered an arrogant presumption refuted by the contradictory opinions of the powerful throughout history, while the second perverted the meaning of the Redemption (Gaustad 1982, 1: 262 ff.).

Virginia's legislature did not pass Patrick Henry's bill, but it did ease the established church's transition in the way previously described. The following year, 1786, it passed Thomas Jefferson's "Bill for Establishing Religious Freedom." This bill clearly stipulated that no one might be forced to join or to support a particular religious community, and that conversely, no one might be disadvantaged because of his adherence to a particular religion. The United States Constitution written in 1787 mentions religion only in specifying that officials are to swear allegiance to the Constitution, but may not be subjected to a "religious test." This referred to the English "Test Act" of 1673, which had been law in the colonies as well and had required public officials not only to participate in Anglican services but also to sign a written declaration regarding dogma—denying transubstantiation, for example.

The Constitution thus has little to say about religion and its legal status. As a result, over the past two centuries the Supreme Court has dealt with this issue more often than with any other. It has repeatedly interpreted the single article in the Constitution that deals with the relationship between church and state, the First Amendment (1791): "Congress shall make no law respecting the establishment of religion, or prohibiting the free exercise thereof." Congress and the Federal Government are therefore prohibited from supporting a particular religious community, for example by requiring participation in its services or conversely by forbidding the exercise of a particular religion. This amendment applies only to federal legislators, however, and does not refer to discrimination against individuals because of their religious affiliation. Moreover, the so-called "wall of separation" often cited in connection with the supposedly required separation of church and state is not mentioned in the Constitution. The expression is found in one of Jefferson's letters, but it does not do justice to either the wording of the First Amendment or the history that led up to it. The goal was "non-establishment," the refusal to grant one religion precedence by requiring membership in it. This meant no more and no less than untrammeled competition among religions and the individual's freedom to choose.

2. The Development of Ecclesiastical Structures

After 1760, the already rather undeveloped structure of the Catholic Church in America fell into ever increasing disorder. In the South, the Mississippi River divided the Bishop of Havana's jurisdiction from that of the equally distant Bishop of Quebec. The latter was also responsible for Catholics in the Ohio Territory, which had since come under British control, and to which he no longer had access. The British Atlantic colonies were under the Apostolic Vicar in London, who had long relied upon the Jesuits' religious superior in Maryland, since at first all Catholic priests in Maryland and Pennsylvania were Jesuits. After the dissolution of the order in 1773 this arrangement could no longer be continued. Moreover, it was becoming clear that British rule in the colonies was also coming to an end, and thus a bishop residing in London would soon find himself in a position as difficult as that of a Canadian bishop.

The papal congregation *De Propaganda Fide*, which was responsible for overseeing all missionary districts, thus began preparations for a reorganization. Apparently it first turned to Joseph Olivier Briand, then bishop of Quebec, asking him to investigate the situation at first hand. He contacted a Jesuit working in Canada, Father Bernard Well, who in turn wrote to his confreres in Maryland and Pennsylvania to find out what the reaction to the appointment of a bishop would be and whether a visit by Bishop Briand was advisable. All this can be gleaned from the reply written from Philadelphia on 22 April 1773 by the German Jesuit Ferdinand Farmer (whose name was probably originally Bauer). Farmer briefly describes the state of the mission in Maryland and Pennsylvania, where, in contrast to the other colonies, the Catholic faith was tolerated, even though Catholics were still forbidden to hold public office. He also states very clearly that a visit by the bishop would not be helpful, and might even imperil the precarious standing of Catholics, since in Maryland the current tolerance was not founded in law, as it was in Pennsylvania. He also cautioned against establishing a diocese by appointing a bishop; while neither he nor his confreres had any intention of withholding confirmation from the faithful, "it is plain to our eyes, being given especially the character of Americans," that the dignity of the episcopal office could not be guaranteed. Farmer clearly echoed the controversy surrounding the appointment of a bishop of the Church of England when he added that it was hardly imaginable how much non-Catholic Americans hated "the very name of a bishop," and that this was true even for "members of the church which is called Anglican." After offering all these hints suggesting that it was advisable to avoid any public attention, Farmer signed his letter "Ferdinand Farmer S.J.," and added a postscript asking that any further correspondence be addressed to Mr. Ferdinand Farmer, Walnut Street, Philadelphia (Ellis 1956, 126 ff.). However, Farmer's concern about the conspicuousness of the initials "S.J." was soon to be rendered moot by the pope.

While the bishop of Quebec could not exercise his authority in the British territories, an American bishop would meet with resistance and would be appointed against the advice of his own clergy. Moreover, the Jesuit order could no longer serve as a substitute for ecclesiastical administration, and even Rome had no ready solution. Thus the situation in America remained unsettled for another decade. Only when Great Britain had recognized the independence of the American colonies in the preliminary treaty of 1782 and France had assumed the role of the American Revolution's advocate in Europe did Cardinal Lorenzo Antonelli, the Prefect for Propaganda, become active again. He asked the nuncio in Paris to intervene, and in 1784, after lengthy discussions in which Benjamin Franklin took part, the course was finally set. An American ecclesiastical administration was established, even though at first the warnings to avoid attracting attention were heeded. John Carroll was named superior of the American missions.

In his letter of 9 June 1784 Antonelli informed Carroll of the appointment, explained his powers as superior, and offered these further reflections: His Holiness and the Sacred Congregation had seen fit to appoint a shepherd to preserve and defend the Catholic Church in the thirteen United States of America, who could devote himself to meeting the spiritual needs of his flock and was to be subordinate to no ecclesiastical authority other than the Sacred Congregation. It was clear, he wrote, that this appointment would please many citizens of the new republic, in particular Mr. Franklin. In the name of the Holy See, the

Congregation conferred on Carroll and the other priests in these states the necessary authority, while reserving the right to approve their decisions. All these regulations were to be regarded as merely preliminary, for his Holiness intended soon to name an Apostolic Vicar. In the meantime, Carroll was asked to submit a *relatio* or report (Ellis 1967, 1: 142 ff.).

The Shortage of Priests, Conflicts between "Old" and "New" Immigrants, Unresolved Legal Issues: John Carroll's 1785 Report

Carroll took his time, submitting on 1 March 1785 a very sober report that nonetheless suggests the structural problems faced by the new church. The first part is subtitled "On the Number of Catholics" and summarizes the limited data at Carroll's disposal. In Maryland there were about 15,800 Catholics, he wrote, and in Pennsylvania about 7,000. He could offer only vague information concerning the small number of Catholics scattered over the areas north and south of this center. He knows of more than two hundred souls in Virginia, for they were visited four or five times a year by priests from Maryland. As for the New York region, he has heard that there are about fifteen hundred. He does not mention New England, and here what John Adams is supposed to have said was probably true: in this part of the world Catholics are as rare as earthquakes or comets (Hennesey 1981, 77). In conclusion, Carroll mentions "many Catholics, former Canadians, who speak French."

As he lists these numbers, Carroll mentions issues with which he and his successors were to struggle for a long time. He reports that Catholics in New York had brought a Franciscan from Ireland at their own cost, and finds it necessary to add that nothing disadvantageous was known about the Irish Franciscan's education or moral conduct. A Carmelite from France was supposed to have appeared among the "former Canadians," but he carried no documents showing whether he had been sent by his superior. Despite a serious shortage of priests, Carroll cautions, one must be careful about priests, mainly members of religious orders, who came to America on their own initiative. They might well be in conflict with their bishop or want to escape their order's discipline. Moreover, rightly or wrongly, Irishmen were reputed to be drunkards and poorly educated.

Aside from the fact that it was already difficult enough to recruit a qualified and disciplined clergy, it often remained unclear who was responsible for maintaining order in an emergency. Thus in connection with the French Canadians and the priests that came to them from France, Carroll mentions that the Bishop of Quebec earlier had jurisdiction over this region. Carroll adds that he does not know whether the Bishop of Quebec still sought to exercise his authority there, since the areas concerned now belonged to the United States.

The second part of Carroll's report—"Condition, Piety and Defects, etc. of Catholics"—attempts to evaluate ecclesiastical life. Here an important difference between Maryland and Pennsylvania emerges. Carroll notes that of the 15,800 Catholics in Maryland, some 3,000 are slaves "called negroes," whereas in Pennsylvania there are about 7,000 Catholics, "very few of whom are negroes."

The developing American church's center was in fact located geographically and figuratively near the borderline between North and South. Carroll mentions this distinction, although he is concerned with something different. Most Marylanders were plantation owners, and some of them belonged to wealthy families that still clung to the Catholic faith of their forefathers. In Pennsylvania, except for the merchants and craftsmen in Philadelphia, almost everyone was a small farmer. Carroll reported that, on the whole, they showed themselves ready enough to practice their religion, for example by receiving the sacraments, but their enthusiasm was dampened by the fact that, because of the shortage of priests and the great distances to be covered, many congregations heard the Word of God only once a month. However, he noted, all this held true only for Catholics born in America, not for those who were coming in great numbers from various European countries. While there were only a few "native Catholics" who did not go to confession and take communion at least once a year, usually at Easter, among the newcomers scarcely any fulfilled their religious duties.

The question as to how one ought to react to the situation of the immigrants was to occupy the church longer than any other. The more immigrants came into the country, the more Catholic congregations showed the social and structural characteristics previously observable in Pennsylvania. Catholic immigrants were among those Carroll called merchants, craftsmen, and farmers. They had neither the opportunity nor the means to establish plantations in Maryland or Virginia, and so they stuck together. They quickly made their presence known as a new element in the already existing parishes, where conflicts between native Catholics and the new arrivals combined with frictions between groups speaking different languages. When Carroll wrote his report, there was still a compelling reason to compromise: the various groups were too small and too poor to establish parishes where their native tongues would be spoken, and not enough priests were available to staff them.

This is the subject of the third part of Carroll's report, "On the Number of the Priests, their Qualifications, Character and Means of Support." According to Carroll, there were nineteen priests in Maryland and five in Pennsylvania, two of whom were already more than seventy years old, and three more only slightly younger. They either derived their income from their "estates" (this was true only for the Jesuits' property in Maryland, where there were slaves) or relied on the generosity of the laity. In this connection Carroll touches on a problem that was to be of great importance, because it could be associated with the previously mentioned conflicts within individual parishes. Strictly speaking, Carroll says, there was no ecclesiastical property capable of paying a priest's expenses. This would be true only for owners who could transfer to new trustees the properties they held in trust. In a concluding section as laconic as the rest of his report, Carroll mentioned the need to establish educational institutions. In Maryland there were two colleges Catholics could attend, and he hoped that some of their students would choose "the ecclesiastical state." Therefore, he said, he was thinking of establishing a seminary (Ellis 1967, 2: 144).

The First College, the First Seminary, the First Bishop

In the thirty years before his death in 1815, Carroll oversaw the development of the American church, pursuing with great persistence two goals that can already be found in his report. The first and most important was the establishment of a separate American ecclesiastical organization that was, to be sure, in union with the bishop of Rome, but comparable to the European churches in independence and self-assurance. Closely connected with this was the question of how to achieve a separate Catholic educational system.

In organizing the church the first task was to accommodate ecclesiastical boundaries with governmental boundaries, that is, to limit the bishop of Quebec's jurisdiction to Canada and to extend John Carroll's responsibility to the whole of the United States. This was sure to be applauded in America, and Carroll could also count on the Vatican's agreement, since accepting political realities corresponded to Rome's thinking and practice. On the other hand, the inevitable next step, the strengthening and differentiation of the American ecclesiastical hierarchy, led to a dilemma, because it revealed the conflict between Catholicism and nationalism that was becoming alarmingly evident in Protestant countries. Thus America's Roman Catholic Church had to assure Americans that it was American and at the same time convince Rome that it would remain Roman.

For Carroll, this meant that the American church had to try to move beyond the status of a missionary church and free itself from the supervision of *De Propaganda Fide.* However, the only argument that might have led the latter's Prefects to give up their authority would have been the assurance that doing so would further the development of the American church. But greater independence meant at least appointing a bishop, and the Americans had already advised against such an appointment.

On the other hand, the only way to prove to the American public that the American church was independent was to appoint an American bishop, whose office would, however, still depend on a foreign authority and represent an ecclesiastical structure that was anything but congregational.

Yet the inevitable consequence of growth appeared to be the continued development of the ecclesiastical organization, and so Carroll concentrated on his second goal, the establishment of a separate Catholic educational system. This involved recruiting priests and thus once again the independence of the American church. In contrast to later times, when a young priest who was ambitious or enjoyed his bishop's protection was likely to complete his training in Europe, Carroll regarded both employment of European priests and training young Americans in Europe as interim solutions. In his view, as soon as possible the training of young priests should take place in America and be adapted to American conditions.

However, from the outset Carroll had in mind an educational system for all Catholics. Separate schools were justified because they provided not only future recruits for seminaries but also an opportunity to improve the social standing of Catholics. If Catholics were already a threatened minority regarded with mistrust by those around them, then they should, in the aristocratic Carroll's view, at least not be inferior. The report submitted by the spiritual leader of American Catholics suggests that he considered Catholic immigrants a dubious blessing—and yet ultimately it was these immigrants who achieved what Carroll had in mind: a unique, private educational system and the Americanization of the American Catholic Church.

In any case, for many years Carroll advocated the founding of a university and a seminary, and he hoped to bring to America religious orders that were willing to establish schools. Already in 1787 he was contradicting some of his priests who like himself were former Jesuits and whose pastoral experience had made them aware of urgent needs other than founding of a university. According to Carroll, their order's most useful contribution had been to the education and rearing of the young. In 1791 he was able not only to found Georgetown University (at first called Georgetown Academy) but also, with the help of the French Sulpicians, to open in Baltimore the first seminary. St. Mary's Seminary began with a teaching staff composed of five French priests and five French seminarians. To raise funds for the seminary as well as for the university, which was from the beginning more expensive, Carroll personally approached his wealthy relatives and other Catholic families, setting an example followed by later American bishops.

Despite their original misgivings, the transformation of the superior into a bishop seemed ultimately inevitable to Carroll and the priests under his jurisdiction as well as to the Vatican. This decision was made easier by the fact that the Episcopal Church had meanwhile proceeded to appoint a bishop without arousing the stormy protest that had been feared. After the Revolution and disestablishment, a bishop no longer represented a threat to civil liberties. The point at issue between Rome and Baltimore was therefore no longer whether a bishop would be appointed, but how, and this was the beginning of a debate that went on for a long time.

At that time, the pope had the right to make direct appointments only for the Vatican City and for missionary territories, which still included America—and this was a further reason for Americans to want to "normalize" their status. A few priests, presumably with Carroll's knowledge, sent a petition to Rome asking that a diocese be established. They also suggested that an assembly of American priests be allowed to elect the first bishop, and that the future process of selection be determined later. Rome granted the Americans' request on both major and minor points: in this case they would be permitted to propose a single candidate and name the city in which the bishop's see would be located. However, the pope's right of selection and the missionary status of America, that is, its supervision by *De Propaganda Fide*, was left untouched.

Thus in May 1789 an assembly of priests finally met, and by a vote of twenty-four to two, decided to propose John Carroll's name. In November, he was appointed the first bishop of Baltimore. For almost twenty years his diocese included the entire territory of the United States, until in 1808, on Carroll's recommendation, it was divided into the dioceses of Boston, New York, Philadelphia, and Bardstown—later Louisville—in Kentucky. Baltimore became an archdiocese. When John Carroll died in 1815, there were six dioceses in his archdiocese, since a sixth was added to the original five when as a result of the Louisiana Purchase the enormous diocese of Louisiana was created, with its see in New Orleans.

The Church between Great Opportunities and the Threat of Power Struggles and Conflicts of Nationalities: Ambrose Marechal's 1818 Report

Carroll's auxiliary bishop Leonard Neele succeeded him, but died only two years later. His successor, the third archbishop of Baltimore, was Ambrose Marechal, a Sulpician born in France who held the office for ten years (1818–1828). Marechal then wrote, as had Carroll thirty years earlier, his report to Rome, where in the meantime Cardinal Lorenzo Litta had become prefect of *De Propaganda Fide*. Unlike Carroll, Marechal seems not to have considered this kind of stocktaking a burdensome duty. He did not limit himself to reporting a few facts such as the number of Catholics, participation in the life of the church, and the number of priests, but offered an analysis from the point of view of an outsider clearly fond of America and Americans. In this respect he resembles his countryman Alexis de Tocqueville, who traveled through the diocese three years after Marechal's death. Many of the observations Marechal communicated to the cardinal in 1818 are so close to Tocqueville's that it is almost as if the latter had read Marechal's letter. In any case, Marechal's report can serve as a retrospective account of the three decades in which, under John Carroll's undaunted leadership, the American church and its future problems took shape.

Marechal begins with the structure of the diocese and a list of the states and territories that still belong to his own bishopric despite the previously mentioned division. In the year of his report, 1818, a significant change took place when the United States acquired Florida and the parts of Louisiana that had been under Spanish control. In addition to Maryland, Virginia, South and North Carolina, Georgia, and Tennessee, the diocese now also included Florida and the adjacent territories all the way to the Mississippi. Marechal emphasizes the great expansion of his diocese in the South, thus preparing the ground for the suggestion made at the end of his report, namely the establishment of a separate diocese for the Southeast with its see in Charleston. This suggestion was acted upon two years later, when John England, whose opinion regarding the French clergy we have already quoted, became the first bishop of Charleston.

Marechal estimates that before the Revolution there had been at most 10,000 Catholics in this area, and now there were at least 100,000, served by fifty-two priests altogether. These priests came from seven different countries: Italy (1), Germany (3), England (4), Belgium (7), Ireland (11), America (12), and France (14). Each had a main church, usually constructed only of wood, but sometimes already of brick or stone. None of these churches were sufficient for the increasing numbers of faithful, and therefore Marechal hoped that in the next ten years new ones would be dedicated. After describing the four churches in the city of Baltimore, Marechal also mentions the cathedral begun by Carroll. No doubt the size and splendor of this cathedral would far surpass what Protestants or Catholics had thus far achieved in the way of church construction, and even Baltimore's Protestants were proud of it.

There follows a description of the educational system, in which it becomes evident that in the meantime the seminary had been organized on the French model of "major" and "minor" seminaries. In Emmitsburg, outside Baltimore, the Sulpicians now ran both a minor seminary with eighty students—fifteen of whom had already been

tonsured, while the spiritual vocation of the others was not yet sufficiently clear—and a major seminary where more advanced candidates
studied philosophy and theology. The major seminary was connected
with a college, then the only one in Maryland. In addition, there was
Georgetown, "a magnificent college . . . directed by the Fathers of the
Society of Jesus." The Jesuits, whose order had been restored, had in
the meantime also officially taken over Georgetown. Thus Marechal
reports that at Georgetown there were two main buildings; one housed
the secular students, the other the order's thirty-three novices. Hence
the Jesuits were also trying to associate their own seminary with a
college. They all wondered, the prefect of *De Propaganda Fide* was told,
why the Jesuit superiors in Rome did not send six or eight members of
their order to Georgetown, for nowhere in the Catholic world could
members of the Society of Jesus live and work with greater success.

Already in Carroll's time Carmelite nuns had settled in Maryland.
The bishop had welcomed them, though he was disappointed because
he had hoped for teaching nuns. The Ursuline nuns he wanted had in
the meantime established themselves in Philadelphia, and Marechal
reported that in his diocese there were, in addition to the Carmelite
convent where twenty-three nuns lived, a Visitandine convent with
fifty nuns and a Vincentian convent with thirty; both had begun establishing schools for girls. The archbishop concluded his statistical and
institutional overview by announcing that during the coming winter
he planned to establish in Baltimore schools for girls and boys that
could be attended by Protestants as well as Catholics, so long as parents did not object to their children being given religious instruction.

Finally, Marechal came to the unresolved problems of the American church. First he described the mentality and religious culture of
Americans in a way also found in many later authors. American Protestantism cared little about Luther's or Calvin's doctrines, he said, and
now that the Anglican church no longer had any power a clear tendency to Socinianism was developing. (Marechal, a former professor of
theology, was alluding to Faustus Socinus, a sixteenth-century Italian
theologian whose doctrines influenced the rationalistic, unitarian tendency that split off from New England congregationalism in the course
of the nineteenth century.)

Somewhat too optimistically, Marechal believed the tolerant mood
that had come in with the Revolution would endure: anti-Catholic

prejudices had been so thoroughly wiped out, he thought, that the few people who persisted in them held their tongues or were immediately contradicted.

There follows a description of the American character that foreshadows many later judgments: Americans have lively minds and a gift for argument, and they make the greatest mental and physical efforts in pursuit of wealth. Everyday capabilities and skills as well as the amenities of life are plentiful, yet hardly anyone is distinguished by exceptional knowledge. Nonetheless it can be said that the majority of Americans far surpass Europeans in education, civilized behavior, and exercise of their minds. They venerate their freedom in an almost religious way.

Marechal considers Americans' pursuit of wealth one of their vices, but in mentioning two remedies he again anticipates later ideas. Americans are eager for religious instruction, and even a preacher of only average eloquence can expect to attract a large number of attentive listeners. The role played by women in America seems to him equally remarkable. Not only are American women distinguished by their impeccable morality (in his diocese, the archbishop claims, adultery and fornication occur seldom if at all), but they take such care about their persons and appearance that it is difficult to tell an American shoemaker's daughters from European ladies of rank. On the other hand, however, this self-assurance does not go so far as immodesty. As later for Tocqueville, for Marechal religion is associated with the American woman, who had to domesticate the inherently moral but acquisitive American male.

Nowhere in the world, Marechal suggested, was the outlook so bright for religion and for the Catholic Church in particular, if only it could provide a sufficient number of qualified priests and avoid schisms. Under these rubrics he then turns to the threatening developments that are becoming increasingly evident in the American church, and that contrast with the rosy picture he has just sketched. These involve on one hand conflicts between nationalities, which first arose in relation to the question of whether it was possible to do without European priests, and on the other hand the first in a long series of controversies regarding the nature and extent of episcopal authority.

The newly appointed archbishop's testiness and defensiveness regarding the selection of priests suggest that he felt pressured both from above and from below. The otherwise exceptionally polite Frenchman bluntly told the Sacred Congregation that he simply could not put Englishmen (he probably meant native speakers, whether British, Irish, or American) in charge of the various missions. He had only a few at his disposal, and did not see how he could get more. He was also well aware that Americans preferred American priests who were familiar with their ways and customs, and all he could do was to promote the development of a native clergy by establishing seminaries. In the meantime, they must thank God for the European priests who "crossed the ocean." The Belgians, French, and Germans had proven the best missionaries, distinguishing themselves through their zeal in the battle for souls, the purity of their way of life, and their partiality to ecclesiastical discipline. A few had trouble with the English language, but not with the Word of God. The small number of priests who had already been trained in America were equipped with the necessary knowledge, but were so deeply involved in their pastoral duties that they had no time to continue their education. Thus they found it difficult to deal with ideas that required a certain level of knowledge. The Irish were zealous and gifted rhetorically, and he would therefore welcome more Irish priests with open arms—but that would require a careful examination of each individual case, because too many of them were afflicted with the vice of drunkenness. Moreover, he had noticed that the Irish were not only drunkards but troublemakers, and these two vices went hand in hand. If for instance one tried to remove from office an Irish priest who had become a problem, one found that he was often able to get his compatriots to defend him. It was amazing, Marechal wrote, how much authority such priests enjoyed among their compatriots, to the point that they sometimes left the church. In internal dissensions, it was never the other ethnic groups that disturbed the peace, but always priests from Ireland, who were given to ambition and to drink.

Once again Marechal insists that he is not fundamentally prejudiced against the Irish. He has, after all, ordained ten Irishmen as priests, and most of the students in his diocese's seminary are Irish. But his feeling is deeply rooted, for he sees a connection between the two main problems facing the church, the qualification of the priests and the danger of schisms.

The previously mentioned conflicts in Charleston, Norfolk, and

Philadelphia, and other cities had to do with control of the congregations' assets and the right to appoint or suspend pastors. Marechal believed that control of the congregations' assets could be handed over to lay people or their trustees, but in no case could control over the priests be surrendered. To his later regret, Bishop Carroll had initially been too lenient in this matter. Marechal saw quite clearly that unresolved legal issues could lead to power struggles between influential lay people and their bishop. But he shows understanding for rebellious lay people and blames the priests. The lay people, who share the well-known American love of freedom, are used to choosing through democratic elections those who are to fill the highest and most important government offices, and thus American Catholics, with the Protestants' example before their eyes, are tempted to apply the same principles to ecclesiastical offices. Clever and impious priests, Marechal suggests, have persuaded American Catholics that they have the right to elect their pastor and to dismiss him at will.

With this hint, Marechal dismisses the reader as well (Ellis 1967, 1: 202 ff.). Whether or not the rebellious trustees were seduced by refractory Irish priests or the other way around, the problem of "trusteeism," that is, the laity's claim to control over more than the congregation's assets, anticipates both of the controversies that were to determine the internal development of Catholicism in the course of the nineteenth century: the struggle to establish episcopal authority—that is, the Catholic ecclesiastical structure—on one hand, and the conflicts between nationalities on the other.

Controversies regarding Trusteeism and the Establishment of Episcopal Authority

It is obvious why the problems the archbishop reported could at first emerge only in very specific places. Only a few Catholic parishes were sufficiently wealthy to be able to use church assets as a lever, and few were large enough and ethnically or socially diverse enough to invite the formation of splinter groups. Thus these problems emerged, if at all, only in the East Coast port cities. There the initially small waves of immigration had left behind ethnic centers, and there as well commerce and trade had been concentrated over the past century and a half. Hence the oldest and most diverse congregations were found in cities such as Baltimore, Philadelphia, and New York, as well as in

Richmond and Norfolk, the port cities of Virginia. These old congregations were in a position to develop self-confidence and initiative, and
already in 1785 John Carroll heard that New Yorkers had hired an Irish
Franciscan at their own expense.

The power struggles between the established lay people and the
bishops that ensued can be explained in part by the American cultural
climate. Americans were naturally congregationalists, and inclined
to organize the church from below. This irritated not only Catholic
bishops but also others, such as the German Lutheran bishop Heinrich
Melchior Mühlenberg, who under the name Henry Muhlenberg put his
mark on Pennsylvania—for example, the college named after him in
Allentown. But the democratization of religion had not yet taken hold
in all ethnic groups and all denominations, and least of all Catholic
immigrants from Eastern Europe. Probably more important than "the
heady wine of their newly won religious freedom" that, according to
John T. Ellis, went to some Catholics' heads (Ellis 1967, 1: 150) was the
temporal coincidence of an unusual ethnic and cultural diversity in a
few cities and an equally novel legal situation that initially emerged
only in a few states.

The Catholic Church's ethnic and cultural diversity was ensured by
the presence of French priests, a clergy without congregations, and the
first Irish immigrants, then still a congregation without a clergy. The
church's new legal situation in relation to the state, on the other hand,
was a byproduct of the first steps in disestablishment, that is, of the
decline of the Anglican church.

It was not clear that after the lifting of the monopoly it was necessary to regulate the legal status of religious communities. Virginia's
Baptists, for instance, believed that by incorporating the Episcopal
Church the State of Virginia had once again exceeded its authority.
However, several states enacted so-called laws of general incorporation. The 1784 New York law, which became a model for later laws in
other states, provided for elections in which all male adults in a congregation or parish would elect trustees and in this way form a corporation with administrative powers. This included the "right of patron-
age," that is, the right to select ministers (McNamara).

As archbishop Marechal later explained to the congregation in Norfolk, under canon law this responsibility was an inalienable right of
bishops (Ellis 1967, 1: 220). However, his warning had little effect, for

since the 1780s, when the legal groundwork had been laid, discontented groups had been trying to resolve their problems by founding new, more homogeneous congregations. But this way of gaining independence, which emerged in American Protestantism as a way of overcoming conflicts, had the opposite effect in the Catholic Church. The bishops were forced to enter a battle that they had to fight to the end if they wanted to adhere to the Catholic conception of the church.

The first incident in which the trustees played a role took place in New York. An Irish Capuchin, Charles Wheelan, who was probably the Franciscan Carroll had heard about, had served the parish of St. Peter since 1784. The following year another Irish Capuchin, Andrew Nugent, also came to New York, and soon the congregation was divided into two factions. The trustees dismissed Wheelan and engaged Nugent, who was said to be a better preacher (Ellis 1956, 150).

Carroll was at first spared a direct confrontation with the trustees, for Wheelan retired, and soon thereafter the trustees who had hired Nugent made documented personal accusations against him, with the result that Carroll suspended him. However, Nugent still had the support of part of the congregation, and announced that he would not yield to the pope or anyone else except Christ and the secular authorities of New York. His followers prevented the superior and the trustees from entering the church, and the matter ended up in court. The court convicted Nugent of disturbing the peace and declared him unfit to hold any clerical office in the Catholic Church, since he declined "its doctrines" (Hennesey 1981, 77).

Whether intentionally or unintentionally, this 1787 decision by the New York court revised the law of incorporation by acknowledging that individual religious communities had a right to protect themselves. If one was fit for service in a religious community only if one agreed with its "doctrines," then the decision would be made by an authority independent of the priest and the congregation, assuming the religion concerned had such an authority that it recognized as competent to interpret its doctrines.

At the same time, German Catholics in Philadelphia decided to declare their independence. For thirty years they had been served by Father Ferdinand Farmer, and when Farmer died in 1786 they no longer felt at home in St. Mary's Church, where Father Robert Molyneux now preached his sermons in Gallicized English. The German majority of the parish, including most of the long-established wealthier families, therefore decided to found a new congregation. However, they sought Carroll's permission before electing trustees and applying for incorporation. Similarly, they did not simply hire the German Capuchin they had found and whose name has come down to us as Charles Helbron; instead, they asked the superior to do so.

Whereas the New York case petered out only because the trustees were ultimately happy to dismiss the priest they themselves had engaged, the German trustees in Philadelphia did not challenge the bishop's rights, so that Carroll was not forced to oppose the plan. He could have rejected the principle of an ethnic parish, but apart from the fact that in the American missionary region parishes did not yet exist as ecclesiastical entities according to canon law, it was chiefly a question of authority and power, and not yet a choice between Americanization and maintaining the ethnic subculture. Thus there emerged in Philadelphia a new German-speaking congregation that Pennsylvania officials incorporated as Holy Trinity Church in 1788.

The Irish immigrants who were now pouring into the country were not able to resolve their problems in this relatively quiet way. They relied not on their wealth but on their numbers, and they did not ask permission to separate off, but rather fought for power. They had not only a tactical advantage but also a good conscience, because their interest as a group could also be described as the objective necessity of Americanizing the church. The Irish thus sought to prevail over the French in Charleston and New Orleans, and over the Germans in Buffalo. Moreover, as Patrick W. Carey has shown in his book on the social aspects of trusteeism, these clear interethnic boundary lines were later blurred by intraethnic contradictions. In Philadelphia's Holy Trinity Church a difference between social levels soon became noticeable. High Germans, the wealthy older families, tended to adopt an anticlerical attitude and insisted on the rights of the trustees, while Low Germans, the so-called ordinary people, were more prepared to recognize the bishop's authority and therefore to elect as trustees candidates who were loyal to the bishop. It is reported that among Germans in Cincinnati the most important question was whether one had emigrated before or after 1848, and similar structures developed even in the older Irish congregations, for instance in Philadelphia's St. Mary's, where the Irish took over after the Germans moved out.

This social differentiation offered the bishops an initial advantage: they could win over the majority and turn their own weapons against those who defended the rights of the trustees. For instance, the New York bishop John Dubois, like Marechal a Sulpician born in France, had to battle throughout his term of office (1826–1842) with his cathedral's trustees, who finally threatened to cut off his salary. Dubois did not give in, but it never occurred to him to intimidate or act against the trustees himself. In 1839, however, after he had suffered a stroke, John Joseph Hughes, who later succeeded him, was appointed as his coadjutor. As if to test Hughes, soon after he arrived in New York the trustees denied a Dubois-appointed catechist entry to the cathedral. Hughes responded by inviting members of the congregation to a meeting that he himself led and brought those present to vote out all the current trustees. Thus New Yorkers got a foretaste of this fiery bishop's style, but a long-term solution to the trustee problem probably could not consist in the bishops using democratization to defend themselves against democratization.

However, few other means of defense were at hand. In his Charleston diocese John England tried out an episcopal constitution that adhered to the procedures required by canon law. But such appeals were effective only among those who were prepared to respect such rules. The problem was that the trustees appealed to extra-ecclesiastical law; for example, in dealing with the catechist who was supposed to run the cathedral's Sunday school, they insisted on their property rights, which could be enforced by calling in the police. Help was thus to be sought only by bringing about a change in the relevant laws, but the bishops hesitated to take this step. That their prudence was justified was shown when the short-lived American Party (also known as the Know-Nothing Party) introduced a bill whose aim was to legally prescribe incorporation and the trustee system (Billington 1938, 39).

Not until the 1860s, after the high-water mark of nativism and after the Civil War, when the mood had shifted and it became clear that Catholic bishops were a political force to be reckoned with, were individual states' regulations concerning incorporation gradually changed. Then the situation changed completely. For instance, an 1863 New York state law stipulated that the committee of trustees in Catholic congregations consisted of the bishop, the vicar general, the parish priest, and two lay persons, the three ex-officio members retaining the right to vote out the two lay members (McNamara). Ultimately the struggle between the bishops and the trustees showed who was master of the house, in both the property rights sense and the figurative sense. However, this outcome simply shifted the problem to another level. For many non-Catholics it merely confirmed that "American freedoms" and Catholicism could not exist under the same roof, and even within the church a controversy over the compatibility of Catholicism with America was brewing.

However, it was a long journey from Marechal's description of the schisms he blamed on rebellious Irishmen to the controversies within the church at the end of the nineteenth century. It led through a whole century of American history, and yet in many areas similar developments emerged that could be described in a general and paradoxical way as the Americanization of America. Above all, not only a new style, but also a new representative type emerged that had been prepared by the European structures transplanted into the New World. As the United States expanded toward the west and, after the 1862 Homestead Act, the prairies were divided up into countless family farms, the farmer replaced the planter. In John Carroll's terms, a Pennsylvania-type society drove out a Maryland-type society. In 1835 Tocqueville had already noted that quite independently of the moral attitude toward slavery, even superficial observation showed clearly that the two sides of the Ohio River were different, and that only farms worked by people who owned them had a future. Long before Jefferson's Monticello and Washington's Mount Vernon were transformed into huge outdoor museums, as a social type and an economic style the Maryland type was already ready for a museum. However, this also meant that populist politicians replaced the gentleman politicians from Virginia, and just as the common man determined economics and politics, so he now also dominated culture. Here religious and political populism intersected, and neither ever tired of praising the competence and virtue of the common man.

American religion was no longer simply the continuation of European religious history under other circumstances. Instead of theologians trained at Harvard or Yale, the nearby Baptist preacher or the Methodist preacher on his horse was dominant. Instead of French professors of theology, Irish bishops resided in Catholic dioceses, seeing themselves as autocratic leaders and defenders of the Catholic common man. Protestantism and Catholicism did not in any way become interchangeable, but within their respective traditions they assumed an American form.

Since the American Revolution this Americanization of America has become evident in various domains and it has even become the theme of American culture, ranging from the literary representation of Americans as a type and the historical emphasis on America's uniqueness and unmistakable singularity to the aggressive rejection of anything allegedly un-American.

3. The Americanization of American Religion

A New Religious Style and New Religious Institutions

Despite the unreliability of the statistics available, there is general agreement that in the first half of the nineteenth century America underwent a religious upswing. Before the Revolution, religious affiliation was recorded, but in federal censuses made after 1790 this question could no longer be asked. It has been estimated that at the beginning of the nineteenth century only about 7 percent of the population belonged to a religious community, and that this proportion reached 15 percent by 1840 (Caplow 1983, 29).

Of course, we must remember that church membership was defined in various ways. For instance, in contrast to the New England Congregationalists from whom they had split off, Baptists maintained a very exclusive admissions policy and yet their numbers rose significantly. Thus Winthrop Hudson estimates that around 1830 "three times as many people" attended a given congregation's services as actually belonged it (Hudson 1981, 136 ff.). The increasing importance of religion is shown by the so-called "Second Awakening" that was centered in the West and reached its highpoint in the 1830s, and by the revival movements of the 1850s that occurred chiefly in the cities of the Northeast. We should also mention Unitarianism and Universalism, small but intellectually influential movements within contemporary American Protestantism that were to become important for understanding religion in America.

Frontier Religions: Methodists and Baptists

The Second Awakening followed the settlement of the Midwest and has been described as the latter's Christianization (Marty 1984, 169). The first reports on this new religious movement came in the 1820s, from Kentucky. Such reports became more numerous around 1830, and were concentrated in the area west of the Ohio River. In contrast, the revivals of the 1850s took place in the cities of the Northeast, and the descriptions of them given by observers and participants—for instance, the preacher Charles G. Finney—emphasize that they attracted a "refined" audience. Preachers like Finney or Lyman Beecher found the greatest response to their novel, emotionally rousing style in places where religious establishment disintegrated most slowly and structures long remained unchanged. In New England, for instance, Baptists had long offered an alternative, but in these dissenting congregations it was an alternative that consisted in a simple style and simple people. In the meantime, however, the social value of belonging to the formerly established church had diminished for the established strata of society, so that they too were now open to the individual, emotional religious style.

Although in New England structures had to be loosened up in order for this individual and enthusiastic religiousness to develop, farther to the west there were no structures, and religious communities that were adequately flexible or just beginning to develop their ecclesiastical organization profited most from this situation. For the most part, the Baptists still had no ordained ministers, relying instead on lay preachers who carried out their duties alongside their regular work. They needed only the Bible and a suitable place "down by the riverside." Thus camp meetings developed—a kind of popular evangelizing that lasted several days and drew interested people from the surrounding area.

In contrast, the Methodists, whose ecclesiastical structure was more firmly established, did not invite people to assemble by the river but rather sent their chief preacher from farm to farm, and these "circuit riders" became a general symbol of the Midwest. When the weather was particularly bad, people said that only the Methodist preacher was still on the road.

Thus both these frontier religions improvised in differing ways predetermined by their respective organizational structures. At the same time, however, they both resorted to practices suited to the situation in the recently settled regions. Moreover, they sought common solutions to some problems, and in so doing provided the impetus for a common national organizational structure that spanned the increasing diversity of American Protestantism.

One familiar institution that gained a new meaning among Baptist and Methodist congregations in the Midwest was the Sunday school, in which even the Methodists were willing to employ lay teachers. Sunday school thus became not only an early form of the local church community, but also laid the early groundwork for women to assume a prominent role.

The more important voluntary service and lay participation became, the more need there was not only for Bibles but also for supplementary instructional materials, and this led to the establishment of Protestant organizations at the national level. The American Bible Society (1816) raised funds to send Bibles and printing plates west, and the American Sunday School Union (1824) and the American Tract Society (1825) also provided money and religious tracts for distribution.

The situation in the Northeast looks at first quite different. There farmers did not preach to other farmers, but well-known figures such as Charles G. Finney and Lyman Beecher, who both came from long lines of preachers, addressed urban audiences in the new enthusiastic style. When Finney was in Boston during the winter of 1857–1858, an experimental "businessmen's prayer meeting" was held at noon in the Old South Church, and drew such a large attendance that it was held daily from then on (Gaustad 1982, 1: 403).

In 1854, Philipp Schaff, a theology professor from Berlin, described his impressions of America in a report addressed to his colleagues in Berlin. His report shows his reservations regarding an excessively narrow literalism and his opposition to the emotional and individualistic tendency of the revivals, but at the same time he is full of admiration. For him, the United States is clearly the most religious and Christian country in the world, and church membership cannot be separated from moral and social respect. In Berlin, he noted, forty poorly attended churches served 450,000 residents; in New York 250 always well-filled churches served 600,000 residents (Hudson 1981, 170 ff.).

Religious Individualism and Moral Consensus

Despite the differences between a Mississippi camp meeting and a businessmen's prayer meeting in downtown Boston, and between the theological starting points of the various religious communities, the style and content of preaching now became similar. The emphasis was not on doctrine but on religious experience; doctrine was subordinated to the immediate encounter with God and to the individual experience of conversion. Even Congregationalist preachers in New England participated in the new movement, playing down the Calvinistic tradition and stressing the element of individual choice that had not been prominent in this tradition. Even for them the individual stands in an immediate relation to God, and like the revival movements they emphasize the importance of self-observation and self-perfection. However, their sermons lack the populist flavor of Baptist sermons that present the common man, that is, both the preacher and his audience, as having the capability and the right to assume responsibility for self-perfection and for solving all problems. Nonetheless, there is general acceptance of the principle that every individual is chosen, and that it is possible not only to improve the individual but also to reform society. It is this belief in the perfectibility of the individual and of America, which had in the meantime become widely shared among Protestants, that explains the impact of Harriet Beecher Stowe, Lyman Beecher's daughter, and her book *Uncle Tom's Cabin*. Just as Protestant relief efforts became a common organizational bond, the duty to improve conditions acted as a moral and ideological bridge spanning the multiplicity of denominations. The crusade-like battle against social evils such as slavery, as well as alcohol and people identified with drink, developed into a common moral cause for American Protestants, who thus identified themselves with American culture.

The principle of individualization and a moralizing tendency, although not their emotional emphasis, linked the revivals with the opposite end of the theological spectrum, namely liberal Congregationalism, which had sought to replace revivalist fervor with rationalistic theology. This surprising rapprochement became possible because elitist liberals promoted a revision of Calvinistic doctrines, with results quite similar to those of the adaptive efforts made by the revivals. With the Universalism of the Boston Congregationalist preacher Charles Chauncy, this revision takes a path already discernible in Stoddard. In 1784 Chauncy published *The Salvation of all Men—The Grand Thing Aimed at in the Scheme of God*, in which he emphasized not God's justice, as in the Calvinist tradition, but rather God's goodness. It is unimaginable, Chauncy wrote, that God did not predetermine a universal salvation of man and the world. Why would He have created humanity if He did not intend "to make them finally happy"? This argument was subsequently elaborated by the Unitarians, whose name indicates that they deny the Trinity; however, their impact consisted rather in taking a further step in the transformation of Calvinism into a positive, edifying doctrine. Instead of original sin, they emphasized human reason and the ability to progress, and favored expressions such as "the brotherhood of men" and "the fatherhood of God," which already in the nineteenth century invited the jibe that they believed above all in "the neighborhood of Boston" (Hudson 1981, 154). This kind of joke was repeated by journalists in this century when New York Governor Nelson Rockefeller all too often spoke of the "brotherhood of men under the fatherhood of God." The corresponding acronym, "bomfog," was made into a verb, and "bomfogging" came to mean "spouting humanitarian clichés."

Both Unitarianism and Universalism evolved into distinct denominations, from which two influential groups of intellectuals emerged. On one hand, there was the Free Religious Association, which promoted a "religion of humanity" and was strongly influenced by French positivism (Lears 1981, 120 ff.). On the other, there were the so-called Transcendentalists, a loosely organized group whose name was simply meant to indicate that its members did not see things materialistically or naturalistically. Among the Transcendentalists were Ralph Waldo Emerson, who had begun as a Unitarian minister in Boston, and initially Orestes Brownson as well.

4. Catholicism as an Immigrant Church

At first glance, American Catholicism looks quite different. It seemed concerned not with developing new institutions adapted to the circumstances, but rather with maintaining the old, familiar, unalterable structures. The controversy over the status of trustees was an example of this, and many people's prejudices concerning Catholicism and "American freedoms" were confirmed by the newsworthy spectacle of bishops and laity calling in the police to enforce their right to enter churches. In fact, a new kind of bishops now emerged whose image corresponded quite precisely to the task of establishing Catholic ecclesiastical structures. That is, they were well-suited to construct the ecclesiastical organization, to administer it, and even to defend it intellectually if need be; sometimes administrative and political talent predominated, sometimes a gift for quick-witted apologetics, but both were obviously important for advancing an episcopal career. These self-assured bishops aware of their power relied on a church that was growing and increasingly shaped by immigrants, and whose members were for the time being largely immune to congregationalism and other expressions of the American conception of freedom. One of the two antidotes against an Americanized conception of religion and church was produced by the hostile way in which contemporary American Protestantism reacted to the mass immigration of Catholics. Anti-Catholicism became the major common point characterizing an otherwise unmistakably diverse Protestantism. Conversely, Catholics developed a sense of being a minority that had to overcome resistance to win a place in America. This also meant that the bishops were expected to provide strong leadership and dignified representation for a group demanding recognition.

Ethnic Parishes as Sanctuaries and Agents of Americanization

A second antidote against an Americanized conception of religion arose from the later, nostalgically transfigured identification with a native national culture, including a traditional church affiliation. People from the Palatinate and from Sicily, who often had emigrated before the ideology of nationalism had swept over Europe, now realized for the first time that the language they spoke made them Germans or Italians. The hostile environment these immigrants encountered made it clear to them that the un-American religion they had brought with them was also part of their identity, no matter how weak their church affiliations in the old world might have been. Thus on one hand immigrants were inclined to see the church as the representative of their claims and hopes, and to accept the authority of the Irish bishops. On the other hand, however, they expected that the language and customs of the old country would be preserved in their parishes.

John England, John Hughes, John Martin Henni, and John Martin Spalding: A New Kind of Bishop

Nonetheless, institutions such as ethnic parishes and separate schools ultimately proved to be not merely sanctuaries, but also at least equally effective instruments of integration and gradual Americanization. The characteristic marks of an American religious style became increasingly evident; both Roman observers and some American bishops began to ask how American American Catholicism could become and still remain Catholic, and how American it had to be in order to survive in America. From these questions emerged the conflicts of the decades following the Civil War. At first, however, the issue was how to incorporate the growing influx of immigrants while preserving unity inside the church and seeking equality before the law outside it. Bishops John England and John Hughes were more determined and better prepared to accomplish these tasks than were their French predecessors, whose time, as even Marechal agreed, was now over. England and Hughes are forerunners of a new kind of bishops who after the Civil War were increasingly recruited from a network of American institutions. This growing institutionalization of a separate career path began when individual bishops, who often still came from the generation of the French bishops, sponsored a young man by sending him to the European seminary they themselves had attended. However, American bishops soon established their own institutions in Washington and Rome, through which more and more future American bishops passed.

John England, who had grown up in Ireland and was ordained there, came to the United States in 1820 as the first bishop of Charleston. He was thirty-four when he arrived, and he engaged tirelessly in activities reaching far beyond his diocese. He sought to advance the establishment of unified ecclesiastical structures to counter anti-Catholic prejudices by means of an intensive public relations campaign. Thus he introduced a diocesan constitution that left the bishop's jurisdiction untouched but allowed the laity to be represented. However, this did not resolve the trustee problem.

The first Conferences of Bishops were convened at John England's urging, but for the time being they remained limited to the ecclesiastical Province of Baltimore. Not until 1852, after England's death, did the first national Conference of Bishops take place. Such common assemblies had seemed to him important not only for unifying pastoral care but also for the church's relations with the surrounding society. He founded the first Catholic newspaper and took every opportunity to address non-Catholic audiences such as Boston businessmen and New York journalists, commenting ironically on anti-Catholic propaganda (Gaustad 1982, 1: 451 ff.). He died in 1842, the year in which the less subtle John Hughes became bishop of New York.

Hughes, who had also been born in Ireland, came to Pennsylvania when he was twenty. There he applied for admission to the Sulpicians' St. Mary's Seminary in Emmitsburg. At first there was no room for him, and so he worked as a gardener until the rector, Father John Dubois (later bishop of New York) hired him as the seminary's gardener. Finally, he was admitted as a student, and after completing his studies, ordained in Philadelphia in 1826. He served as a pastor there for the next twelve years, but did not limit himself to his pastoral duties alone. He conducted a public debate with a Presbyterian pastor who maintained that Catholicism was an obstacle to religious and civil liberties, and he founded a newspaper that was later taken over by the diocese. However, what was particularly characteristic of his style and his taste for provocation is the way in which he exposed *The Protestant*, a weekly newspaper published by Protestant ministers in New York that specialized in anti-Catholic agitation and publicized the most abstruse conspiracy theories and reports of scandals. Hughes dreamed up some particularly crude revelations and sent them, under a pseudonym, to the publishers, who fell into the trap and printed everything. Later he led the fight for Catholic schools in New York and at the height of nativist excesses displayed his well-known fearlessness.

In 1842 Hughes succeeded as bishop of New York the rector of his old seminary, Dubois, and shortly afterward two other bishops were appointed who are less well known but in many respects worthy of attention. In 1843, John Martin Henni (1805–1881) became the first bishop of Wisconsin, with his see in Milwaukee, and in 1850 John Martin Spalding succeeded his sponsor Benedict Flaget, another Sulpician, as bishop of Kentucky. The lives of these two bishops have much in common—similar tendencies and styles—and yet, without being directly involved and in an entirely unavoidable way, both became trailblazers for the next generation's conflicts and promoters of some of the leading figures in these controversies.

Henni, born Johann Martin Henni in Switzerland in 1805, began his studies in Lucerne and Rome, but completed his training in Bardstown, Kentucky. In 1829, at the St. Thomas Seminary in Bardstown, he was ordained to serve in the diocese of Ohio. It is not clear whether the young man already found the situation in Switzerland not promising for a Catholic theologian with intellectual interests, or during his studies in Rome had been enlisted to care for the German-speaking immigrants in Ohio.

John Martin Spalding, who was born in Kentucky in 1810, followed the opposite path. He came from an old Maryland Catholic family that had moved on to Kentucky twenty years earlier. Forty years later he had so many relatives in Kentucky that questions were raised regarding his appointment as bishop—and these become comprehensible when one reads that he grew up with twenty sisters. He first attended St. Thomas Seminary and was then sent by Bishop Flaget to Rome, where he studied at the college of *De Propaganda Fide*. He was the first American to receive a degree in theology there. When he returned home, he was ordained a priest in the diocese of Kentucky in 1834, five years after the ordination of Henni, who was five years older than he.

As young priests, both men made a name for themselves through publications, although they had already assumed wide-ranging pastoral and administrative tasks in their respective dioceses. Henni first spent five years as a supply priest, making the circuit of the German Catholics in Ohio and earning the name of "Apostle of the Germans." In 1834 he became vicar general of the diocese, and yet found time to write a history of the Catholic Church in America, which was published in Munich in 1836 under the title *Ein Blick ins Tal des Ohio* ("A View of the Ohio Valley"). He also founded the newspaper *Der Wahrheitsfreund* ("The Friend of Truth"), whose direction he determined for many years through his own contributions to it. The position of the *Wahrheitsfreund* reflected the difficult situation of a German-speaking Catholic liberal. Unlike Carroll, England, or Spalding, Henni and the *Wahrheitsfreund* were unequivocally opposed to slavery and prohibition, as well as to Prussian or any other autocratic regime "that makes foot fit the shoe instead of the other way around." On the other hand, Henni later fought the immigrants who were among the German revolutionaries of 1848 and who confused liberalism with anti-religious propaganda. In any case, the *Wahrheitsfreund* played a major role in the so-called German triangle of American Catholicism, which had emerged since the 1830s in the area between Cincinnati, St. Louis, and Milwaukee, and it continued to be important even after the Civil War.

Meanwhile, after a time as president of a college in Bardstown, Spalding worked in various wide-ranging missions of the Kentucky diocese, and in 1844 became its vicar general. Before taking up the latter post, he wrote a *History of the Great Reformation in Germany and Switzerland,* which first appeared in 1844 and was later revised and reprinted as *The History of the Protestant Reformation.* In addition, like Hughes and Henni he founded a newspaper; its name, *The Catholic Advocate,* made it particularly clear that in Kentucky, if not in the relatively peaceful German triangle, Irish immigrants encountered "native Americans."

Both vicars general eventually became bishops, Spalding in the diocese of Kentucky, whose see had been moved to Louisville, and Henni in the newly established diocese of Wisconsin, with its see in Milwaukee. Both constructed the ecclesiastical structures for Irish and German immigrants on what was then the western frontier of America, emphasized education, and, with the help of religious orders they encouraged to settle in their dioceses, founded schools and colleges. But in certain decisive respects they also set quite different courses, since they were reacting to differing conditions in the areas for which they were responsible.

The difficulties Henni had to resolve turned around the problem of language. On one hand, he understood that the new immigrants would gain a footing in America only to the extent that they truly mastered English, and this led him to set up English courses for adults. On the other hand, he greatly feared that immigrants would lose their faith along with their native language. And so Henni himself wrote a catechism in German for children. He saw clearly that it would not be possible to maintain an independent German subculture, and pinned his hopes on bilingualism.

As bishop and later archbishop of Milwaukee, he founded not only the *Seebote* but also the *Catholic Citizen;* ultimately, the German language was less important to him than the mutual complementarity of Catholic institutions. Just as he had done when he was vicar general in Cincinnati, in Milwaukee he saw to it that Catholic schools were established in all parishes, making exceptions only for poor rural parishes. Separate schools were established even in the urban parishes of Cincinnati and Milwaukee, where Catholics were in the majority and thus in theory could have controlled the public school boards. For the obedient faithful, this meant that they could send their children to their own schools but had to support these private Catholic schools as well as the public schools.

Henni founded the St. Francis Seminary where a new generation of priests was educated, and not only for his own diocese; in 1869, thirty-six graduates from twelve dioceses were ordained there. He promoted the founding of colleges and universities, chiefly by making land available or by helping to buy it, but otherwise did not intervene in any way. Thus the Jesuits founded Marquette University, and Swiss Benedictines from Einsiedeln, who had earlier founded the abbey of St. Meinrad in Indiana, established themselves in Greenbay, which was later renamed Collegeville (White 1989, 116).

Spalding did not invest as much energy in founding new institutions, for he had found some already established, including the seminary he and Henni had attended. In addition, in 1863 he was appointed Archbishop of Baltimore, where he had an opportunity to further emphasize his priorities, one of which was certainly not bilingualism. Spalding and the bishops of the next generation he promoted directly or indirectly and who were all of Irish descent, were convinced that the church must shed any French or German accent as quickly as possible—and initially they also believed that other Americans no longer distinguished between an Irish and an American accent. Like John England, Spalding considered it important to create central institutions that could ease and accelerate the Americanization of the church. Thus while still in Louisville he had taken part in the preparations for the first national Conference of Bishops convened in 1852, and when he arrived in Baltimore he immediately began laying the groundwork for a second American Conference of Bishops, which took place under his direction in 1866.

Similarly, Spalding helped create a second level of education for the next generation of priests that slowly emerged from the institutions which American bishops had established in Europe and America and which they maintained in common. Spalding was deeply involved in discussions regarding an American college in Rome, and together with Peter Lefevere, the Belgian bishop of Detroit, he founded in 1857 an American College in Louvain. This college in Belgium came into being through a Roman detour. Lefevere and Spalding had asked the Jesuit Peter Kindekens to investigate the possibility of establishing

an American college in Rome. In the Eternal City, which had been occupied by the French since 1854, Kindekens found it impossible to
achieve anything. On his way back Kindekens, who was Belgian and
had gone to school in Louvain, visited his alma mater, where he found
people interested in establishing an American college. And so from
1857 on young American clergymen were sent to Belgium. When the
college's fiftieth anniversary was celebrated in 1907, seven hundred
Americans had completed their studies there. The American College,
founded in 1859, was no doubt of still greater significance (Ellis 1969,
1: 315).

One of the first students sent to Louvain was John Lancaster Spalding, a nephew of the co-founder, and later on, as the first bishop of
Peoria, Illinois, this younger Spalding pushed hard for the establishment of a university run in common by the American bishops. After
lengthy negotiations, this university was eventually founded in 1887
as The Catholic University of America. From the 1860s on, the career of an American bishop usually began when his bishop sent him to
Rome or Louvain to continue his education and take a degree, ideally
in canon law. Later on, it was also possible to go to the Catholic University of America in Washington; this was sometimes an alternative
to further study in Europe, and sometimes combined with it. Thus a
"main road" for recruiting bishops developed, alongside which for a
short time there was still a German "secondary road." Henni, who
came to America from Rome just as Spalding was leaving for Europe,
was guided by the logic of his own recruiting efforts to take a path that
led not to Rome but to Munich and Vienna. The Ludwigs-Missions-
verein (King Ludwig Missionary Association) in Munich, which with
the help of the Royal House of Bavaria sought to provide pastoral care
for German-speaking Catholics in America, increasingly focused its
aid on Henni's diocese. The missionary association supplied whole
groups of religious who were prepared to establish settlements in Wisconsin and in the neighboring prairie states, and it repeatedly provided
funds and helped send young priests. One of these Bavarian priests was
Michael Heiss, who was ordained in 1840 in Eichstadt. From 1844 on,
he worked as Henni's secretary; starting in 1844 he directed the newly
founded seminary. In 1878 he was appointed the first bishop of the
diocese of La Crosse. Henni finally managed to have Heiss named as

his coadjutor with the right to succeed him, and in 1881 Heiss took over as archbishop of Milwaukee. In this capacity Heiss became leader of the so-called German bishops' group.

In Baltimore, the young priest James Gibbons had been working as Archbishop Spalding's secretary since 1875. Thanks to Spalding's sponsorship, Gibbons' career advanced with unusual speed, and in 1877 he became archbishop of Baltimore. He represented American Catholicism for more than four decades, and during his exceptionally long tenure millions of European immigrants flowed into America.

The Three Waves of Immigration

Since 1790, the United States has conducted a census every ten years. From 1820 on, port authorities noted down the country that provided the incoming passengers' identification papers, so that immigration statistics were produced, although they were still inexact in many ways. In any case, they did not show the relatively small numbers of immigrants who came by way of land, they did not distinguish between travelers and immigrants, and they inferred ethnic affiliation from nationality alone, so that a Macedonian could become a Turk and a Pole a Russian.

Even in the 1860s, when transatlantic steamship lines came into being, the port authorities' statistics were refined only insofar as they began to distinguish among travelers, immigrants, and emigrants. Here we need only note the magnitude of the immigration, its role in the growth of the general population, and the date at which it peaked. Table 2 summarizes the official figures on which Hertling and other authors have relied (Hertling 1954, 158 ff.).

This table shows that in the second half of the nineteenth century expansion to the west was followed by an increase in population resulting primarily from immigration. Between 1850 and 1900 the population more than tripled, growing from 23 million to 76 million. The greatest increases took place after the turn of the century, and massive immigration continued during World War I and after it, until restrictive immigration laws went into effect in 1921 and 1924.

If we consider the relative magnitude of the immigration, that is, the relationship between the current population and the newcomers, we find a curve with three peaks in the 1850s, the 1880s, and at the

Table 2
A Hundred Years of Immigration

General Population		Immigration	
1820	9,638,000	1821–1830	140,000
1830	12,866,000	1831–1840	600,000
1840	17,069,000	1841–1850	1,700,000
1850	23,192,000	1851–1860	2,600,000
1860	31,443,000	1861–1870	2,300,000
1870	39,818,000	1871–1880	2,800,000
1880	50,156,000	1881–1890	5,200,000
1890	62,948,000	1891–1900	3,900,000
1900	75,995,000	1901–1910	8,600,000
1910	91,972,000	1911–1920	1,900,000

Source: Hertling 1954, 158 ff.; Moltmann and Lindig 1985, 90.

beginning of the twentieth century. In these peak periods the number of immigrants rises to more than 10 percent of the total population at the beginning of the corresponding decade.

The first wave, which peaked around 1850, consisted primarily of immigrants from northern Europe. A significant proportion of the English and French immigrants went to Canada. Irish and German immigrants constituted the largest groups entering the United States, and the proportion of immigrants from Ireland doubled after the Irish famine of 1847. It may be assumed that German immigrants were less impoverished and better trained as farmers or craftsmen, and thus more prepared to move west. The Irish, in contrast, were for the most part forced to remain in the eastern states where they might be able to work for wages. In time another characteristic of life in the city appeared: only there could the numerical size of a group of people be turned into employment opportunities, if they knew how to make use of the instrument of political organization. Very soon, almost all the thousands of New York policemen were Irishmen.

The second wave saw an increase in German immigration at the end of the 1870s and the beginning of the 1880s. Most of these German immigrants settled in the already existing German triangle, that is, in cities such as Cincinnati, Toledo, and Milwaukee. However, they also moved into the rural areas around this triangle, and their farms extended it to the south along the Mississippi past St. Louis and to the north beyond Minnesota and into the prairie states.

The third wave, some 20 million strong, came in between the turn of the century and the enactment of legal restrictions on immigration, primarily from southern and eastern Europe. They came at a time when settlement of the Midwest and the West was complete, but industrialization was still continuing. Even more than the Irish, these impoverished Europeans were therefore concentrated in the cities of the Northeast and the Atlantic seaboard. Jews from Galicia and Russia began working in New York's textile factories, Slovaks in Pittsburgh's steel industry or Detroit's automobile industry, and Poles in Chicago's wagon factories.

For the Catholic Church, these hundred years of immigration meant huge growth in both absolute and relative terms, because the proportion of Catholics among the immigrants was significantly greater than among the American population in 1820, although here again the lack of precise figures is a problem. In 1790, when the first census showed a population of four million, John Carroll estimated his flock at 35,000 people, which corresponds to a proportion of less than 1 percent. When in 1853 Archbishop Gaetano Bedini, at the Vatican's request, undertook a journey through America, American bishops mentioned a figure of about two million, which already amounted to about a tenth of the total population of the country at the time. Hennesey believes that by the beginning of the Civil War the number of Catholics had risen to three million, a third of whom had come in during the preceding decade (Hennesey 1981, 159).

In trying to determine the ethnic composition of this group of three million Catholics we are forced to rely on estimates, because neither immigration officials nor census-takers asked about religious affiliation. Once again we have only approximations inferred from nationality, and as a result authors such as Fitzpatrick (Fitzpatrick 1987) and Shaughnessy (Shaughnessy 1925) somewhat prematurely conclude that all the Irishmen were Catholics.

Nonetheless, it can be assumed that the Irish, who were in any case the largest group of immigrants, were about 85 percent Catholic. In contrast, among German immigrants the proportion was probably less than 40 percent, and German immigration did not peak until the end of the century.

The Irish thus long determined the development and image of American Catholicism. They attracted even more attention than their already considerable numbers deserved, and there were two main reasons for this. One was that the English had unintentionally prepared the Irish by providing them with the English language as well as political consciousness. Another reason was that the Irish settled primarily in the cities of the Northeast, where they competed economically with the already established underclass and became a subject of discussion for journalists representing this underclass.

After his journey, even Archbishop Bedini reported that the only Catholics the average American had ever met were poor, uneducated Irish. Several decades had passed since Catholics had profited from John Carroll's reputation as a polished gentleman, and it is conceivable that the Irish gave American Catholicism a plebeian cast. But even in Carroll's time a general anti-Catholic feeling was discernible in the turbulent history of Maryland, and this can surely not be blamed on the Irish.

5. Cultural War in America

Nativism and Anti-Catholic Cultural Propaganda in the Decades preceding the Civil War

Between 1834 and 1855, this general anti-Catholic feeling erupted in the form of violent riots in Boston, Philadelphia, and Louisville. An already Americanized Protestant mob was surely involved in these riots, and it may have been angered by the growing Irish Catholic proletariat. However, behind these events organizational structures were discernible, and without them the attacks would hardly have been so concentrated.

A network of anti-Catholic propaganda organizations was involved that has been described in Ray Allen Billington's *The Protestant Crusade, 1800–1860.* In addition, however, political organizations connected with nativism also emerged at this time. Nativism is not inherently anti-Catholic, but by combining with anti-Catholicism it became a political force in the 1850s. The foundation of this propaganda network consisted in weeklies such as *The New York Observer* and *The Recorder*, which specialized in scandalous stories about life behind monastery and convent walls. They throve on the same material that Maria Monk's book and Rachel McCrindell's novels (for example, *School Girl in France*) successfully exploited. Monk's *Awful Disclosures of Maria Monk* first appeared in 1836, going through twenty reprintings and selling more than 300,000 copies in all. It was produced, as was soon revealed, by a young woman who had earlier escaped, with the help of a young man, from a home for delinquent youth run by nuns. In her book she represented herself as a novice at a convent in Montreal. She claimed that she and other nuns were forced to have sexual intercourse with priests. Because she wanted to keep her child from being killed immediately after it was baptized and buried in the cellar, as was common in the convent, her only option was to escape. A group of ministers sent Maria Monk on a lecture tour to tell her story to Protestant church congregations (Cogley 1986, 38).

This campaign took on a somewhat more sophisticated, more political quality in *The Protestant*, the rag Bishop Hughes had unmasked with his fictitious story. It had been founded in New York in 1830 by a group of Protestant ministers, and although it did not forego stories of Maria Monk's kind, its main goal was expressed in its masthead by the subtitle "Expositor of Popery." It was concerned with alleged assaults on American freedoms and American institutions, and its concern could be shared by many people who had a reputation to preserve.

Samuel F. B. Morse, the inventor of the telegraph and the son of the Congregational minister Yedidiah Morse ("the father of American geography"), was also the inventor of the notion that there was a foreign conspiracy against American democracy. In his 1834 book—whose title, *A Foreign Conspiracy Against the Liberties of the United States*, virtually exhausts its content—he describes a plot directed by the Vatican and the Habsburgs, with the intention of using Catholic immigrants to infiltrate American democracy.

Along the same line are the Protestant associations founded to organize and support the corresponding publications. In 1840 the American Society to Promote the Principles of the Protestant Reformation was established, which had as its goal to disseminate information concerning the differences between "protestantism and popery," and to "convert the papists to christianity." In addition, lecture series were to be organized and tracts distributed (Gaustad 1982, 1: 464). Two years later a hundred Protestant ministers founded the Protestant Association. They declared that papism undermined civil and religious liberties and therefore a concerted effort had to be made against it. Members were not only to alert their congregations to the danger, but also to appeal to the public at large and promote the dissemination of anti-Catholic books (Billington 1938, 183).

Cultural war waged through propaganda of this kind had thus long ceased to be limited to a few fanatical outsiders; in the course of the 1820s and 1830s it had clearly become respectable. Lyman Beecher adopted Samuel Morse's conspiracy theories and in his sermons he warned that the United States could be pushed out of the Mississippi valley. Horace Bushnell, the leader of the liberal school of theology, considered the greatest peril to be "barbarism," that is, the influx of foreigners, but the papist peril was not far behind (Hennesey 1981, 119 ff.).

All this came to a head, however, only when religious nativism joined forces with political nativism. The combination was in no way necessary, as we have said. Before 1841 attempts were made even in New Orleans to found a nativistic American Party that was to advocate legal limitations on immigration. This group separated from the corresponding organizations in New York and Philadelphia when their anti-Catholic orientation became apparent (Uthmann 1992).

In 1842, the periodical *The Native American*, which was to give the movement its name, appeared on the East Coast. In 1843, the American Republican Party was formed, and won a majority in the elections held the next year in the state of New York. The party's chief demand was that government offices be held only by native-born Americans. In addition, the King James Version of the Bible was to be used in public schools, despite the protests of Catholics and their bishop Hughes (Billington 1938, 38).

The Know-Nothing Party

The success of the American Republican Party remained limited to New York, the neighboring states of New England, and New Jersey, but in the following years a secret patriotic association was established that excited great public interest precisely because of its allegedly secret nature. This "Order of the Star-Spangled Banner" was not supposed to get involved in politics directly, but rather to gain influence within existing parties in order to work for nativist and anti-Catholic candidates. The association's statutes specify that the Order's goal is to oppose the Church of Rome's underhanded political activities and other threats to republican institutions, and to ensure that public offices come into the hands only of "native born protestant citizens." Whereas in its public statements the New York party had still limited itself to the specifically nativist demand that only second-generation immigrants be considered eligible for election to public office, a denominational criterion like that in the old "anti-popery laws" of the seventeenth century was now invoked. If they were asked about the goals of their organization, members were to explain that they knew nothing about them. Thus they became famous and popular under the name of "Know-Nothings" rather than under the pompous name of their Order. In the 1850s there were brands of matches and varieties of tea labeled "Know-Nothing," and even ships were christened with this name. When the American Party was eventually founded at the national level in 1854 it was known not by its official name, but as the "Know-Nothing Party," like the secret order that preceded it.

Lincoln soon sealed the party's doom when he changed the political priorities. By breaking up the existing party system through their success at the polls, the nativists unintentionally helped Lincoln construct his Republican Party. Up to this point, however, anti-Catholic propaganda combined with nativist party politics resulted in a turbulent period that continued to affect American Catholics for many generations.

Street Fighting in Boston, Philadelphia, and Louisville

In the young republic, which still saw itself as threatened by reactionary forces all over the world, public opinion found reason for concern in all sorts of events. As had already happened in relation to the trustee problem, controversies involving bishops and school officials provided ongoing publicity that left the impression that the Catholic Church was in fact incompatible with the American political system. In New York, where Bishop Hughes was always good for a news story, almost all the city's school budget was allocated to a "Public School Society" whose name did not suffice to convince the bishop that this society represented everyone's interests. The fact that in the schools this society supported with public funds, the Bible was the basis for a kind of instruction described as "nonsectarian" did not make the whole operation any more palatable to the bishop and many Catholic parents. But in order to understand that "nonsectarian" still did not mean nondenominational, but rather the lowest common denominator of Protestantism, or to understand how Christians could have seen a problem in instruction based on the Bible, experience with other kinds of religious instruction would have been necessary. In any case, Catholic positions had little standing in public opinion. But that was not enough; at the same time xenophobia was also growing. Thus in the 1830s there were ever more frequent reports of connections between immigration, the rising cost of caring for the poor, and increasing crime (Billington 1938, 35).

At this time it didn't take much to provoke a serious incident. A series of such incidents began in Charlestown, now part of Boston, in 1834, when fifty men stormed an Ursuline convent and set it and its school afire. A large crowd cheered as the buildings burned, but the nuns and their pupils managed to escape just in time. The disturbances in Philadelphia ten years later had graver consequences. In May 1844 the newly founded American Republican Party, which wanted to make itself known outside New York, held a meeting in Kensington, an industrial and residential neighborhood where Irish immigrants lived, and succeeded in provoking a brawl. The nativists thereupon announced that a few days later they would hold another meeting at the same place, and invited the public to support them. They got the support they asked for, and the second meeting ended in even more serious street fighting, in which one person was killed. The dead man and some of the injured became known as the "Protestant martyrs of Kensington." Soon afterward a silent march was organized to honor the memory of the martyrs. When it was learned that the militia was prepared to protect the Catholic churches from attacks, and that for this purpose weapons from the city armory had already been moved into one of the churches, several of the marchers tried to storm it. This attempt resulted in street fighting that lasted all night and left fourteen dead.

The bishop of Philadelphia, Francis Kenrick, did what he might have been expected to do. He pleaded for peace, urged everyone to obey the authorities, and tried to mediate. In New York, Bishop Hughes, who was forced to assume that the violence would not remain limited to Philadelphia, reacted in his own way. He demanded a meeting with Mayor Morris and with Harper, the mayor's designated successor, who had been elected with the help of the nativists. Alluding to the conflagration that had accompanied Napoleon's occupation of Moscow thirty-two years earlier, Hughes told the two men that if one of the Catholic churches in New York were set afire, New York would become another Moscow. Finally, he saw to it that the churches were guarded by volunteers and warned the latter not to allow themselves to be provoked and not to provoke anyone. In the end, the hot summer in Philadelphia was not replicated in New York, and Hughes could interpret this as a further confirmation of his bold way of handling matters.

The Know-Nothing Party's influence was at its peak in the 1850s, when it had more than seventy representatives in Congress, and yet it was once again involved in an outbreak of violence. A Know-Nothing was elected mayor of Louisville, and when he organized the city's next election he tried to exclude immigrants. This resulted in the riots known as "bloody Monday," in which more than twenty people reportedly died. Like his colleague Kenrick, all Bishop Spalding could do was call for moderation and wait until the storm blew over (Cogley 1986, 37 ff.; Marty 1984, 274 ff.; Cohalan).

6. North and South, White and Black, Progressive and Conservative

The whole nightmare ended with the Civil War. Although as a hereditary illness of American culture, anti-Catholicism was still far from overcome, there were no more openly anti-Catholic campaigns that were organized by Protestant ministers and lent respectability by prominent Protestant theologians' endorsement. Moreover, there were no longer any publicly active political organizations that combined religious and political nativism. The latter were once again taken up by secret societies; the secret Order of the Know-Nothings was succeeded toward the end of the century by the American Protective Association, and in the 1920s by the Ku Klux Klan. There were, however, two enduring consequences. One was that nativism strengthened Catholics' mistrust and sense of being special, their tendency to rely on members of their own faith and on their own institutions; in short, their socalled ghetto mentality—which was, to be sure, also one of the sources of American Catholicism's great achievements. A second consequence was that from these conflicts there emerged a problem in American political culture that remains unresolved today. The cultural war that

since the end of the Civil War had been relegated to the gray zone of secret societies, still repeatedly crops up in secondary arenas and proxy
battles. This was true for Prohibition (which was not only supposed
to save the American family's morality but also to counter what was
seen as Irish and German culture) and especially for educational policy. The public schools increasingly became a symbol of the American
institutions that had to be protected from foreign influence. For example, in the 1920s the Ku Klux Klan tried to make a controversy over
educational policy in Oregon into a national issue, and to re-align anti-
Catholic feelings politically by claiming to defend the public school
system. In any event, in American politics even today a division of
labor between private and public schools cannot be discussed without
ulterior motives and historical memories.

Lines of Demarcation in the Religious
Landscape after the Civil War

With the North's victory not only the political but also the religious
landscape was altered, and American Protestantism was particularly
affected by this change. It is true that the culture retained a certain
Protestant coloring, insofar as even non-religious language was determined by Biblical images and by the Calvinistic rhetoric of original sin, conversion, and testing. However, since anti-slavery and anti-
popery, the negative common ground of the 1840s and 1850s, were no
longer the primary issues, the contradictions that were internal to
Protestantism and marked all its denominations became increasingly
clear. Thus while the emotional style of the revivals was still predomi-
nant, it by no means always met with unqualified approval, and this
depended on more than taste or temperament. Differing kinds of evangelizing were connected with differing modes of theological thought
and argument. An enthusiastic, emotional style was bound up with a
simple, narrow theology based on the Bible; conversely, criticism of
the revivals was the expression of a rationalistic, "liberal" theology. In
these conflicts a conservative, individualistic camp and a progressive-
political camp were already becoming discernible. After the Civil War
two further distinctions emerged. Since blacks withdrew from the
churches controlled by whites and founded their own congregations,
there developed, particularly among Baptists and Methodists in the
South, separate black and white churches co-existing alongside each

other. This made it easier for whites in the Protestant churches of the South to leave everything else as it had been, and to see themselves as defeated but not conquered. In the North, however, the enmities that had developed were still strong. Thus separate northern and southern branches of the same denomination were often formed. In any case, three lines of demarcation now cut through the multiplicity of Protestant denominations: conservative vs. progressive, black vs. white, North vs. South.

For the Catholic Church, the Civil War did not represent this kind of turning point. The attitude of Catholic bishops, like that of Protestant colleagues, in large part depended on whether they came from the North or the South, and in particular, their support for a war to maintain the Union was considerably stronger than their generally negative but somewhat hesitant judgment concerning slavery. Apart from the fact that the structure of the Catholic Church did not allow any of its parts to become independent, differing political sympathies had left behind a few touchy issues but no deep contradictions.

Thus the Catholic Church found it easier to preserve its unity, although there was a price to be paid. The centers of American Catholicism already lay primarily in the North and in the cities, to a greater extent than the average distribution of Catholics would have indicated. This meant that African-Americans, who still lived almost exclusively in the South, had less contact with the Catholic Church. But even where there was such contact, as in Maryland and Louisiana, the Catholic Church offered neither the degree of autonomy nor the corresponding freedom of liturgical forms that were necessary to make it attractive to African-Americans. In England a new order, the St. Joseph's Society, had been formed, and at Archbishop Spalding's request the Josephites, as they were called, also became involved in pastoral care for blacks in America. Hennesey reports that in 1888 the first black American priest was ordained for work among blacks, in following studies in Rome. However, most bishops probably thought the church already had its hands full in trying to cope with the differences among European immigrants. In any event, the Catholic Church never became a church for African-Americans. It remained for a long time shielded from many developments in American culture because its marked institutional form set it apart, and also because as a community of different immigrant groups it was chiefly concerned with its own internal problems. Nonetheless, the two antidotes against Americanization mentioned earlier eventually lost their power. Militant anti-Catholicism was no longer an organized political force, and immigrants' attachment to old world culture was transformed, in their children at least, into a desire to bring their own heritage into harmony with an American future.

The debate over Catholicism's compatibility with America thus necessarily followed from the inner development of American Catholicism, but it could not take place so long as a hostile majority of Americans considered the two traditions irreconcilable. However, when external pressure diminished, debates internal to the church could be conducted openly, and even the suspicion that had long been directed against Catholics in general—namely, that they were not really American—became a topic in discussions within the church. This did not mean that public confrontations had ended and been replaced by internal discussions; rather, an entirely new climate prevailed, since the same theme was discussed on several levels at once, and the previously unquestioned identification of Protestantism with America was challenged for the first time.

3

THE STRUGGLE TO DEFINE
CATHOLICISM'S OWN POSITION
The "Great Crisis"
1865–1908

THE CATHOLIC CHURCH had to learn to explain itself both outwardly and inwardly, that is, to explain itself both to immigrants coming from very different religious backgrounds and to a general public shaped by Protestantism. Suddenly it seemed possible not only to challenge the identification of Protestantism with America but even to present the association of Catholicism with American democracy as the cultural formula of the future. This way of thinking was of course by no means typical, and took by surprise both American cultural understanding and the Catholic Church itself. Yet it is worth noting that such ideas came out of intellectual discussions in New England, and were thus taken seriously. In any case the new cultural climate was increasingly reflected in a different kind of Catholic self-image, in which Catholicism and America, the church and democracy, were seen as compatible and in mutual need of complementation.

Thus there emerged not only a message addressed both inwardly and outwardly, but also a new criterion of selection. Leaders of the church were to be those who could communicate its message most effectively. Intellectual critics such as Orestes Brownson and Isaac Hecker, who were masters of the new apologetics, became representatives of the original American Catholicism that first developed in the second half of the nineteenth century, and at first they seemed alien elements within the church. But we must also count among such men the second generation of Irish bishops, who undertook to Americanize the church, and especially the later Cardinal Gibbons, whose explanation of Catholicism (*The Faith of our Fathers*, 1876) sold two million copies in his lifetime.

1. Apologetics and Precursors of the Conflict: "Becoming a Catholic and Remaining an American"

Brownson, Hecker, and the Paulists

Born in Vermont in 1803, Orestes Brownson joined the Presbyterian Church when he was nineteen, and left it two years later because of its doctrine of predestination. He then joined the Universalists, because they proclaimed "the salvation of all mankind." Two years later he had already become a Universalist minister and was bringing out the periodical *The Gospel Advocate*. Because of his increasingly liberal views on theological issues, he gave up his office and henceforth worked only as a free-lance writer. He took part in founding a short-lived political party, the "Workingmen's Party," and after a time returned to pastoral work, this time as a Unitarian minister, serving for two years congregations in New Hampshire and Massachusetts. In 1836 he established his own church in Boston, the Society for Christian Unity and Progress. In 1838 he founded the *Boston Quarterly Review*, which for a short time he combined with the *New Yorker Democratic Review*, only to later resume publishing it in Boston as *Brownson's Quarterly Review*.

In these Boston years he knew everyone connected with so-called New England liberalism—the Thoreau family, Emerson and the Transcendentalists, Channing and Bancroft. He was also acquainted with the Transcendentalists' Brook Farm, which evolved from an intellectual commune into an elite boarding school. Thus it came as a surprise when in 1844 he became a Catholic, and the *Dictionary of American Biography* suggests that his conversion produced a shock similar to that produced by Newman's conversion the following year. However, Brownson's decision had been intellectually prepared by his opinions regarding the connection between democracy and religion, which were crucial in changing his religious views.

In a series of articles written for the *Democratic Review* Brownson argued against popular sovereignty in a manner radical readers found difficult to accept, which also explains why the two periodicals later parted ways. Brownson emphasized that the notion of a social contract lacked the elements of self-limitation and self-control characteristic of the English Common Law tradition. From this it was only a short step to the delineation of two democratic and two religious traditions, which Brownson then opposed to each other. "Protestantism," he insisted, "though it may institute, cannot sustain popular liberty." Depending on the country, Protestantism expressed either the government's will or popular opinion, and therefore had to obey one or the other. In order to preserve a democratic form of government, however, a religion was required that was "above the people, exempt from their control" (Brownson 1972, 375, 378 ff.).

Compared with this career of an intellectual from New England, Isaac Hecker's itinerary seems at first wholly different. The son of German immigrants, he was born in 1819 in New York, where he was brought up without religious training and received only minimal education. At the age of eleven he was taken out of school in order to help his brothers in their bakery. Then began his apprenticeship in two senses, characterized by recurrent escapes from the bakery and returns to the rhythm of the family's work. The young Hecker joined the Workingmen's Party and in this way soon came into contact with Brownson. As a result, Hecker was invited to Brook Farm, where he studied philosophy for a semester before finally returning to his brothers in New York. About a year later Hecker joined the Thoreaus and lived with them for some time. New England transcendentalism, which then set the intellectual tone, seemed to him too individualistic. After lengthy discussions with Thoreau, who thoroughly disagreed with him on this point, he decided to become a Catholic. He converted to Catholicism in 1844, the same year as Brownson.

He applied for permission to join the Redemptorists, who were active in pastoral work among German immigrants in New York, and was accepted. Now calling himself Isaac Thomas Hecker, he entered a Redemptorist seminary in Belgium, and returned in 1851 an ordained priest. In America, like most of his confreres he worked in German parishes for a few years. During this time he wrote two books (*Questions of the Soul* and *Aspirations of Nature*) intended to explain Catholic belief to English-speaking non-Catholics. This task seemed to him increasingly important, and the four confreres with whom he was working strengthened him in this conviction. And so he conceived the idea of proposing to his superiors that an English-speaking mission house be opened. He secured the backing of Archbishop Hughes and set off for Rome. When he arrived, however, he was expelled from his order because he had come without having asked permission to make the trip. However, he found a sponsor in Cardinal Alessandro Barnabo, the prefect of *De Propagande Fide,* who persuaded the pope to support Hecker's plan. Pius IX released Hecker and his four New York confreres from their original vows and allowed them to establish a new order. The latter, the Missionary Priests of St. Paul the Apostle, known as the Paulists, was founded in 1858, and Hecker served as its first superior until his death in 1888.

During these thirty years he not only organized the new American order but also founded the newspaper *Catholic World* and the Catholic Publication Society. Together with Brownson he tried to set a powerful American tone, and in the correspondence they conducted with each other and with others, we can glimpse the coming crisis that was to result from the controversy about so-called Americanism. Hecker tends to describe his vision in rather emotional terms, whereas Brownson constantly sharpens the issues polemically, though in doing so he often succeeds in formulating them more clearly and succinctly.

In a letter written in 1859 Hecker describes his hopes for his order and explains why the Americanization of the Catholic Church seems to him so important: the combination of Catholic faith and American civilization would give both an opportunity to renew themselves, and at the same time offer the church the prospect of a future more glorious than anything in its past. This is, in sum, his credo (Gower and Leliaert 1979, 280 ff.). A long letter he wrote to Brownson in 1870 shows that he also sees America as a model for future European development. Political changes in Europe need not be to the disadvantage of religion, Hecker insists; on the contrary, Divine Providence may intend them to win European peoples back to religion. Hecker predicted that the church would be compensated for the loss of state support because in the future religion would be placed on "the foundations where our maker intended it should be, on the convictions of each individual soul and on personal sacrifices" (Gower and Leliaert 1979, 280 ff.).

Whereas Hecker believed in progress and in the American principle of voluntarism, Brownson argued polemically from a more contemporary point of view. He was convinced that the anti-republican tendencies of a large proportion of Catholics and of the clergy in particular had been strengthened by "these silly Know-Nothing-movements" and by French influence. This was especially true, he said, of "the European party among us." Therefore Rome had to decide what its attitude would be toward those who loved America and desired its conversion, "without being brought under the political system of Europe." His question was: "Can our people become catholics without ceasing to be Americans?" (Gower and Leliaert 1979, 199 ff.).

Becoming American and Remaining Catholic

Of course, the primary question was not how to make it easier for Americans to become Catholic. More and more Catholics kept coming into the country, and to keep them Catholic the church had to adapt to the immigrants. That meant that in the West an already relatively wide net had to be further extended, whereas in the Northeast, and especially in Pennsylvania, New York, and Ohio it was drawn increasingly tight. Since America had become independent, the distribution of dioceses had tended to correspond to the divisions among states, so that eventually each state had its own diocese. But where the numbers of Catholics were particularly great, several dioceses were established within a single state, so that the history of the establishment of dioceses more or less reflects the history of immigration.

During the first fifty years after the appointment of John Carroll as bishop of Baltimore, seventeen dioceses were established, eight in the North and nine in the South and Southwest. Between 1840 and 1860 twenty-nine dioceses were added, three-quarters of them in the North (22 out of 29). By 1890, thirty-eight additional dioceses were founded, five-sixths of them in the North (32 out of 38). Catholics were thus increasingly concentrated in the North, but there were significant differences between the densely settled Northeast and the Midwest and Northwest. In 1843 the dioceses of Illinois and Wisconsin were established with their sees in Chicago and Milwaukee, and in 1850 the diocese of Minnesota with its see in St. Paul. At the same time, however, a second diocese was founded in Pennsylvania and Ohio and a fourth diocese in New York (Hertling 1954, 148).

In contrast to the older and more populous dioceses in the Northeast—which had acquired what they needed to carry out their work, but for that very reason were often in debt—things were going very poorly in the Midwest, and that is why the bishops there depended for the time being on European missionary societies. Not every bishop's relations with these societies were as good as Henni's with the Bavarian King Ludwig Missionary Association. When the Belgian Jesuit James O. Van de Velde was appointed bishop of the new diocese of Chicago in 1849, he found 80,000 Catholics and 57 priests. However, these priests had to serve not only Catholics in Chicago but also those scattered all over the state of Illinois. The bishop turned to a French missionary society based in Lyons (*La Société pour la Propagation de la Foi*) and his report gives some idea of the situation in the interior of the country, even if in this case the author was tempted to make his diocese look even poorer than it was. He claimed that a single priest had to serve as many as eight churches, and since many of them lacked liturgical vessels, the priest had to carry them with him. There was no need, he wrote, to describe his official residence, because it was equally humble (Ellis 1967, 2: 301).

The First and Second Plenary Councils of Bishops

In 1852, thirty-two bishops came to Baltimore for the first plenary council of American bishops. This council issued no formal statement, which was wise, considering the lack of consensus regarding slavery and school policy. It proposed that ten new dioceses be established, a proposal on which the Vatican acted the following year. The archbishop of Baltimore functioned as a de facto primate, although strictly speaking there was no such office in the American missionary region. In 1864 the pope asked Spalding, who had been appointed bishop of Baltimore the preceding year, to call a plenary council as soon as possible—that is, immediately after the Civil War. Forty-seven bishops attended this second plenary council, held in Baltimore in 1866. They sought to put their program into language that Americans could understand and once again recommended, as they had in 1852, the establishment of further dioceses. In this case as well the Vatican followed their recommendation.

The second national Council of Bishops laid particular emphasis on its own authority and that of its members. The bishops stressed that "the gift of inerrancy" was granted bishops "from on high," no matter "whether they are gathered in general councils or dispersed throughout the world." Of course, they claimed infallibility only when the bishops agreed among themselves and with the pope, for with the pope they were called upon to rule the church of God: "agreeing and judging together with its head on earth the Roman Pontiff" (Hennesey 1981, 160).

There was thus no question of pitting the bishops' collegial authority against that of the pope. Rather, the bishops assembled in Baltimore hoped with Rome's help to strengthen their own position with regard to their subordinates. The conflict with the trustees had been decided in the bishops' favor, but the contending interests of various ethnic groups within the church that had played a role in this matter now emerged even more clearly and provided an additional reason for strengthening the authority of the bishops. The bishops' cause was aided by the fact that many issues in the American church were still undecided and many rules of canon law did not yet seem applicable. In a church that still had the status of a missionary region, there were no parishes and thus no parish priests that could not be removed, with the result that the clergy's claim to participate in decision-making was based on very weak grounds (Curran 1980; Trisco 1988).

Bishop Hughes liked to point out that the bishops' authority came from on high, not from below, and he told the converted Brownson that he would not tolerate anyone in his diocese who was not under his control and yet sought to have a say in ecclesiastical decisions. "I will either put him down, or he shall put me down," he wrote (Gower and Leliaert 1979, 228).

Most bishops probably expressed themselves less directly, but they would surely have agreed with Hughes concerning the origin of their authority. Hughes was the first and perhaps most colorful in a long succession of autocratic bishops who gradually replaced French bishops almost everywhere in the country, and dominated the American church for a century. Setting his personality aside, Hughes is the prototype of this kind of bishop, and in the tense relationship between him and Brownson we can already glimpse a dilemma that is independent of the two antagonists' personalities. It was precisely this authority deriving from "on high" rather than from the people that Brownson and other intellectual admirers of the Church of Rome expected to find in Catholicism, and they tended to see Hughes's blunt directness as typical Irish crudeness. Appealing to American principles, however, they rebelled against an unconditional and uncompromising position that obviously cannot be seen as resulting from personal characteristics or national character.

Hughes died in 1864, before the end of the Civil War and the beginning of better times for his American church, whose Roman nature he never questioned and which he served with tireless devotion. Although he was not only the archbishop of the largest ecclesiastical province but also the dominating figure among the American bishops of his time, he was never made a cardinal, despite Lincoln's intervention in Rome on his behalf.

The second plenary council of 1866 was attended by John McCloskey, then archbishop of New York; he had worked as Hughes's coadjutor before serving him as auxiliary bishop of Albany. In 1875, McCloskey was made a cardinal, after Spalding's death; now the Vatican could underscore the importance of the New York archdiocese without giving satisfaction to either side in the Civil War by honoring Spalding or Hughes. Moreover, during the Reconstruction period ecclesiastical policy was guided by a logic of transition and protective consolidation. Where growth resulting from immigration was greatest—for instance in Baltimore and New York, which were then the only ecclesiastical provinces in the East, and in the archdiocese of Cincinnati and in Wisconsin, which was then the outpost of settlement in the Northwest—power was held by men over sixty to whom the institutional growth of the church offered an opportunity for personal politics. Archbishops like McCloskey (New York), Spalding (Baltimore), Purcell (Cincinnati), and Henni (Milwaukee) had at their disposal ample means of supporting their protégés. In an ideal case, the archbishop could send a young man to study in Rome or Louvain, make him a secretary on his return, recommend the secretary's appointment as bishop in one of the auxiliary dioceses of his province, and finally get Rome to appoint the bishop as his coadjutor with the right to succeed him.

Thus Gibbons, who was sponsored by Spalding, became the latter's secretary and his auxiliary bishop in Richmond. Spalding's successor, Bayley, made Gibbons his coadjutor and his own successor. Corrigan, whom Bayley had sent to study in Rome, moved up from his former bishopric in Newark to succeed his mentor, Gibbon's protégé Keane succeeded him in Richmond, and Keane in turn sponsored a young priest by the name of O'Connell. In Cincinnati, Purcell's coadjutor

Elder succeeded him, and as already noted, Henni trained his secretary Heiss as his successor.

2. The Antagonists and the Issues

The support given by the senior bishops led in the 1870s to the emergence of a new group of younger bishops, who were predominantly of Irish descent; about a fifth came from German-speaking countries, and the rest from France, Belgium, and Holland. Most of them had been born in America or at least grown up there, and were under forty when they became bishops. This generation controlled the American church until the beginning of World War I. Three factions grew up within it that played a role in the conflicts of the 1880s and 1890s.

Three "Factions" in Church Politics

The first of these three factions, generally known as the "Americanists," clearly dominated the stage, though strictly speaking it consisted of only three major players and two secondary ones. Gibbons, Ireland, and O'Connell formed the core of this group, dividing their work in accord with their temperaments, ranks, and functions. In addition, we must mention John Lancaster Spalding, although he was essentially an intellectual who went his own way. John J. Keane, because of his loyalty to Gibbons and his later function as the first rector of the Catholic University of America, also belonged to this group. The label "Americanists" or "Americanist party" is more accurate than that of the "Irish party," which is also used to designate this group.

The second faction was Irish and conservative. It consisted of only two active clergymen, namely Michael Corrigan, bishop of New York, and Bernard J. McQuaid, bishop of Rochester. It is nonetheless appropriate to treat them as a group, because that is how the Americanists saw them. The latter's attention was focused chiefly on Corrigan, whom Ireland in particular regarded, in a way difficult to understand, as the "enemy." Occasionally McQuaid took over this role by apparently acting as Corrigan's alter ego; like Ireland on the other side, he was responsible for making the stronger statements. In matters of church politics, where a distinction between traditionalist and progressive positions could be drawn, the conservatives could generally count on a diffuse majority of the bishops and especially on the German bishops' block to support them. However, as we shall see, such distinctions were not always possible. In addition, we must keep in mind that only about ten of the more than seventy bishops actively participated in the controversies that clarified the American church's sense of its own identity as the nineteenth century drew to a close.

The third group is generally called the "Germans," and in fact it consisted of bishops who had come from Germany, Switzerland, and Austria to continue Henni's pastoral work among German-speaking immigrants. Thus they appeared to be a group whose behavior was quite independent of the active participants' individual characteristics.

The "Crisis" in Studies on Church History

In an attempt to sort out the tangle of hopes for the future, positions regarding politics and church politics, and personal characteristics, let us examine more closely the persons involved, and then the causes of the disputes that took place toward the end of the century. It is not difficult to learn more about the participants, since American church historians long devoted themselves almost exclusively to writing biographies. The dominant mode is represented by studies such as John Tracy Ellis's *The Life of James Cardinal Gibbons* (1952), James Moynihan's *The Life of Archbishop John Ireland* (1953), and Patrick H. Ahern's *The Life of John J. Keane* (1954). Such biographies are particularly useful when, like Frederick J. Zwierlein's *The Life and Letters of Bishop McQuaid* or the same author's edition of Corrigan's letters to McQuaid, they offer a perspective on the disagreements among the three parties that differs from that of the Americanists and the biographers who endorse their views. The same can be said of Colman Barry's *The Catholic Church and German-Americans*, on which all other authors rely when discussing the so-called German party and its writings.

Not until the 1970s did a large number of studies going beyond the description of exemplary lives begin to appear. The social historian's perspective was then also brought to bear on religion and religious history. After the relationship between immigration and ethnic culture had been rediscovered by historians such as Oscar Handlin and Kathleen Conzen, and sociologists like Nathan Glazer and Daniel P.

Moynihan, and social history flourished, a perspective on church history "from below" also emerged. Jay P. Dolan's studies are good examples of this kind of church history. In *The Immigrant Church* he described Irish and German parishes in New York around the middle of the nineteenth century, and in his later books he sought to portray the development of American Catholicism as a history of social milieus. In the 1970s a series of biographies appeared that tried to understand earlier crises and the ideas of the people who participated in them as forerunners of present-day ideological polarization. Thus the subtitle of Robert E. Curran's biography of Corrigan is "The Shaping of Conservative Catholicism in America 1878–1902."

This method is completely legitimate and can also serve to organize complicated developments around the career of someone involved in the events concerned. That is precisely what Gerald P. Fogarty achieves in *The Vatican and the Americanist Crisis*, which is described as a biography only in its subtitle: *Dennis J. O'Connell, American Agent in Rome 1885–1903.* Fogarty offers the best account of this important time, because he analyzes and evaluates both American and Roman sources and uses O'Connell's activity as an "agent" as a reliable image of the so-called Americanism crisis.

The Americanists: James Gibbons, Dennis J. O'Connell, John Ireland, John Lancaster Spalding, and John J. Keane

James Gibbons was at the center of this crisis from the time he was appointed bishop of Baltimore in 1877 until his death in 1921. In Rome and in American public opinion he was regarded as the representative of the American Catholic Church, and these four decades are often called "The Gibbons Era." Although he was born in America, Gibbons still became an Irish immigrant. In 1834 he came into the world in the shadow of his later cathedral, his parents having emigrated from Ireland a few years earlier and settled in Baltimore. James was the fourth of six children and the first son of Thomas and Bridget Gibbons. His father had prospered in his work for a trading company, and the family lived near the cathedral in what was then considered a good neighborhood. But Thomas Gibbons found the climate exhausting. He finally bought a farm in Ireland, and the family moved there when James was three years old. In Ireland James attended a private "classical school," but when he was thirteen, his father died. His mother at first tried to carry on with the farm, but after a few years she gave up and took her children back to America, this time to New Orleans. James found a job in a grocery store, and like his father he showed such business acumen that the owner wanted to make him a partner. But in the meantime James had made the decision to become a priest, and so when he was twenty-one he went to study at a college in Baltimore. Eventually he was accepted by the seminary run by the Sulpicians. In 1861 he was ordained a priest, and worked for four years in various churches in Baltimore before Archbishop Spalding made him his secretary in 1865. His first assignment was to organize the second Conference of Bishops, which was to take place the following year. This work, which he carried out before and during the conference, was recognized, and Spalding recommended that he be made vicar of the Apostolic Diocese of North Carolina, which had been established in 1868 along with eight other new dioceses. Gibbons was appointed the same year.

In subsequent years Gibbons made long journeys through North Carolina, delivering sermons in courtrooms, in the open air, and often in Protestant churches. He gained an idea of the world outside the Catholic circles in which he had previously moved. In 1870 he was the youngest Catholic bishop to take part in the Vatican Council, and mindful of his age, he remained silent. In the balloting concerning papal infallibility—the central issue on which the bishops gathered in Rome focused from May until July—he joined twenty-five other Americans in voting yes. About the same number of American bishops considered such a declaration conceivable but untimely, and went home before the balloting, in order to avoid having to vote no. Only Bishop Edward Fitzgerald of Little Rock cast one of the two opposing votes. In 1872 Gibbons was appointed bishop of Richmond, and this was probably the last such decision in which Archbishop Spalding was able to take part.

In contrast to the situation in North Carolina, in the fifty year-old diocese of Richmond Gibbons found established relationships already in place. He spent less time traveling, and instead used the impressions gained over the preceding years in writing his catechistic work *The Faith of our Fathers*, published in 1877. The book's sales may have been increased by its author's subsequent fame, but its style no doubt played a still more important role in its exceptional success. Gibbons presupposed nothing, laying out in the Scholastic manner the common objections to Catholic faith and the structure of the Catholic Church as seriously and soundly as he could. Then he replied to these objections in a temperate way, drawing on analogies to American institutions, customs, and ways of speaking. For instance, he tried to explain the recently confirmed doctrine of papal infallibility by reference to the function of the Supreme Court in the American system of government.

Meanwhile, in 1872 James Roosevelt Bayley succeeded Spalding, who was only four years older, as the resident bishop of Baltimore. Having converted in 1842, he led the newly created diocese of Newark from 1853 to 1872, and sponsored both McQuaid and the younger Corrigan. In Baltimore he adopted his predecessor's habit of consulting on all difficult questions young Bishop Gibbons who, having served as a diocesan priest in Baltimore, was fully familiar with the situation and was, moreover, an agreeable, prudent man. When his health began to fail, Bayley convinced Rome to make Gibbons his coadjutor with the right to succeed him. Thus Gibbons had half a year to prepare himself before being appointed at the end of 1877, at the age of forty-three, archbishop of the oldest see in America.

In Baltimore, Gibbons acted like someone who thought he had plenty of time. He took advantage of the proximity of Washington, which was then still part of his diocese, developing good personal relationships with all the presidents in office during his long term. Within the church he was quite willing to promote further uniformity and to make use of a conference of bishops—the means most readily available to him—to achieve this end. However, he preferred to secure in advance Rome's approval of the decisions of such a national council, since the Vatican's policy was not yet sufficiently clear. Immediately after Gibbons' installation the Vatican had sent the Irish Bishop Conroy on an inspection tour of America. But Conroy's report had not been analyzed and its consequences were still unclear when Pius IX died. As a result, in 1880 Gibbons went to Rome for the first time. There he established a good relationship with Leo XIII, and was relieved to learn that the new pope recognized that the old European order was moribund, and, so it seemed to Gibbons, was doing his best to keep the church from dying with it.

The third plenary council of Baltimore, which took place in 1884 after extensive preparations, consolidated Gibbons' standing in America and in Rome. A year later, after McCloskey's death, Leo XIII made Gibbons America's second cardinal. In Rome, on the occasion of his installation at his titular church of Santa Maria in Trastevere, Gibbons delivered an address in which he set forth a programmatic credo, asserting that the great progress made by the Catholic Church in America was due in large measure to American liberty. He went on to say that he was thankful to live in a land in which the government protected the church without meddling in its affairs, and where there was "liberty without license and authority without despotism" (Ellis 1952, 2: 65).

Gibbons' standing was not disturbed by the controversies of the following years. The pope had a high opinion of the American cardinal. Moreover, within the Americanist party work was divided up in a way that was not only prudent but also in accord with the personal qualifications of its members. John Ireland was responsible for making provocative public statements, and O'Connell was active in ways that went far beyond his official assignment (which was limited to directing, on behalf of all the American bishops, the American College) and that were often authorized neither by decisions made by the bishops nor by any consensus among them. Nonetheless, when Ireland and O'Connell inevitably got into trouble, they were able to count on the cardinal's help. This division of roles was not merely clever, but also corresponded to Gibbons' personality. The cardinal believed in the program he had outlined in Santa Maria in Trastevere, but unlike the constantly aggressive and grandstanding Ireland, he was a benevolent spiritual leader who enjoyed his position and did not see the "Germans" or the "conservatives" as his enemies.

Dennis J. O'Connell's career, from its promising beginnings to its relatively disappointing end, was constantly bound up with Gibbons' favor. He was born in Ireland, but three years later his parents emigrated to Columbia, South Carolina, where his father's brothers were already serving as priests. The latter encouraged the young Dennis and put him in touch with Gibbons, who got him admitted to the American College in 1872. Four years later, he completed his studies with distinction and was admitted to the doctoral program, which he completed in one year. In 1877, while still in Rome, he was ordained, and then returned to his home diocese of Richmond. At that time, this diocese was still partly administered by Gibbons, who had already been named archbishop of Baltimore and was supposed to travel to Rome in order to receive the pallium as a sign of his episcopal authority. Instead, O'Connell was asked to go immediately to Rome to handle all the formalities, and in this case as in later ones, John J. Keane, who had just been appointed bishop of Richmond, did not hesitate to grant his young diocesan priest leave. Over the following years, O'Connell was given many similar assignments until Gibbons finally succeeded in getting him stationed in Rome.

In 1884 O'Connell returned to the American College, which he had left not quite seven years earlier, as its rector. He remained in this position for eleven years, until he and Ireland had a falling-out, and his own garrulity got him in trouble. After the pope had personally demanded that he resign as rector, O'Connell was once again wholly dependent upon the support of his patron, who first made him curator of his titular church in Rome, and then got him appointed rector of Catholic University in Washington. No doubt Gibbons also had a hand in O'Connell's appointment, in 1912, as bishop of Richmond, where like Keane he was one of Gibbons' successors, and where he died in 1927. If we consider only these highpoints, O'Connell's career was entirely respectable for a son of poor Irish immigrants. Nonetheless, Fogarty is probably right in seeing O'Connell as a tragic figure. Seldom in the history of the American church had anyone aroused such great expectations and exercised so much influence, while at the same time achieving so little of lasting value (Fogarty, 317).

John Ireland, the most colorful figure in the Americanist triumvirate, was born in Ireland in 1838, and at the age of fourteen he arrived, after brief stays on the East Coast and in Chicago, in St. Paul, where a diocese had been established only two years earlier. The contradictory nature of these frontier days can be discerned in the fact that St. Paul was still described as a trading post, but was also building a cathedral, and the cathedral parish was already running a school. Young John attended the cathedral school, after delivering milk early in the morning and then often serving as acolyte. In any event, he was noticed by the first bishop of St. Paul, a Frenchman named Joseph Cretin, and the latter sent him to France, where John Ireland completed the four years of the *Petit Séminaire* and the subsequent four years of the *Grand Séminaire* (the bipartite structure that served as the model for

American seminaries). In 1861 he returned to Minnesota and was soon ordained by Bishop Thomas L. Grace, who had been bishop there since Cretin's death in 1857.

Ireland at first became a military chaplain, serving in Mississippi with the Fifth Minnesota Volunteers until he fell ill with yellow fever. As often happens among military veterans, his military service later grew in duration as well as in significance, and Ireland spoke of this relatively short time as "the happiest and most fruitful years of my ministry" (O'Connell 1989, 106).

Back in St. Paul, Ireland first was assigned to several congregations, and then became pastor of the cathedral parish in 1867. During this time he made a name for himself by the clarity with which he expressed himself and by his support for the Catholic Total Abstinence Union. Although he constantly advocated abstinence and demanded that no alcohol be served at church functions such as first communion or ordination, he always remained opposed to prohibition. At this time he also gained prominence as a supporter of Lincoln and of the Republican Party.

In 1870 Bishop Grace sent Ireland to Rome, and two years later got him appointed as his coadjutor. Ireland served in this capacity for nine years, until he finally succeeded Grace in 1884. Then he was in a position to satisfy more fully his desire for travel, and especially to cultivate relations with his French colleagues. In the same year the third plenary council took place in Baltimore, an occasion that for the first time brought all the members of the Americanist faction together for an extended period.

St. Paul was made a separate church province in 1888, and included both North and South Dakota. As a result of this reorganization, which occurred after Gibbons had O'Connell repeatedly press the case in Rome, Ireland became independent of the "German" archdiocese of Milwaukee, with which he had previously been associated as auxiliary bishop. In 1881, Michael Heiss's appointment as Henni's successor was strongly criticized outside the German triangle. When the historian John G. Shea complained that there was not a single American bishop in the whole of the Western United States, his observation met with wide public approval (Barry 1953, 112).

Now, however, there was an American bishop in the West, and he constantly emphasized that he was American and fought to Americanize his church. Moreover, he belonged to the group of archbishops that had gained increasing power as the number of bishops increased.

The Americanist party's disintegration in 1895 affected Ireland less severely than O'Connell. Ireland was reduced to his function as archbishop and enjoyed, precisely because of his defeat within the church, a certain popularity outside the church, where he was seen as a defender of American institutions, particularly public schools. Thus in 1901 the Yale University Law School awarded him an honorary doctoral degree, a distinction one would hardly expect a Catholic bishop to receive at this time. Actually, he was not really a liberal in either theology or church politics. His addresses and writings leave no doubt as to his support for the pope, and he acknowledged the pope's authority while making every effort to strengthen the position of the bishops in the United States. As he wrote in a letter to the prefect of *De Propaganda Fide*, this was the only way to bind together the extremely diverse elements of the American church (O'Connell 1989, 111).

John Ireland resembled John Hughes in his authoritarian mode of thought and expression, in his delight in controversy, and his political views. However, the situation had changed: it was no longer the alliance between political and religious nativism but rather the allegedly anti-American forces within the church that now appeared as the obstacle to integrating Catholics into American life. Like Hughes, Ireland remained pugnacious and controversial, and like Hughes he never became a cardinal, despite his fame—or perhaps because of it. Here, however, the resemblance ceases. For while Hughes was only an eager warrior who lacked any trace of *Romanità*, and Rome, to his disadvantage, did not want to take sides in the Civil War, Ireland disqualified himself through his choice of methods and arguments in controversies within the church. For instance, his references to German-speaking Catholics as "Prussian Agents" and "Bismarck's henchmen" were not merely absurd but blunders carefully noted down by German Jesuits in *De Propaganda Fide*.

And so after the end of the controversies Ireland was limited for the following twenty years to the role of a prince of the American church. He was able to complete the building of a second, still larger cathedral, and in 1910, when the second diocese in North Dakota and the fifth one in Minnesota were established, the number of dioceses within the jurisdiction of his church province, which had been created only in

1888, rose to nine. One may see a certain irony in the fact that now there was a diocese of Bismarck, North Dakota, within Ireland's archdiocese.

John Lancaster Spalding was born in Kentucky in 1840. After completing his studies in Louvain and being ordained a priest, he first returned to Louisville as secretary to the bishop, and then assumed the direction of Catholic schools in New York. At this time he published a biography of his uncle, *The Life of the Most Reverend M. J. Spalding* (1873) and at the age of thirty-six put together a collection of his own work under the title *Essays and Reviews* (1876). In 1877 he was ordained the first bishop of the new diocese in Peoria, Illinois, and held this position for over thirty years. In 1908 he suffered a stroke and retired, remaining in Peoria until his death eight years later.

During his tenure as bishop he was particularly active in promoting the building of Catholic schools, whose number he increased from twelve to seventy, and he also discussed the issue in theoretical terms. Like the New England Congregationalists, he published almost all his sermons and addresses. The titles of these volumes—*Education and the Higher Life* (1890), *Means and Ends of Education* (1895), *Thoughts and Theories of Life and Education* (1897)—show the significance he attached to educational theory and educational policy. In his later years as bishop, he was more engaged with political questions and with the social order.

In his high regard for the American republic, Spalding was surely an Americanist, but he did not consider public schools an indispensable American institution. Unlike Ireland, he had been involved in school issues both practically and theoretically, and he rejected Ireland's argument that separate schools could be foregone if religious instruction were accepted in public schools. Spalding, having found his niche in education, concentrated on it. He introduced the notion that Catholics were deficient in the area of education, an inexhaustible theme that was also taken up in the 1950s by his biographer, John Tracy Ellis. Spalding constantly referred to the "intellectual weakness" of Catholics, and for a long time he continued to promote, as had his uncle, the establishment of a Catholic university, to be supported by all the bishops. It was because of his efforts that such an institution finally came into being. He not only constantly called for its foundation but also secured the first substantial donation, which forced his episcopal colleagues to follow suit. However, he declined to become the first rector of Catholic University.

Spalding suggested instead John J. Keane, the bishop of Richmond, who had succeeded Gibbons there in 1878. Keane had to assume this rather thankless task, since otherwise there was a danger that the (then) conservative Jesuits would gain control of the new university. The Jesuits, many of whom were German, and who maintained in direct contact with Rome, would then be in a position to recruit the most crucial professors from their own ranks.

Keane's term as rector also came to an end with the defeat of his "party." In 1897 the Vatican did not reappoint him, explaining simply that in such matters it was wise to make changes occasionally. As we see in the directory of American bishops, from 1897 to 1900 Keane served as advisor to *De Propaganda Fide* ("Consultor of the Congregation for the Propagation of the Faith"), a post that suggested that he was no longer of any use (*Catholic Almanac* 1991, 472). In 1900 he was named archbishop of Dubuque, Iowa, and for eleven years he led, as Ireland had, the life of a bishop in the new farming states of the Northwest.

The Americanists had no explicit program, and as we have already said, they were not "liberal" in either the European or the American sense of the term; neither did they have any discernible modernist theological tendencies. As the term "Americanists" suggests, what bound them together was their common demand for a consistent Americanization of the church. Ireland's and Keane's response to the so-called Abbelen memorandum therefore comes closest to a programmatic statement of their position. In the spring of 1887 Gibbons, Ireland, Keane, and O'Connell had spent several weeks together at the American College, and during this time they had discussed the memorandum written by German-speaking priests from Cincinnati and Milwaukee, which called for a guarantee that pastoral work in the native languages would continue. Their response noted that the battle for the rights of the German-speaking Catholics was being waged with the stubbornness typical of "Bismarck's compatriots," but argued that the church's own interest demanded that it not yield. They went on to say that in America there was a clear movement toward the church, and that in order to take advantage of this trend, the church should present itself in a way attractive to Americans whenever it could do so without compromising its principles. Since the church had been portrayed as an alien institution and as a menace, it was unreasonable to expect that such prejudices would disappear if the church impeded the Americanization of immigrants' children by choosing as its chief representatives men who had no sympathy for the customs and legitimate ideas of the country, and who were not in full command of its language (Barry 1953, 296 ff.; Hertling 1954, 189).

The Two-Member Party of the "Conservatives": Michael A. Corrigan and Bernard J. McQuaid

Just as the bishops of French descent had earlier been accused of lacking allegiance to American ideas, so now the nativist argument emerged again in controversies within the church. It was used not only against those who supported the concept of a bilingual American church, but also against bishops of Irish descent to whom it was more important that the church be Roman than that it be American.

If we consider the two persons usually mentioned as the representatives of the "conservative" faction, however, their conservatism seems just as vague as the liberalism of the Americanists that is supposed to be its opposite. Corrigan and McQuaid's interpretation of the catechism and their office was just as traditional and authoritarian as that of other bishops, including the Americanists. If one is determined to find indications of liberalism or conservatism, McQuaid is ultimately more liberal than Gibbons, because he opposed the declaration of papal infallibility. Moreover, Corrigan's and McQuaid's backgrounds are similar: both grew up in the New York area, and both clearly supported the Americanization of the church.

Michael Augustine Corrigan was born in Newark in 1839, the fifth of nine children. His father, Thomas Corrigan, had emigrated from Ireland eleven years earlier and opened a grocery store in Newark, which proved so successful that he soon became one of the wealthiest men in town. He was able to give his family a comfortable middle-class life and invested in the education of his children. Michael graduated with honors from the college in Emmitsburg connected with St. Mary's Seminary in Maryland. On the recommendation of the first bishop of Newark, James Roosevelt Bayley, he was among the first twelve students sent to the American College, where he studied from 1859 to 1863 and was ordained a priest. A year later he completed the doctoral program, whereupon his bishop sent him to teach at the newly established seminary in Seton Hall, New Jersey. This seminary—which was connected with a college, as was then usual—was directed by Bernard J. McQuaid, who had also grown up in New York the son of an Irish immigrant, though his family had been somewhat less well-off than Corrigan's. Like Bayley, McQuaid had been sponsored by John Hughes, and Bayley called him back to New Jersey when he founded his own seminary.

Corrigan proved to be an especially conscientious teacher and won the friendship of McQuaid, sixteen years his elder. When McQuaid was appointed bishop of Rochester in 1868, he recommended that Corrigan succeed him. In addition to directing the college and the seminary, Corrigan soon became vicar general as well, so that in practice he was already running the diocese while Bayley was in Rome in 1871 to attend the council. Finally, when Bayley went to Baltimore in 1872, the vicar general was appointed his successor, because Cardinal McCloskey and Bishop McQuaid both insisted that their candidate's youth be overlooked. The thirty-five-year-old Corrigan was appointed bishop of Newark. Soon afterward the cardinal conferred with his auxiliary bishops about how to handle his succession. The consensus was that Corrigan should be named his coadjutor. In 1885, after serving in this capacity until McCloskey's death five years later, Corrigan became archbishop of New York. McQuaid had for the third time helped advance his friend's career, with the result that the younger man moved ahead of him.

In New York, Corrigan, who persistently advocated separate Catholic schools and demanded that the clergy show restraint in political matters, soon clashed with a group of politically active clergy who identified with Henry George and his combination of Irish nationalism and socialism, and who opposed the idea of Catholic schools. It did not help that the leader of this group, Edward McGlynn, had studied with Corrigan in Rome. From the outset, public controversies cast a pall over the otherwise indisputably successful career of Archbishop Corrigan, who died in 1902 at the age of sixty-three.

For this reason many authors, such as Robert E. Curran, see the controversy surrounding McGlynn and the clerical radicalism of the 1880s and 1890s as the first step in the formation of two political camps within American Catholicism. It is in fact in this arena, rather than in church politics, that two conflicting tendencies emerged. While Canadian bishops and some American bishops sought to dissociate the church from socialistic ideas, labor unions, and the secret order of the Knights of Labour, in Rome Gibbons was opposing the Canadians' efforts to have such organizations condemned and membership in them prohibited. However, in this case as in others, Gibbons was acting out of pastoral prudence rather than ideological persuasion. Although Corrigan and McQuaid were close to the New York Democratic party machine, and although Ireland annoyed them by participating as a Republican in New York educational politics and in this way stirring up conflict between McGlynn and Corrigan, this had less to do with later ideological alignments than with the personalities involved.

The German "Faction"

The German-speaking bishops were an entirely different case. Like the bishops from France, they were suspected of lacking allegiance to American ideas and institutions. If we take the list of participants in the third plenary session in Baltimore as a guide, it seems that a French faction did not exist. In 1884 sixty-nine bishops gathered in Baltimore. Hennesey divides them as follows: 35 Irish, 15 German, 11 French, 5 English, and one each Dutch, Scottish, and Spanish (Hennesey 1981, 194).

The French bishops, most of whom were in what was then the southwestern part of the United States, had not come from France to care for French immigrants, and seldom had French protégés. Instead, they sponsored ambitious young Irishmen, as Bishop Dubois had sponsored Hughes and Bishop Cretin had sponsored Ireland. In contrast, a bishop of German descent was just as likely to be a son of German immigrants, who spoke only broken German or none at all, as he was to be a priest trained in Germany, who had been sent to America to help out the American church.

Thus we must examine this question more closely, and here once again the directory of American bishops provides a starting point. If we look up all the American bishops who were appointed in the second half of the nineteenth century and who, according to the directory, came from Germany, Switzerland, Austria, or Luxembourg or have German family names, we find twenty-three in all. Only four of the "German" bishops of this time had been born in America, namely Thomas Becker (appointed bishop of Wilmington in 1886), Ignatius Horstmann (appointed bishop of Cleveland in 1892), William Gross (appointed bishop of Savannah in 1873), and Josef Rademacher (appointed bishop of Nashville in 1883). In the first half of the twentieth century we find among the increased number of American bishops about the same number of bishops who are in the broad sense of German descent—so that the proportion is reversed. Only a few had still been born in Europe, but we find names such as Henry Moeller, and Moeller is typical in that he was first archbishop of Columbus, Ohio (1900) and then archbishop of Cincinnati (1904). Even in the 1880s, when the controversy over the Americanization of the church was going on, there were only a few bishops of German descent active outside the German triangle. Among these were, however, three of the four who had been born in America—Becker, Rademacher, and Gross. Half of the others, in contrast, served in the ecclesiastical province of Milwaukee (*Catholic Almanac* 1991, 472).

Thus even within the German triangle, bishops who were still recognizable as immigrants were dominant only where German immigration was heaviest toward the end of the nineteenth century. In Ohio, on the other hand, to which many Germans had long emigrated, the Irish controlled the church hierarchy, even though as an ethnic group they were in the minority. For example, in the Cincinnati diocese, which had been founded in 1821 and became an archdiocese in 1850, bishops of Irish descent were in control throughout the whole of the nineteenth century, although they sought to appoint German auxiliary bishops or vicars general like Henni. Even in the dioceses later established in this province, attempts were made to make it clear that the balance between the two major ethnic groups was being maintained. Before and after the turn of the century, the names of the bishops in Cleveland were Gilmour, Horstmann, and Farelly, while in Columbus they were Watterson, Moeller, and Hartley.

False Alternative on All Sides

With the emergence of these three factions the stage was set for the controversies of the 1880s and 1890s, which have been described by American church historians as the "great crisis" (McAvoy), the

"Americanist crisis" (Fogarty), or the prelude to later ideological polarizations (Cross). In fact the various developments referred to in the titles of such studies all influenced each other.

Initially it is possible to speak of a developmental crisis insofar as it had become necessary to resolve long-standing issues that had in no way been settled by the creation of additional dioceses. The internal constitution of the church was involved, and therefore power. In addition there was the so-called Americanist crisis, which was only superficially about the Americanization of the church. None of those involved had any doubt that Americanization had long been in full swing. The church would have been ill advised to posit an opposition between Catholic belief and American culture and ask immigrants to choose between them. Moreover, like Henni many German bishops considered the assimilation of immigrants into American society not only inevitable but desirable, because they were convinced that religion's future lay in America rather than in Europe. There was therefore no alternative to Americanization. More precisely, the only remaining issue was the proper mix of identity and difference, that is, what degree of adaptation egalitarian American society required and how much distance Catholicism had to maintain in order to remain distinct within a modern culture less differentiated than any other.

This question regarding the possibility of cultural pluralism and the autonomy of the religious realm was at first connected only with the situation of immigrants and therefore constantly confronted by false alternatives. One side maintained that if Catholicism rejected any foreign character as quickly and decisively as possible it would not only be accepted but might even hope to attract new members from long-established groups and from non-Catholic immigrant families. The other side insisted that as soon as immigrants lost their language they were lost for the church. This argument seemed to suggest that language, instead of being subservient to religion, was to serve as a means of preserving German, or later on, Polish, subculture. Whenever there was any hint of Germanization, conservatives like Corrigan and McQuaid agreed with the Americanists in rejecting the corresponding demands.

Thus nationalistic simplifications of the problem dominated the views of both sides, but there was little anyone could do about it. At a time when nationalism was associated with progress and Rome and

Vienna were seen as representatives of the opposite principle, the Catholic Church was not immune to this epidemic. Yet discussions concerning the need for separate Catholic schools should finally have led to the realization that the issue was neither Germanization nor Americanization, but whether Catholicism's further development was dependent upon the support of its own institutions. This was the original function of the ethnic parishes (including the English courses they offered), and it was later taken over by a separate school system that was no longer ethnic but not yet denominationally defined, either.

Finally, the third crisis was brought about by the gradual development of two ideological political camps, what Cross, and also Curran, interpret as the emergence of a progressive, left-liberal Catholicism (Cross 1968; Curran 1978). At this time, the only evidence for this interpretation is the radical priests in New York, represented above all by McGlynn. In other respects, these political developments show chiefly how much the different battle lines overlap. The bishops considered progressive were in fact as authoritarian as Corrigan was, but the latter's episcopal authority was challenged by priests with Irish nationalist and socialist tendencies, who agreed with John Ireland regarding schools. Most bishops did not side with Ireland on this issue, though they were unsure whether the "Germans" were chiefly concerned with language or with faith. On one hand, the events involved in the so-called "great crisis" did not add up to a unified picture, because three unresolved problems, namely discipline within the church, cultural pluralism, and the church's political stance led to the formation of differing coalitions. On the other hand, the controversies were rendered more complex by the fact that all the participants constantly acted with one eye on Rome, where differing tendencies and considerations were also at work. Thus their behavior was often clearly determined by an intention to discredit the opposing party in Rome. At the same time, however, their constant maneuvering did not enable either party to gain full and lasting control over the American church. Therefore this period of conflict within the church, so decisive for the latter's future, did not proceed like a Greek tragedy, in which everything moves relentlessly toward a clarification. Rather, it proceeded like a novel of development, one episode following another, and resulting not in the victory of one side and the defeat of the other, but in the movement of the problems to another level.

The report on America submitted to the Vatican in 1878 by the Irish bishop George Conroy looks in retrospect like a prelude. Because he lacked sufficient knowledge of the country—and presumably also because his hosts went to great lengths to make his stay a pleasant one—Conroy limited himself to the classical viewpoint of an internal audit, focusing on administration and finance, the qualifications of the clergy, and the relationships between bishops and clergy. However, even in this limited perspective certain problems came into view. Gibbons had assigned Dennis O'Connell, who had just returned from Rome, to serve as Conroy's companion, and the two traveled for weeks throughout the United States. Conroy was impressed by the general development of the American church, but did not fail to see the problems as well. Thus he pointed out the relation between the church's financial constitution and its staffing policies. Because of its rapid expansion and the relative poverty of the immigrants, Conroy wrote, the church had fallen deeply into debt. For this reason priests constantly had to ask for money, instead of devoting their sermons to other subjects. Moreover, business ability played too great a role in the choice of bishops, and the bishops themselves took similar considerations too much into account in judging and promoting the priests under their jurisdiction. All too often the candidates recommended to the Holy See were better qualified as bankers than as shepherds for souls. Among the sixty-eight bishops there were perhaps ten very talented ones; the rest were mediocre, and "in theological knowledge they do not even reach mediocrity." Conroy also described the tensions between bishops and priests as a burden on an otherwise positive development. The selection of bishops, he noted, was purposely kept secret, thereby favoring the appointment of protégés, and the rules of canon law, which granted the clergy certain rights, were ignored by the bishops (Fogarty 1974, 27 ff.; Hennesey 1981, 178 ff.).

This report played a role when Cardinal Simeoni, the prefect of *De Propaganda Fide*, invited the twelve American archbishops to come to Rome. (To the four archdioceses that had emerged from the first archdiocese along the East Coast—Baltimore, Philadelphia, New York, and Boston—as well as the old archdiocese of New Orleans had been gradually added the church provinces of Cincinnati, St. Louis, Chicago, Milwaukee, Santa Fe, Portland, and San Francisco.) Eleven of the twelve American princes of the church went to Rome in 1883, and some brought with them a secretary or theological advisor. Thus Cardinal McCloskey was accompanied by Bishop Corrigan, and the already indispensable Dennis O'Connell accompanied Archbishop Gibbons. The archbishops stayed in Rome for several weeks, and among the most important subjects they discussed were regulations concerning the constitution of archdioceses and educational policy. The Vatican suggested that each diocese appoint a council of priests with permanent membership whose consent would be required to establish or dissolve a parish, and to purchase or sell church property. However, the archbishops felt that the bishops should have the right to dismiss diocesan councils. On the other hand, they accepted the suggestion that Catholic schools should be established wherever possible.

The Third Plenary Council of 1884 and the Constitution of Dioceses

A year later, in November 1884, in the Sulpician seminary in Baltimore, the third plenary council of American bishops took place, and lasted almost a month. It was decided that in each diocese there should be arbitration panels and a set quota of pastors who could not be dismissed. However, the council of priests was weakened still further: the bishop had to consult it only when business transactions or the establishment or dissolution of parishes were involved.

It was further decided that within two years, every American parish should establish its own primary school. In addition, the bishops agreed to found the Catholic University of America and appointed a committee charged with this task. Regarding pastoral care, the bishops decided to appoint another committee to prepare a unified catechism and a prayer book, and they approved guidelines calling for regular, brief, prepared sermons on Sundays and holidays (Fogarty 1974, 42 ff.).

These decisions had to be defended in Rome in order to keep them as intact as possible. To this end a few bishops were sent to Rome, and Dennis O'Connell was asked to accompany them. While this delegation was in Rome, the Vatican approved the nomination of O'Connell as rector of the American College. As a result, O'Connell no longer needed the cabin booked for his voyage home.

From this time on O'Connell served as the American representative in Rome, as Fogarty calls him, but this description is justified only because for much of this period the Catholic Church in America was equated with Gibbons. The new rector's initial assignments show that his work consisted less in caring for American students and administering the American College than in explaining the statutes of the newly-founded Catholic University and getting them approved. In addition, he had to see to it that St. Paul became a church province and that Ireland joined in this way the archbishops' club.

The Knights of Labor and the Distinction between Labor Unions and Socialism

Meanwhile, in America it had become clear that the political conflicts that had long polarized American Protestantism were now becoming discernible in the Catholic Church as well. Particularly in the controversies regarding the role of labor unions and the meaning of socialist ideas, which culminated in the mid-1880s, the Catholic Church found it impossible to remain neutral because Catholic labor unionists and politically active Catholic priests were among the chief participants. A preview of what was to come was provided by the dispute over the Knights of Labor, who were organized into lodges, but whose spokesmen brought their views to the attention of the public. Most of the members were said to be Catholic like their leader, Terence Powderly, even though the latter's name seemed to associate the organization with the smell of gunpowder. The Knights of Labor had been involved in many violent, long-running strikes, and especially with the Haymarket riots in Chicago on May Day, 1886, during which several policemen were killed. Thus Powderly's constant assertions that they did not engage in violence and were not socialists were of little help. In Rome, the Canadian bishops had argued that the Knights should be condemned, and most of the American bishops probably agreed. In any case, James Augustine Healey, bishop of Portland, Maine, the first African-American bishop in the United States, threatened to excommunicate members of the Knights. Basing himself on the way they presented themselves, Healey treated the Knights as freemasons, and invoked the consequences foreseen in the Vatican's instruction *De Secta Masonum* of 1884.

However, Gibbons emphasized in a memorandum for Cardinal Simeoni that the Knights did not constitute a secret society in the sense of the Vatican instruction, and argued that the church should not give the impression that it wanted to prevent workers from representing their interests. Thus Rome decided to tolerate the Knights for the moment (*Societatem Equitum Laboris pro nunc tolerari*), so long as they did not act like a secret society or propagate any socialistic ideas (Hertling 1954, 201).

By the time Rome came to this decision, the Knights had already ceased to play a significant role. But in the long run Rome's tolerance of this movement was very important, because it introduced a distinction between the representation of labor union interests and socialism that not only lent moral support to Catholic labor union officials but was also interpreted by lay people and by the Catholic clergy as encouraging them to participate in labor unions in order to prevent the latter from falling under socialist control. Together with the lack of a real socialist party, this shift helped the American church, which in the first half of the twentieth century was largely shaped by urban industrial workers, exercise a formative influence on labor unions that the church lacked in all other industrial countries.

Irish Nationalist Socialism and Clerical Radicals in New York

The conflict with supporters of Irish nationalist socialism in the clergy was far more difficult to resolve, even though it is often described as though it amounted to nothing more than a conflict between an authoritarian bishop and a progressive clergyman. The new archbishop Corrigan had little in common with McGlynn apart from their student years at the American College. His active promotion of Catholic schools while serving as Cardinal McCloskey's coadjutor had already made this clear. In 1886 their antagonism headed for a climax when McGlynn, despite Corrigan's warning not to get involved in politics, took every opportunity to support Henry George and in 1886 backed George's bid to become mayor of New York.

Henry George maintained that ownership of land was the root of all evil, and in particular of Irish poverty. He therefore urged that real estate be taxed so heavily that private land ownership would become unattractive and no other taxes would be necessary. McGlynn adopted these ideas and in his speeches presented them as the quintessence of Christianity. Walter Rauschenbusch, at this time minister of the Second German Baptist Church in New York and later the leading figure in the Protestant Social Gospel movement, recalled that in his public lectures McGlynn described social justice as the true heart of all religions, and made a great impression on his audiences by explaining that this was the meaning of "Thy will be done on earth" (Rauschenbusch 1912, 91; Marty 1984, 350).

The more McGlynn saw it was not only New York newspapers that were paying attention to him, the less he was inclined to submit to his bishop, who emphasized the importance of property ownership. Finally McGlynn was ordered to appear in Rome, but claimed he could not comply because of poor health, lack of money, and family obligations. In a letter to Corrigan he said that so long as he lived he would spread the doctrine that private ownership of land violated natural justice, no matter what civil or canon laws justified it, and no one, neither "bishop, propaganda nor pope" had the right to punish him for political opinions that the church had not condemned as heretical. However, he himself provided other grounds for disciplinary action, and despite the threatened consequences, he ignored a second order to come to Rome. The news of the Vatican's ultimatum led in 1887 to a demonstration in New York in which, according to newspaper reports, 75,000 people took part. For the time being, the affair came to an end with McGlynn's excommunication. Five years later, however, he was absolved by the papal legate, Satolli, and when he died in 1900, Corrigan himself celebrated the mass for the repose of his soul (Curran 1980, 189 ff.).

The McGlynn affair, which made headlines for more than a year, and the debate over the Knights of Labor both had the same unexpected consequence. Politics did not stop at the church door, and the strengthening of church discipline did little good when it became impossible to distinguish matters of order that involved Catholic principles from individual, concrete political issues. Intentionally or not, Rome had set the example when Gibbons' tactical argument was broadened to suggest that in defense of their interests Catholic workers had the right to organize however they saw fit, so long as they did not come into conflict with church doctrine. In this case the motto was: unions yes, socialism no.

Things were more difficult in the case of Henry George's clerical sympathizers, not only because his teachings were a hodgepodge of the most diverse ideas borrowed from Karl Marx and Herbert Spencer, but also because the clergy's role was a matter currently under discussion. At least three distinct points of view were involved here. To the extent that the issue was whether a condemnation of private property was compatible with Catholic doctrine, Corrigan was on solid ground and no doubt felt vindicated by the positive evaluation of ownership in the encyclical *Rerum novarum* (1891). On the other hand, Catholics might well have very different opinions about Henry George's idea of a single tax. For this very reason, however, a third question arose: to avoid limiting the autonomy of the laity and to prevent the church from being identified with the private opinions of politically active priests, was a bishop justified in requiring a clergyman to refrain from getting involved in such matters? Curran's assessment that in these controversies two politically ideological camps had emerged within American Catholicism is accurate insofar as the New York clerical radicals around McGlynn became the forerunners of the Protestant Social Gospel movement, which in turn influenced later Catholic social ethicists.

However, there were still not clearly delimited conservative or liberal factions within the church. Inside the church, the McGlynn affair chiefly altered the atmosphere: Gibbons, who was at that time in Rome because he had been made a cardinal, urged that ideas he described as somewhat confused not be taken too seriously. However, Corrigan, who had studied in Rome and still had connections there, concluded from the reports he received that the cardinal had stabbed him in the back (Hennesey 1981, 190).

3. Distance and Closeness to American Culture: The Key Issue in the Conflict

Between 1887 and 1891 conflicts concerning Catholic schools and ethnic parishes, that is, ones in which the parishioners' native language was used, moved to the front of the stage. At the same time the strife took on a new quality, because both sides were not only maneuvering in corridors of the Vatican, where one could easily go through the wrong door, but also trying to get the public involved. One side was interested in internationalizing the discussion, and thus sought the cooperation of Catholic organizations in Italy and France in order to show that it was not a matter of the German language, but of ministry in one's native language. The other side presented this internationalization of the discussion within the church as foreign meddling in

American affairs, and tried to mobilize non-Catholic public opinion in America against it. Ireland, who went furthest in this direction, seemed not to care what kinds of people he mobilized to support him.

The Ethnic Ministry Issue: The Abbelen Memorandum and the Congress of Lucerne

The opposing views were first clearly formulated in a memorandum written by Peter M. Abbelen, a priest from Milwaukee, together with other priests from the German triangle. This memorandum laid out all the ways of promoting ministry in German that had long been discussed. The authors had the support not only of Archbishop Michael Heiss, but also that of Gibbons, whom they kept informed and who at first agreed that Abbelen should represent these ideas in Rome. The memorandum pointed out the extent to which the two large Catholic immigrant groups, the Irish and the Germans, were shaped by differing ways of life, liturgical styles, church holidays, and other traditions. In time the two subcultures would necessarily become assimilated, but "God forbid" that this process be accelerated through the suppression of German language and customs (Gaustad 1982, vol. 2; Barry 1954, 295). The two conceptions of ministry were thus divided over the question as to whether an admittedly inevitable development should be slowed down or speeded up, and they were obviously battling for power within the church as well.

By working with groups that spoke other languages, those who wanted to preserve the ethnic milieu sought to counter the objection that they were ultimately concerned only about "Germanness" (*Deutschtum*). In order to do so, it was necessary to correct the development of the preceding decades, in which national missionary enterprises supported by lay people, such as the Bavarian King Louis Missionary Society or the Austrian Emperor Leopold Foundation, operated independently of each other and had severed their ties with the church-wide Society for the Propagation of the Faith, which was based in Lyons, and which concentrated on promoting missionary work in French. In several countries, a certain counterweight to this nationalistic missionary fervor was provided by "Raphael Societies," which considered themselves an international alliance. In 1890, these Raphael Societies convened in Lucerne, where they passed a petition that was to be delivered to the pope by the Italian Count Volpe-Landi and Peter Paul Cahensly, a German politician who belonged to the Center party.

Later known as the Lucerne Memorial, the petition begins by noting that 400,000 Catholics emigrated to America every year, and that as a result some ten million "souls" had been so far lost to the church. Even if we accept this dubious figure, it has implications that could not have been foreseen by those who proposed it. The American Catholic Church would then have nonetheless succeeded, despite the circumstances in which it grew up and despite freedom of choice, in winning the allegiance of 60 percent of twenty-five million nominal Catholics. These figures thus provided little foundation for the associated demands for native-language parishes and schools, equal treatment for American and immigrant priests, and more attention to national origins in appointing bishops.

The Lucerne Memorial was not a very persuasive presentation of the argument—in itself simplistic—that belief depended on the native language. Nevertheless, it resulted in an unexpected consequence: Ireland and O'Connell saw it as a gift, and accordingly exploited it. O'Connell funneled information to a correspondent working in Rome for the ABC news agency. The latter's reports mention only Cahensly and the Germans, and the Lucerne Memorial's demands are made to seem still more extreme. Ireland, who in a letter to O'Connell wrote that he had recognized the hand behind the news agency reports (Fogarty 1974, 140), gave one interview after another in America, going almost wild. "Send more, send everything; what a miraculous way to promote the good cause," he telegraphed (Hertling 1954, 217), adding, as a justification, that they were after all at war and had to use all the weapons at their disposal (Fogarty 1974, 146).

O'Connell, however, warned Ireland not to go too far. In Rome there was a growing suspicion that the whole affair had been staged by Ireland. As he had previously done in writing to Gibbons, O'Connell pointed out to Ireland that further progress depended upon getting the American administration or Congress involved. As a matter of fact, the issue was raised in the Senate, and Cushman C. Davis, a senator from Minnesota, stated that there had never been a more infamous attempt to misuse religion for political ends than Cahensly's plan. For the senator, it sufficed to know that Cahensly had been a member of the Prussian legislature (Hertling 1954, 218). The Cahensly affair ended as quickly as it had begun, and had no immediate consequences. Among its indirect consequences, however, may have been that Ireland did lasting damage to his standing in Rome, and that in America the demand for native-language ministry was discredited.

The Controversy over Catholic Schools: Ireland's Speech and the Responses to It

The delight of the inner circle of Americanists was short-lived, however, because now the controversy over Catholic schools moved to the center of the stage. In contrast to the case of the Lucerne Memorial, here Ireland was fighting a losing battle against the majority of his episcopal colleagues as well as against the Vatican's repeated reminders. O'Connell's efforts in Rome also fell on deaf ears. In his letters he reported that he had emphasized the financial burdens involved in establishing Catholic schools and pointed out that similar demands were not made on French or Italian Catholics, even though American public schools were better than those in France or Italy. But despite all this, the Vatican persisted in requiring that a private Catholic school be established in every parish (Fogarty 1974, 197 ff.).

Nonetheless, Ireland tried to find a compromise between the public schools' claim to monopolize education and the demand for separate Catholic schools. At the same time, Ireland's political convictions were mingled with pragmatic considerations. On one hand, he wanted the church to be relieved of the financial and staffing burdens involved in establishing its own schools, so that it could concentrate on its central mission. On the other hand, Ireland's American nationalism was reflected in his opinion that public schools were the epitome of "American institutions." When in the summer of 1890 the National Education Association held its annual meeting in St. Paul, Ireland had an irresistible opportunity to present his views. In his typically passionate style, he praised the public schools as "our pride and glory (. . .) Blessed (. . .) the nation whose vales and hillsides they adorn and blessed the generations upon whose souls are poured their treasures" (Reilly 1943, 237). Ireland made it clear, however, that this praise applied only to "secular instruction," and that church-approved religious instruction must be guaranteed before Catholics could forego having their own schools.

These reservations were not included in reports on the meeting, and the non-Catholic press either took Ireland's speech as an unqualified endorsement of public schools or regarded his comments as a clever attempt to bring the public schools under Catholic control. Catholic newspapers, in contrast, and especially the German-language ones, suspected treason and in reporting on Ireland's speech quoted primarily his flowery praise of public schools. Thus in a letter to Gibbons, Ireland set forth his reservations and consequent demands more clearly than he had done in his speech before the teachers and school administrators.

He began by complaining about the inadequate reports and suggesting that they reflect not merely the ignorance but also the "dislike which so many Catholics entertain for American institutions or American ideas." He assured Gibbons that while he defended "compulsory education," this did not entail a government monopoly. Every parish has the right, he went on, to decide "what is required in the state school to make it acceptable to us." And he demanded a "positive Catholic dogmatic teaching" that could not be replaced by "mere moral teaching" or instruction in so-called "common Christianity." When these conditions were met, however, there would no longer be any compelling need for parochial schools, for the church had not been "established to teach writing and ciphering but to teach morals and faith" (Ellis 1967, 2: 474).

Ireland's explanations, which were intended to help the cardinal answer questions from the Vatican or the press, did not lay the subject to rest. Both Catholics and Protestants were too aware of the past history of debates over educational policy, which could only excite mistrust, and Ireland had made himself too prominent in controversies within the church.

Thus ideas and experiments that in themselves were neither original nor scandalous attracted particular attention. For instance, when in 1891 the parishes of Faribault and Stillwater in Minnesota signed a contract with the local school authorities, it became a national issue, even though in 1873 a similar arrangement had been negotiated in New York, under Archbishop McCloskey, between the pastor of St. Peter's Church in Poughkeepsie and the city schools. Following the New York example, the parishes of Faribault and Stillwater leased their school buildings to the local authorities for one dollar a year, while the public school system took responsibility for hiring teachers and maintaining the buildings. In exchange, the public school authorities agreed to allow Catholic religious instruction in the same school buildings, but outside regular school hours.

As Daniel F. Reilly has shown in detail in his book on this so-called school controversy, Ireland now found himself caught between the criticism that the state of Minnesota had gone too far in accommodating the church and the corresponding fear that the church had made too many concessions to the state. In addition, theologians addressed the issue or were called in to help, and in the process the institutions with which they were connected were identified with one side or the other. Thomas Bouquillon, a moral theologian at Catholic University, came to Ireland's assistance with a pamphlet titled *Education: To Whom Does It Belong?* Bouquillon granted the family, the state, and the church all the right to take part in education. In contrast, René Holaind, S.J., who taught at the Jesuits' Woodstock College, upheld the priority of the family, as is made clear by the title of his pamphlet: *The Parents First.*

O'Connell, Satolli, and "the Enemy"

Ireland went to Rome in the summer of 1892 to explain his position on the school issue. The discussions he had there tended to confirm the impression O'Connell had already mentioned in a letter to Gibbons. Despite the American bishops' reservations, Leo XIII seemed determined to appoint a legate. Therefore O'Connell and Ireland apparently agreed to stop resisting the inevitable and instead to work as closely as possible with Archbishop Francesco Satolli, who was to be sent to America as the papal legate.

Satolli's real mission was at first kept secret. He went to America toward the end of 1892, supposedly to deliver valuable old maps that the pope had agreed to lend to the World's Columbian Exposition—although the latter was not scheduled to open until May 1893. To those in the know, this pretext seemed to have its advantages; as O'Connell wrote to Ireland, the "enemy"—that is, Corrigan—should be kept in the dark as long as possible, so that he could not influence Satolli's travel plans and the selection of the people with whom he was to speak (Fogarty 1974, 231).

At first it seemed that they might be able to limit Satolli's contacts. He stayed at Catholic University as Rector Keane's guest, was constantly accompanied by the helpful O'Connell, and brought the ex-communicated McGlynn back into the church community. In the long run, however, it was not possible to keep Satolli from meeting "the enemy," particularly since he had explained to the assembled bishops that he had come with the mission of establishing a legation among the American bishops and to exercise certain papal powers.

O'Connell's and Ireland's hopes were not fulfilled, and the establishment of a papal legation led to the downfall of the Americanist party. Satolli's relatively progressive views, on which O'Connell had counted, turned out to be not very stable, but that was not really the issue. What mattered was that the Vatican now had an independent source of information that was no longer controlled by Gibbons and O'Connell.

The difference made by direct communication between Rome and individual American bishops soon became clear when Ireland once again caused a stir by provoking a public dispute with McQuaid. In 1898, McQuaid was a candidate for a seat on the board of trustees of the State University of New York, and among his rivals was Sylvester Malone, a priest who was one of the clerical radicals around McGlynn. The archbishop of St. Paul came to the diocese of the bishop of Rochester and recommended that Malone rather than McQuaid should be elected. In turn, McQuaid criticized from the pulpit Ireland's meddling in New York politics, and was reprimanded by Rome, probably at Satolli's instigation, and asked to explain himself. McQuaid seemed to have been waiting for such an opportunity. In reply, he described in detail Ireland's role in American ecclesiastical intrigues. McAvoy sees this exchange of letters as the turning point in the Americanist crisis. According to him, McQuaid's description "tipped the scales" against the "club of four" (McAvoy 1957, 123).

Satolli was hardly living up to expectations. He developed good contacts with Corrigan and publicly praised German-speaking Catholics who, as he said, had recently been the object of unjustified suspicions and accusations (Fogarty 1974, 249).

In addition, O'Connell and Ireland did a great deal to weaken their own positions. O'Connell, who had long used his knowledge of gossip in Rome to the advantage of the Americanists, blundered by spreading the rumor that Satolli was Leo XIII's son. Called to account by the pope in 1895, he could only ask to be relieved, on the pretext that he was in poor health, of his office as rector of the American College. In the following year Keane's term of office as rector of Catholic University ended, and although he was recommended again by the relevant committee, Rome declined to reappoint him on the general ground that in such cases occasional changes were desirable (White 1989, 207). Finally, at the ordination of a bishop attended by Satolli, Ireland elaborated on one of his favorite themes, praising the secular clergy and asserting that monastic priests were outdated (Hennesey 1981, 201).

Satolli, who in the interim had been made a cardinal, soon returned to Rome, where he worked together with those whose functions had to do with America or who had worked in America for an extended time. These included the Polish Cardinal Ledochowski, then prefect of *De Propaganda Fide,* and the Italian Jesuits Camillo Mazzella and Salvatore Brandi, both of whom had taught at Woodstock College. Mazzella had been appointed cardinal of the Curia for Catholic educational institutions, and was thus responsible for the Catholic universities, while Brandi directed the important newspaper *Civiltà Cattolica.* Thus in Rome there was now an influential group of people who knew America and who were particularly suspicious of Ireland's activities and prepared to call him to account when the occasion presented itself. Two events that occurred at the same time increased their inclination to do so.

"Work As Though All Depended on Us, and Pray As Though All Depended upon God"

In 1897 French progressive Catholics affiliated with the Institut Catholique commissioned a translation of a biography of Isaac Thomas Hecker, the founder of the Missionary Society of St. Paul the Apostle, that had been published in America in 1891 by Walter Elliott, a member of the Paulists. In the following year the United States went to war with Spain in order to appropriate the latter's remaining American colonies. The events surrounding this war were followed with particular interest in Rome, because disturbing implications could be perceived in them. In official American propaganda, Spain stood for the decadence of the Old World and for everything that stood in the way of human progress, whereas America represented the future, and this division of the world into two parts had denominational undertones that could hardly be missed. Nonetheless, criticism was as muted within the American Catholic Church as among the general public. With the exception of Spalding, who signed an anti-imperialistic declaration, most Catholics supported the war, a few with excessive zeal. Dennis O'Connell wrote that now was the time to give the English-speaking population the recognition owed them by the church. He described the war as a conflict between everything that was old, mean, decrepit, and wrong in Europe and everything that was free, noble, open, and humane in America (Forgarty 1974, 218; Hennesey 1981, 205). In Rome, however, these events were observed with concern, because the future of the missions in the Philippines and in Cuba was in danger.

The biography of Hecker seems at first to have nothing to do with all this, and to offer no grounds for controversy. It is an uncritical, completely unpolemical account of the founder of the Paulist order, written chiefly for the common reader. Only John Ireland's introduction made the book interesting in relation to the controversies within French Catholicism. Ireland, otherwise known to be no friend of monastic life, called the father of the most American of all monastic orders the prototype of American priests, and drew, with a few characteristically bold strokes, a clear portrait of him. According to Ireland, Hecker had the qualities that are necessary in every priest, but which alone are not sufficient. No one need remind him, Ireland went on, that without immigration the American church would have remained insignificant. But that did not alter the fact that priests whose attitudes and practices remained alien to American culture did not make a favorable impression on non-Catholic Americans and on Catholic immigrants' children born in America. In this respect, he maintained, there was no distinction to be drawn between Irish priests and other foreigners.

In contrast, Ireland went on, Father Hecker understood and loved the country and its institutions, and found nothing to deplore or change in them. Accordingly, he had emphasized the natural and social virtues that Americans treasure most. Americans judge a religion first of all by its contribution to social life—"the order of social existence"— and this in no way contradicts Catholic doctrine, since Christ did not come to destroy human institutions but to perfect them. To be sure, Revelation led just as much "to the elevation of the life that is no less than to the gaining of the life to come." As a contrast, Ireland mentioned a well-meaning old priest who faithfully said his rosary, but whose sermons were so bad that he "made a desert around his pulpit." In opposition to this image of pious simplicity Ireland sets the active understanding of the world and of the faith characteristic of the American progressives (who within the church defended contemporary American life against the conservatives). Sometimes people leave more to God than God wishes, Ireland suggested, and sometimes piety serves as an excuse for laziness and cowardice. God does not wish to work any miracles in order to make up for our failures. Our task is to "work as if all depended on us and pray as if all depended on God" (Gaustad 1982, 2: 385 ff.).

This powerful formulation of an Irish-tinged Protestant ethic was now available in French to cardinals to whom the New World was known only by hearsay and who had not read Tocqueville. When after the Spanish-American War a Vatican team (under the leadership of Cardinals Mazzella and Satolli, with Brandi as advisor) was given the assignment of assessing the situation of the American church and the formerly Spanish colonies that had now come under American control, the Hecker biography served as evidence of Americanism's spiritual tendencies. The subsequent encyclical directed against Americanism seems to have resulted from the preparatory work of this team.

All sides regarded Elliott's book as supporting their views. Those critical of the Americans could act as if they were merely warning against certain ideas, without connecting them with anyone in particular, while the Americans being criticized could hide behind the contention that certain ideas discussed in Europe were being lumped together under the name of "Americanism." The Vatican went so far as to encourage this game of hide and seek. That, at least, is the view held by Ireland, who in this situation could only play the role in which he had been cast. Ireland claimed that Cardinal Rampolla, the Vatican Secretary of State, had let him know about the encyclical against Americanism, telling him that it referred to the Hecker biography in order to avoid the harshness of a direct criticism, and that the targets of the encyclical could still evade the issue by insisting that it dealt only with the French translation and a debate that was actually taking place only in France (McAvoy 1957, 281). Ellis is still following Rampolla's advice when he begins his discussion of the text of the encyclical in his collection of documents by noting that "a careless

French translation" led to a crisis in French Catholicism (Ellis 1967, 2: 537).

The encyclical *Testem Benevolentiae,* issued in January 1899, takes the form of a letter to Gibbons. In it, Leo XIII emphasizes his good will and his admiration for America and the American church, which he says he has already expressed, probably referring to his apostolic letter *Longinqua Oceani* of 1895. This time, he went on, he was not concerned to repeat his praise, but rather to offer admonitions and thereby put an end to the discussions that had recently taken place "among you," and which had disturbed the peace of the church. However, in the next sentence these controversies are blamed on those who translated the Hecker biography into another language. In any case, the pope writes that he is taking these controversies as an opportunity to correct certain opinions regarding the conduct of Christian life. These newfangled ideas can be reduced to a single principle: in order more easily to win over those who are not in agreement with Catholic teaching, the church should more fully adapt itself to modern civilization, and for many people this holds not only for ways of life but also for doctrine.

In opposition to this view, Leo XIII maintains that while the rules concerning the conduct of life recognized by Catholicism are in no way inalterable, adaptations to differing circumstances cannot take place in accord with individual whim. In particular, it seems to him important to observe that the previously mentioned new opinions proceed from good intentions, but lead to objectionable consequences. He names two such consequences, which he deals with in the rest of the encyclical. The first, which he discusses only briefly, is that all sorts of help and mediation are made to seem superfluous if not actually harmful, and that people expect the Holy Spirit to act wholly without mediation.

The second consequence of this kind of thinking, which Leo discusses more fully, he describes as the priority of natural virtues over supernatural virtues and the opposition between active and passive virtues associated with it. This opposition depends on a lack of conceptual clarity, because there is no such thing as a passive virtue, and sooner or later it would lead to a depreciation of religious orders. No one who knows the history of the church, he goes on, would seriously maintain that religious orders had made little or no contribution to the church, and to ensure that the hint was taken in Minneapolis, the pope adds that the history of the American church can serve as an example of their significance.

In his conclusion, the pope leaves yet another door open by distinguishing between political and religious Americanism: if Americanism refers to the polity, laws, and customs of the United States, then there is no reason to demand that Americans dissociate themselves from it. However, if it is interpreted to mean the previously mentioned doctrines, then American bishops would certainly be the first to protest, because otherwise it might be suspected that "there are some among you" who want an American church that is different from the church in the rest of the world (Ellis 1967, 2: 539).

The objects of this criticism replied as Rampolla, and indeed the encyclical itself, had suggested. Ireland declared that he rejected the conceptions that were the target of the encyclical, and that in America no one had yet heard of them; accordingly, he regarded it as "an insult to America" to lump such extravagant views under the name of "Americanism" (McAvoy 1957, 281).

For his part, Gibbons wrote that these so-called Americanist doctrines, which he prudently described as extravagant and absurd, had nothing to do with the opinions, hopes, doctrinal beliefs, or even the practical behavior of Americans (Ellis 1952, 2: 71). However, the bishops of the church province of Milwaukee objected to the suggestion that the pope had attacked a straw man—"had beaten the air." The opinions in question, they maintained, had been spread far more by word of mouth than by the written word (McAvoy 1957, 293).

Americanism: An Early Form of Modernism?

There is general agreement that the long series of conflicts in the 1880s and 1890s mark a decisive turning point in the history of the American church and that one may therefore speak of a "great crisis." It is much less clear how this crisis is related to other crises, for example those in Europe, how the participants should be characterized, and what the point at issue was—if, in fact, one can assume that these episodes are all related to each other.

The question of what the relationship between Americanism and European modernism was and whether there actually was any connection between the two movements has been debated since the turn of the century. The first opinions were clearly influenced by partisan points of view. The Americanists themselves sought to establish contacts with progressive European groups—Dennis O'Connell, who continued to live in Rome after his retirement as rector of the American College, was particularly active in this regard—but otherwise they gladly adopted Rome's prescribed phraseology, since like all American nationalists, they were convinced of Americans uniqueness and understood American history more as a break with European tradition than as its continuation (Zöller 1992, 244 ff.). O'Connell's previously mentioned assessment of the Spanish-American war is only a particularly crass expression of the American philosophy of history that was then dominant and that was hardly compatible with the Roman Catholic Church's understanding of history and of itself.

The comparability of Americanism and modernism was emphasized more by those who saw modernism as a necessary reaction to the unified development of modern societies and therefore classified Americanism as one of its forerunners. This kind of interpretation can already be found in the work of Albert Houtin, one of the French modernists (Reher 1980, 89).

Against this interpretation it can be argued that despite superficial similarities (for example, the wish to reconcile the church with contemporary realities), the situations in France and America, for example, were too different, and that in addition Americanism lacked the tendency to approach history critically, and indeed any sort of philosophical and theological ambition. The Americanists' opponents were better versed in theology, and in particular the former theology professor McQuaid, who, as bishop of Rochester, had founded a seminary that soon came to be regarded as one of the best (Hennesey 1981, 179). The small group of Americanists, on the contrary, consisted of men with political talents of various kinds. They were guided by a cultural-political idea, and therefore could take the hand the pope offered them. The real issue was whether the distinction between political and religious Americanism was compatible with America's self-image, and whether a democratized culture could tolerate a certain group's demand to remain different in certain ways. "America" is a normative concept, and to be an American means sharing a set of basic convictions that goes beyond mere loyalty to include a significant degree of conformity, and aggressively resists ideas and ways of life deemed un-American.

Thus it seems that foreigners have to either adapt or withdraw into an ethnic ghetto that allows them to preserve their own heritage, but marks them as outsiders. If they want to give their children an opportunity for integration and advancement, however, there are only two ways of reacting to the pressure for assimilation. The first consists in evading the dominant norms by taking them literally, and at the same time formulating one's own identity differently. A lack of adaptation can be transformed into similarity if ethnic characteristics are presented as an expression of religion (the Irishman as a Christian who happens to be Catholic, the Eastern European Jew as an Orthodox Jew). Religion as a source of social virtues is a distinctive feature that immigrants must not give up if they want to be considered respectable citizens. The second tactic consists not in evading the demands for assimilation but rather in beating them at their own game by presenting Catholicism not only as a particular culture that is entirely compatible with America, but also as a fully Americanized form of Christianity that may in fact be more in tune with the future of American culture and American institutions. This way of pushing Tocqueville's argument further is found in Brownson and Hecker; it leads the pressure for Americanization inward and transforms it into a challenge addressed to those who would like to distinguish more clearly between political and religious Americanism.

This more inward expectation of assimilation necessarily moves the battle over American culture and the nativistic mode of argumentation into the church. On one hand the Americanists thought they were already fully participating in American society and in its hopes for the future; on the other, their belief that they "had made it" was constantly contradicted by other Catholics' obvious lack of adaptation. The more the Americanists insisted that only real Americans could instruct Americans in the Catholic faith, the more emphatically they confirmed the norm that Ireland had described as Father Hecker's advantage: he understood and loved the country and its institutions, and found nothing wrong with them (Ellis 1967, 2: 537).

Thus within the American church two groups with differing cultural politics and conceptions of ministry opposed one another. One believed that to be a good American it sufficed to honor the republic and its laws and, if necessary, to defend it by force of arms, and that anyone who fulfilled these duties of a citizen had thereby earned the right to preserve the specificity of his own heritage and to make himself at home in his own subculture. The other group insisted that America was more than a geographical concept, and even more than a political system, and therefore one became an American by adopting the country's way of life and its fundamental convictions. Hence they acknowledged society's right to exert pressure to assimilate on immigrants and accepted public schools as a logical consequence of this legitimate demand.

It is no accident that this Americanist position was first formulated by converts like Brownson and Hecker, who were Americans before they became Catholics. Later on, this view was espoused in particular by Irish clergymen who had made their careers in America, such as John Ireland, who no longer appeared to be hampered by anything that prevented their incorporation into American society. To them it seemed obvious that one could become an American through a conscious, voluntary decision, a free act of belief.

Retrospectively one can choose to say that both sides were right, or that later developments were not in accord with the ideas of either of the two "parties." On one hand, the Catholic Church not only gained a footing in America but also Americanized itself and confirmed Tocqueville's prediction that Catholicism was entirely compatible with democracy and with American culture. On the other hand, American Catholicism's success was directly connected with the fact that the ethnic subculture in which it was anchored had both integrating and distancing effects. This ethnic subculture proved to be an effective vehicle of integration, because it offered an intermediate support system that relied upon immigrants helping themselves in an organized way. At the same time, by keeping alive the memory of a cultural heritage, it made available an element of distancing and thus self-respect, even if what was preserved as the culture of the "old country" often owed a great deal to the New World, that is, was often already a product of the American situation. Nonetheless, this notion of a subculture served initially as the underpinning for Rome's insistence that even an Americanized Catholicism had to be more than an expression of American society.

This mixture of integration and distance provided the recipe not only for American Catholicism's success but also for its enduring internal conflicts. How much adaptation was possible and how much distance was necessary was a question that in the subsequent history of American Catholicism has repeatedly arisen in two forms, both indicated in *Testem Benevolentiae.* In his apostolic letter, Leo XIII speaks of the tendency to consider any kind of help or mediation superfluous or even harmful. Looking back on modern American religious history, we can see this as concern about how a culture that is favorable to religion but also populist—and that means anti-elitist and anti-institutional—can accept the concept of an ecclesiastically organized religion, that is, a magisterium independent of society. In addition, Leo XIII was also worried about the inherently problematic distinction between active and passive virtues.

4. The Catholic Milieu

Immigration at Its Height

While a cultural war was being waged within the American Catholic Church, the number of immigrants constantly rose, and the proportion of Irish and German immigrants fell. Instead, immigrants now poured in from southern and especially eastern Europe. The immigrants were increasingly concentrated in the northeastern states, and around the Great Lakes, where there were many jobs in industry. In 1880 the population of New York had already reached a million, and yet by the turn of the century it had risen to three and a half million; during the same twenty years Chicago experienced a fourfold increase, the population growing from 410,000 to 1.7 million (Hertling 1954, 155).

These demographic developments were more noticeable within the Catholic Church than among the general population, so that a large Eastern European element was added to American Catholicism. It further differed from the American average by its high proportion of industrial workers and city-dwellers as well as by its concentration in the northeastern states. In New York and Chicago, as well as in cities such as Pittsburgh, Detroit, and Cleveland, this resulted in conditions favoring the development of ethnic subcultures. Many national associations of all kinds were formed (Conzen 1976; Doerries 1986), yet the ethnic church community was by far the most important institution in this initially clearly separate world of the immigrants. It did not focus on a single concern, but rather played a role in every aspect of its members' lives.

The Catholic immigrant parish thus took on the character of a central social institution, for above and beyond the network of associations and volunteer activities available in all American religious communities, its parochial school gave it a milieu-building capacity that reached into the heart of every family. Despite their relatively clear demarcation from the outside world and despite their dense networks of internal relationships, in the long run parishes dominated by a single ethnic group did not function as reservations protecting German Catholic or Polish Catholic identity, no matter what might have been expected. They did not do so first of all because this kind of identity was not nearly so developed and manifest as the Raphael Societies' Lucerne Memorial had assumed. The often-quoted passages insisting that it was necessary to preserve the immigrants' faith or to use their language in order to maintain their belief obviously presuppose that the immigrants had brought with them a national culture bound up with their native language and that this culture was essentially religious. Neither of these presuppositions is self-evidently true.

Religion as an Accepted Form of Nonconformity

The later immigration from a given country began, the more likely immigrants were to be conscious of their national identity. Yet in the second half of the nineteenth century, when a million Europeans had already emigrated to America, the ideology of national integration had not yet spread to every part of Europe, and neither had official national languages. Among the German lower and middle classes, mastery of High German could not be assumed; in Hamburg, for instance, witnesses swore oaths in Low German as late as the middle of the nineteenth century (Doerries 1986, 205). In the 1860s Garibaldi still relied on interpreters when he made his great march through Italy.

Even the presumed religious orientation of the immigrants and their native countries seems to be largely a retrospective illusion. In the case of Ireland, it has been estimated that before the great famine and the mass emigration that followed it not more than 40 percent of the Catholics regularly attended church. Up until World War I

American priests complained about gaps in immigrants' religious training (Dolan 1975, 54). Reports suggest that in this regard Italians fell beneath even the already low average—a fact that could always be cited with a certain malicious glee when doubts were expressed in Rome regarding the orthodoxy of Americans. Thus the German and Italian Catholics whose faith the commonly cited formula suggested it was necessary to preserve were often not Germans or Italians in terms of cultural socialization, and often not Catholics in terms of religious socialization—even if they were Catholics from the church's point of view.

From Ethnic Parish to Denomination: Stages
in Integration and More Abstract Self-Description

It is important to recognize this fact, because it already shows that from the outset the immigrant parishes preserved and also transformed their self-conception, and that even sheltered in this way, immigrants had to learn how to transfer their orientation and their solidarity to increasingly more abstract entities. Relying on the way people referred to them and on their own observations of linguistic relationships, agricultural workers from the Palatinate and from Sicily learned to define themselves as Germans or Italians. The immigrant's nationality was thus often a result of the American situation. But this in no way exhausted the transformative effects of the ethnic subculture, and immigrants and their descendents were repeatedly called upon to rise to further levels of abstraction. Catholic schools and colleges in particular consciously and unconsciously operated as agencies of Americanization by providing what was required—from the English language to the relevant academic degrees—for professional advancement, and thus also for moving out of the ethnic subculture.

Just as important, but often overlooked, is the fact that it was only in the immigrant parishes that ethnic identity could be repeatedly raised to the next level of abstraction, and this lessened the generational conflict in immigrant families. The first generation defined itself retrospectively, regardless of whether the native culture it looked back to was real or fictitious. The second and third generations could not and would not be satisfied with this; they were not only subjected to much greater pressure to assimilate, but could also hope to take part in the whole range of American life.

The solution was to identify oneself in terms of denomination rather than nationality. Thus it became possible to be American and Catholic, and it was in this way, not as a Pole or a Croatian, that one was connected with the preceding generation, whose stories of life in the "old country" no longer interested anyone. The sociologist Ruby Joe Kennedy studied the marriage practices of several generations of immigrants and found that the second generation still married chiefly within the same ethnic group, whereas from the third generation on, most marriages crossed ethnic boundaries, but remained within the same denomination (Kennedy 1944).

Will Herberg's description of the corresponding discussions within American Judaism shows the kind of alternatives immigrants confronted and the conflicts that resulted from them. Between 1820 and 1870 half a million Jews immigrated from eastern Europe; they were generally referred to as "German Jews" and like the German Catholics they developed their own institutional network. After 1880, heavy immigration from eastern Europe continued until World War II, and most of the approximately two million additional Jewish immigrants were Orthodox Jews. A controversy regarding the relationship between Judaism, American culture, and European descent quickly developed, and in this case the Germans played the Americanist role—that is, they advocated the concept of the melting pot, whereas the eastern European Orthodox Jews argued for cultural pluralism and insisted on the bond between Judaism and culture. They had only one word for Jewish and Yiddish, and thus tried to preserve *Jiddishkait*. On the other hand, the so-called "German Jews," who were influenced by European biblical criticism, German philosophy, and liberal theology, saw themselves as bound together by their religion, and did not want to distinguish themselves in any other way from Americans (Herber 1955, 172 ff.).

In American Judaism, and still more in American Protestantism, fundamental conflicts led to opposing sides developing their own organizational forms, and even attempts to formulate a compromise usually led to a third, independent organization. Thus Reform and Orthodox Judaism emerged, each with its own synagogues, while the "Conservatives" established themselves in the middle ground between them. Conservative Judaism, to which the great majority of American Jews eventually adhered, adopted certain elements of "liberal theology" but emphasized that despite a positive attitude toward American political structures, Jews still live "in two civilizations," and it therefore insisted on distinguishing between political Americanism and religious-cultural Americanism.

In the Catholic Church, in contrast, it was the course of the institution as a whole that was constantly at issue, as the corresponding controversies make massively and tediously evident. The compromise between Americanism and multiculturalism, which in Judaism became, in the form of the consensus of the Conservative synagogues, the program of the center and the majority, had its counterpart in Catholicism in the practice of the "silent majority," but it had first to be supported by a papal decree.

In the long run this combination of nearness and distance could be maintained, however, only because American Catholicism had its own social form. In order to become American and yet remain Catholic, Catholics had to transform the ethnic subculture into a milieu, and even after the peak of the Americanist crisis this did not happen without frictions, chiefly because the most recent immigrants were not yet prepared to move from the protection of the ethnic community to the Catholic milieu. Thus in 1897 a Polish Catholic Church was founded in America, and in 1906 a Lithuanian National Church was established in Chicago. The latter emerged in part as a reaction to the dominance of Polish Catholicism in Chicago: Lithuanian parents thought Polish nuns were educating their children as Poles. These schisms were made easier by the willingness of the European Old Catholics to ordain their spiritual leaders, Anton Koslowski and Stephan Kaminski, as bishops. However, this sort of thing remained the exception, because it conflicted with the long-term interests of immigrant families. Compared with the drawback of belonging to an expressly un-American religious splinter group, having one's children taught by Polish nuns seemed clearly the lesser evil.

In general, the price the church had to pay for its unification remained small, and the history of this transformation is one of the American success stories. One can therefore distinguish between the events of the Great Crisis, which are in themselves not very attractive, and the results—that is, one can argue that in the end neither of the two sides was right, and yet both were justified to a certain degree. The subculture was not an institution intended to hinder Americanization, but rather a necessary way station. The question whether an immigrant had retained his faith was wrongly formulated, because instead it was necessary to figure out how poor, uneducated immigrants with weak religious ties could become Americans and Catholics. Without the creation of a Catholic milieu this achievement would not have been conceivable, and the special character of this milieu once again consisted in the dual institutionality of the church's cultural community and its own educational system.

Ecclesial Maturity: America's Release from Missionary Status

At the beginning of the new century, this very promising development within the American church was recognized in Rome as well. The achievement was particularly striking when compared with what had happened in other countries. Thus when Leo XIII, who in 1902 could look back on twenty-five years as pope, wrote to Gibbons to thank him for his good wishes on the occasion of his jubilee, he not only praised the American church, whose condition "gladdened his heart," but also emphasized that in contrast, "nations that have been Catholic for many centuries" were giving him cause for concern (Ellis 1967, 2: 547). Leo died the following year, and his successor, Pius X, finally released the New World from its status as a missionary region and thus from the authority of *De Propaganda Fide.* In 1908, after extensive deliberations by Vatican authorities, the pope declared in *Sapienti consilio* that American Catholicism had reached ecclesial maturity.

4

ON THE WAY TO THE
CENTER OF AMERICA
1908–1963

AMERICAN CATHOLICS WERE able to enter the new century confident that Rome would get used to accepting Americans, and that America would learn to respect them as Catholics. This by no means meant that they no longer had to explain themselves inwardly and outwardly and that the nativistic argument was a thing of the past. In 1887 the American Protective Association (APA) was formed; in order to ensure "true Americanism" it demanded that citizenship be denied to anyone "subject to any ecclesiastical power not created and controlled by American citizens." The Populist party, which had already lost all influence, discovered that the Catholic Church was a dangerous, conspiratorial organization, and the Ku Klux Klan called upon people to be vigilant and to defend American institutions, in particular the public schools, against Catholic assault (Gaustad 1982, 2: 262). Resentment directed toward Catholics thus continued, although it could now be exploited only indirectly. The Protestant clergy now seldom participated in actions and organizations whose explicit purpose was to oppose Catholics, for the situation and the mood of American Protestantism had fundamentally changed.

1. The Cultural Climate after the First World War

Protestant Self-doubt and Catholic Confidence

In the meantime, an internal cultural conflict had also evolved within Protestantism. The issue was not the relationship between Protestantism and America but rather what attitude America and Protestant Christianity, which was still identified with America, should adopt toward a modern culture perceived as increasingly non-Christian if not anti-Christian. Protestantism, which was unorganized but culturally dominant, and had for decades possessed the definitional power to determine who was a true American, now had to show whether it was still able to meet the challenges of the time.

In addition, social and cultural changes were threatening to undermine Protestantism's conception of itself, while at the same time apparently leaving undisturbed supposedly un-American, anti-progressive Catholicism. The facts that in 1900 there were more than forty-one cities with populations of over 100,000, whereas in 1850 there were only six in all, and that in the country as a whole the small town, rural middle-class sociocultural milieu had become less influential, were not a problem for Catholicism, which had in any case played a minor role in the latter. Moreover, the great change in the cultural situation, the combined effect of evolutionism and historical and critical Bible research, seemed much less threatening to Catholicism and tended to confirm the Catholic view that the Bible alone did not provide a firm foundation for faith. On the other hand, Protestantism was fundamentally challenged by the new intellectual climate, and had to decide whether it should and could reject it as inspired by German ideas, or should instead emphasize its compatibility with religious belief. Thus in the second half of the nineteenth century two camps were formed within Protestantism. At first they differed chiefly in their evangelistic style and in the associated assessment of contemporary culture, but the longer they existed the more they developed programmatic positions expressly opposed to each other.

The Two Camps within Protestantism

For several decades the representative of the anti-modern and anti-intellectual tendency was the preacher Dwight Lyman Moody, who attracted large audiences and lacked any academic training. The opposite role was played by Henry Ward Beecher, a scion of the Beecher dynasty of clergymen and intellectuals. This descendant of the Puritans not only strove to build bridges between science and faith, but also tirelessly advocated a positive and optimistic outlook on the world. He described the opposition accordingly: whereas Moody thought the world was lost and was trying to save as much as he could from the sinking ship, Beecher believed that Jesus Christ had come to save the world, and he wanted to help Him (Marty 1984, 313).

Increasingly, these two differing conceptions took on the character of partisan opinions. In contrast to the Catholic Americanist crisis of the 1880s and 1890s, here the goal was not to gain dominance within an institution in order to control its relation to the surrounding culture. American Protestants, who had no common ecclesiastical organization, had always been able to consider American culture as an expression of their unity, as a sort of substitute for a church. Now, however, they found themselves on the defensive, not only opposing new cultural forces but also fighting among each other. Like the competing Catholic groups, they appealed to the public, trying to get their views accepted with the help of public opinion and legislative action. The only result, however, was that they involuntarily helped increase the domination of public opinion and politics over culture.

This was what happened in the case of Prohibition, one of the few subjects on which there still seemed to be wide consensus among Protestants. Thus a sociopolitical measure whose effects were uncertain was popularized, with the help of a religious crusade, as a cultural no-confidence vote directed against large groups of immigrants (it "served them right"), and finally pushed through politically. The resulting eighteenth amendment to the constitution remained in force for fourteen years and was American Protestantism's last cultural victory, but a Pyrrhic one. However, even internal controversies were increasingly carried on using modern ways of influencing public opinion, and this ultimately helped further diminish religion's influence on culture and increase the politicization of culture. For example, the revivalists' conception of religion, which involved no clearly formulated dogma and had relied on the individual experience of conversion, was transformed when it was presented to a mass audience. In 1910 the Stewart brothers, who had grown wealthy in the oil business, donated money to have traditional, narrowly Bible-oriented, Protestant religiousness expounded and differentiated in a series of pamphlets that were distributed by the millions under the title *The Fundamentals*. These pamphlets not only gave a new name to Protestant conservatism but also systematized and intellectualized it, and thereby helped transform a traditionalistic religious style into an organized and highly politicized movement.

Fundamentalism was nonetheless different from traditional, non-political literalism. This becomes particularly clear in the fate of a symbolic figure, the moralistically religious William Jennings Bryan. As Secretary of State under Woodrow Wilson, whom he resembled in many respects, Bryan initially played a decisive role in the campaign for Prohibition, but his name is associated above all with the Scopes trial. This spectacular trial, which was held in Dayton, Tennessee in 1925, concerned a teacher who had violated a law passed by the Tennessee legislature that same year, which banned the teaching of the theory of evolution in the public schools. The trial is usually portrayed as a confrontation between religion and science, but other aspects are also noteworthy. First of all, the teacher, John Thomas Scopes, was supported and encouraged by the American Civil Liberties Union, while Bryan was eager to represent the prosecution. Both sides were looking for an effective example to put before the public, and otherwise had little interest in Dayton. The media played along, and in fact the reporting on the "monkey trial" is often counted among radio broadcasting's pioneering achievements. The fundamentalist side also wanted a public debate and even hoped thereby to win victory in the internal Protestant conflict.

American Protestantism was thus deeply divided and unsure of itself, in complete contrast to the optimistic sense of moving forward that characterized American Catholicism at this time. In his history of churches in America, Robert Handy speaks of the "spiritual depression" experienced by Protestantism after World War I (Handy 1971, 398), whereas William M. Halsey describes the intellectual climate in Catholicism at the same point as naïve optimism, and therefore titles his book *The Survival of American Innocence* (Halsey 1980). Although American Protestantism and American Catholicism were confronted by similar alternatives, and although in both denominations two camps were formed, neither their traditions and organizational forms nor their initial situations were the same. This led to an important difference between them.

2. The Emergence of a National Catholic Public Sphere

Catholicism was determined not only by the rule of church unity, but also by its minority status. It therefore directed the pressure inward, and in accord with its tradition, tried to resolve or at least defuse conflicts by internal differentiation. In contrast, Protestantism generalized questions, and tried to transform internal problems into moral challenges to the whole community while defusing conflicts by organizational pluralization, with the result that by the turn of the century there were some three hundred Protestant denominations. In addition, the reactions of others reinforced American Protestantism's assessment of its situation: it gradually came to be, as it was later put, a majority with a minority consciousness (Herberg 1955, 47). American Catholicism, in contrast, had in the interim become a force to be reckoned with, although it represented hardly a fifth of the population and apart from politics, played hardly any role in public life. Nonetheless, it was full of the well-founded feeling that it had "made it." American Catholics showed so much self-confidence that they could have been described as a minority with a majority consciousness. This feeling about themselves was not diminished by the fact that a few intellectuals complained about a cultural deficiency: they held that the intellectual world was meaningless for the everyday life of American Catholicism, and that conversely, the latter played no role in America's spiritual life. Unimpressed, Catholics remained not only optimistic about their own future but also became some of the most fervent champions of America's mission in the world.

At the beginning of World War I about fifteen million Catholics were living in the United States, constituting, according to the 1910 census, about 17 percent of the total population of ninety-two million. In 1920, when the census showed a population of one hundred six million, the *Official Catholic Directory* counted 17,885,000 Catholics, and this means that between the beginning of the war and the beginning of the 1920s the proportion of Catholics in the population had remained constant. Even before the war, with the appointment of a bishop of El Paso, the fifth in Texas, the number of American dioceses rose to ninety-seven, and in 1911 Pius X emphasized the increased importance of the American church by appointing the archbishops of New York and Boston, John Farley and William O'Connell, to the College of Cardinals (Hertling 1954, 155 ff., 165).

The war not only made this significant minority more visible to other Americans, but also led to a new national organizational structure within American Catholicism. Despite the large proportion of Catholics of German and Irish descent, who for different reasons were not very enthusiastic about the war, opposition ceased once America had entered the war. Catholics represented more than a fifth of the 4.7 million American soldiers who served during the war, and a thousandth of those who refused to serve, namely four out of a total of 3,989 (Hennesey 1981, 225). And in their official proclamations, many bishops went far beyond the call of duty (McKeown 1980, 40).

From the Catholic War Council to the National Catholic Welfare Conference: The First Steps toward Centralization

The bishops' willingness to openly support the war and the eagerness with which Catholic organizations took part in caring for the troops seemed to call for a national organization of the American church, and this encouraged those who were in favor of such a centralized organization for reasons apart from the war itself. Father John J. Burke, the editor of the periodical *Catholic World* published by the Paulists, was one of the moving forces behind this kind of union. With Gibbons' help, he had succeeded in bringing together representatives of most of the dioceses, the Catholic lay associations, and almost all the members of the Catholic Press Association, who agreed to found the National War Council. Burke, who was looking beyond the present opportunity, insisted that the group be placed under the authority of the council of archbishops, so that their meeting took on an official character.

The archbishops, who met in November at the annual meeting of the board of trustees of Catholic University, agreed to establish the Catholic War Council themselves, so that the latter might be authorized to speak for the church. While the Council organized care for military personnel and other activities for the troops, the representatives of the national organization began to campaign for a permanent institution.

The war also led to a shift of power within the American system by strengthening the federal government at the expense of the states. For this reason many groups, including the Catholic Church, had begun to have their interests represented in Washington, and no one seriously expected any of the governmental agencies or offices representing a specific group that had emerged as a result of the war to be disbanded once the war was over.

In a letter to his fellow bishops, Gibbons sought to explain why a permanent national organization and a corresponding representation in Washington were necessary. It seemed to him clear that such plans could also be interpreted as the beginning of an effort to weaken the power of individual bishops, and for that reason he emphasized that precisely because such representation was lacking, episcopal authority was imperiled by the increased importance of federal policies, the Catholic laity's self-confidence, and the nationwide influence of the media. In particular, Gibbons went on, there was a danger that un-authorized groups or individuals might claim to speak for the church. The bishops should organize themselves, he said, both to strengthen ecclesiastical authority within the church and to represent Catholic interests in the public sphere more effectively (McKeown 1980, 50 ff.).

In February 1919 the majority of the bishops assembled in Washington to celebrate the fiftieth anniversary of Gibbons' ordination as a bishop, and the occasion was taken to approve proposals to establish a National Catholic Welfare Council* and to hold an annual meeting. Welfare, which was supposed to be dealt with by the annual conference of bishops as well as by its permanent office, was still understood in the older, more general sense of the welfare or interests of Catholics and their church. Benedict XV, who had succeeded Pius X in 1914, gave his seal of approval to these plans, and a conference of bishops was called for September 1919 to discuss the details. Supporters of the conference suggested that seven bishops constitute a central committee with the authority to respond to questions that arose when the conference of bishops was not in session. Initially, the secretariat was to consist of five departments responsible for education, social services, lay activities, the Catholic press, and the propagation of the faith both in the United States and abroad.

The critics of centralization saw these plans as curtailing individual bishops' freedom to make their own decisions, and considered an annual conference of bishops sufficient. In their view, the pope had agreed only to such an annual conference, and not to a new "over-arching authority." However, only a few, including William Cardinal O'Connell of Boston and Archbishop Sebastian Messmer of Milwaukee, made this argument. The great majority voted in favor of the pro-

---

*As Martin Marty points out, after the war a peacetime equivalent was found for the "W" in the acronym NCWC: "Welfare" replaced "War" (Marty 1984, 365).

posal to transform the War Council into a permanent Welfare Council, and appointed seven bishops to take care of the necessary arrangements. Joseph Schrembs, who was then bishop of Toledo, and after 1921 bishop of Cleveland, was the spokesman for this committee for the following three years.

These appointments show two things. First, there was no longer a German faction. German immigrants had been particularly eager to adapt to American society, and moreover anti-German propaganda during the war had led them to conclude that it was better to be inconspicuous. Overt ethnic politics had long been abandoned by German immigrant groups, at least within the Catholic Church. Accordingly, bishops of German descent were now on both sides of the issue. Messmer belonged to the conservative faction, which mistrusted a national organization and supported direct ties between Rome and individual bishops. Schrembs, on the other hand, was for several years the spokesman of the Americanizing, centralizing faction.

However, Americanization no longer meant establishing the monopoly of the English language, but rather further centralizing a unified American church. As a result, the system of three groups was replaced by an opposition between two camps that were nonetheless still defined entirely in terms of church politics. The Americanists, now including a few Germans, worked toward an American church that was as internally unified as possible and conducted itself with regard to Rome as self-confidently as possible, whereas the conservatives gathered around Messmer, O'Connell, and McDonnell (the latter two had begun as Corrigan's protégés) in the more Rome-oriented faction opposing centralization. The next step, the transfer of this opposition between progressives and conservatives to the level of general political issues, occurred in the 1930s. It first became discernible in lay people and in the emergence of a new kind of clergymen associated with national organizations, even before a polarization between right and left appeared in the conference of bishops as well.

The issue itself turned into a long tug of war. The resolutions passed in November 1919 disappeared into Roman file cabinets. In the meantime, members of the Council, which had not yet been dissolved, took steps to show what the letter "W" in the Council's name meant, while critics of the new structure were finding allies in Rome.

John A. Ryan, a social ethicist who ran the Council's Social Action department, published a program for social reconstruction that was subsequently referred to as "the bishops' program," even though the latter were never involved in its elaboration. The members of the preparatory committee therefore warned Ryan and his collaborators to be careful. One of the seven bishops, William T. Russell of Charleston, wrote to Ryan to say that he himself agreed with these ideas, but that that was not the issue: the Council's collaborators must understand that they as well as the seven bishops on the Council would deserve to be "reprimanded" if "without the authority of the hierarchy we seem to commit the whole body to any particular plan." It was even to be feared, he went on, that rushing ahead in this way might result in "a severe, if not fatal blow" to the whole National Council organization (McKeown 1980, 53).

The bishops Russell had in mind were strengthened when upon Gibbons' death Dennis Dougherty, archbishop of Philadelphia, was appointed as the third American cardinal, alongside O'Connell and Farley. In addition, they found a Vatican ally in Cajetan Cardinal de Lai, who was critical of the American plans because he saw in them the first steps toward a separate national church. De Lai convinced the pope and drew up a decretal ordering the dissolution of the Council. When Benedict XV died in January 1922, he had not yet signed the decretal, but his successor, Pius XI, found the order among the unfinished business and gave it his approval (Ellis 1967, 2: 601).

The members of the preparatory committee now showed what a central organization could do and how it could shape a collective will. Within a few days they got ten of the thirteen archbishops and two-thirds of the other bishops to send Rome a telegram asking that the decretal's publication in the *Actae Sanctae Sedis*—which would have put it into effect—be delayed, in order to give the Council's proponents another opportunity to explain their position. This was granted, and Schrembs went to Rome as the majority's representative. The executive committee gave him a petition addressed to the pope, and its style could serve as an illustration of what the opposition feared. It acknowledged that even the majority was subject to criticism and that sometimes this criticism might be justified; "this we understand." However, it went on, the minority of bishops who opposed the continuation of the Council "entertained misconceptions of this work" because they were "not informed" and therefore did not recognize its "true value" (McKeown 1980, 55). Schrembs obtained the pope's approval and at the end of June, sounding like a war correspondent, he telegraphed home: "Fight is won . . . hard struggle . . . complete victory" (Ellis 1967, 2: 608).

The NCWC remained in operation, but now not only the "W" but also the second "C" took on a new meaning. At the Vatican's request, the Council became a Conference, in order to emphasize the purely advisory character of the conference of bishops. Thus from 1922 on there was a National Catholic Welfare Conference, and under the leadership of its general secretary, John J. Burke, it quickly became an institution with its own influence and way of proceeding.

The distinction between advising and deciding did not change the fact that within the Catholic Church there was a redistribution of power similar to the one that had occurred in relations between the federal government and the states during the war. The individual bishops had to accept a loss in influence, and the importance of the church's national representation increased. However, this only confirmed what had already happened independently of the existence and constitution of such a leading organization. Even in the intervals between the three nineteenth-century plenary councils, which the popes had convened after careful preparation by Vatican authorities and the American archbishops, the interests of the American church had been represented in Rome as well as among the American public. This representation was effected through agreements among the archbishops, by individual bishops such as the publicity-hungry John Ireland, and by groups of bishops like the Americanists and their opponents. Compared to what had happened in earlier decades, an annual conference of bishops offered, as Gibbons had emphasized, the advantage of orderly modes of procedure.

So long as the bishops kept to themselves and were the only ones acting, a central committee could ensure both mutual discipline and peace within the church. In fact, the bishops succeeded in establishing this kind of monopoly on power for a few decades. After a long struggle, they had wrested control from the trustees. Lay people like Brownson or groups of priests like the New York radicals were exceptions to the rule, and despite their public notoriety they did not achieve positions of influence within the church. Only religious orders, with the help of the Vatican, were in a position to oppose the bishops, and for this reason they were seen by many bishops as a thorn in their sides.

However, the establishment of the War Council and its transformation into a Welfare Conference had demonstrated that it was ultimately no longer a question of which bishops were authorized to speak for the bishops as a whole, and under what conditions. The War Council had been instigated not by the bishops, but rather by Burke, and although Ryan's program for social reconstruction had been endorsed by the bishops, the latter could only react, whether or not they agreed with the proposals.

Thus between the world wars, the American Catholic Church organized itself on the national level, and this meant not only that ecclesiastical life was further bureaucratized and politicized, but also that the leadership changed. On one hand, a different kind of bishop was selected, and on the other, a whole new type of church official emerged whose chances of having an impact were bound up with the national organizational structure.

Nonetheless, bishops now confronted additional demands as well. A bishop who wanted to exercise influence outside his own diocese had to learn to deal with the new organization and its logic, get used to working on committees and commissions, and engage in shaping public opinion. A bishop who wanted to play a role on the national level thus needed managerial as well as political abilities.

The characteristics of these new ecclesiastical elites suggest that in the course of centralizing unification the Catholic social milieu had once again taken on a more abstract form. While the ethnic protective associations had been transformed into a Catholic milieu, so that loyalty and solidarity had shifted from nationality to denomination, now there emerged along with the central organization a unified mode of communication. Over and above the countless small Catholic milieus developed the structures of a national Catholic public sphere, to which one could still belong when one no longer lived in a Catholic neighborhood. Alongside parishes and dioceses, alongside the bishop and his clergy, a new corps of church officials grew up that was not concerned only to represent "Catholic interests" to the outside world, but rather understood their mission as bridging the gap between internal communication among Catholics and national political debates, working in both directions. However, the more similar the two public spheres became, the less Catholics lived in two separate cultures, and the more clearly the outlines of two political camps appeared within Catholicism as a result of individuals' still more abstract sense of their affiliations. This was a phenomenon that had long been discernible in American Protestantism.

Initially, however, the most striking and consequential changes consisted in the altered mechanisms of recruiting the elites that resulted in a new kind of bishop and a new kind of official, still usually drawn from the clergy, becoming active on the national scene. The bishops in any case controlled one end of the recruiting process, since they decided which young theologians would be sponsored, chiefly through scholarships for study in Rome. During the nineteenth century powerful archbishops had also brought the other end of the process under their control by not only playing a decisive role in the selection of auxiliary bishops but also acquiring a virtually unchallenged right to determine their own successors.

Conversely, under certain circumstances the American College in Rome, as one of the first central institutions created by the American bishops, was able to transform itself into an instrument of an independent Vatican appointment policy, since it provided a choice of particularly well-educated candidates who were personally known in Rome. Since the beginning of the century, a bishop of this new, Roman type had been selected more and more often for appointment in the newer dioceses of the West and Midwest where the structures were not yet firmly established, or in certain dioceses in the Northeast that had long been overshadowed by New York and Baltimore. For example, of the four American cardinals in the period between the two world wars, three had worked in Rome, while only one had spent his whole career in his diocese. The latter, Patrick J. Hayes, was appointed archbishop of New York in 1919 and a cardinal in 1924. Hayes had already served his predecessor, Cardinal Farley, as auxiliary bishop and spent his whole life in New York—a career track that had become typical in New York. Later archbishops made their way by serving the archdiocese, became auxiliary bishops or coadjutors and when they finally took over "the business" they knew it very well. Put positively, this meant that no one could try to put one over on them; put negatively, it meant that they brought to their new positions their own likes and dislikes, and continued to busy themselves with the task of running the mechanism through whose ranks they had risen. On one hand, because of its position as America's largest ecclesiastical province, the archdiocese of New York seemed predestined for the "red hat"; on the other, from Corrigan's death at the beginning of the century to World War II, when Spellman began his career, it played no role on the national level. Instead, other dioceses gained power, particularly the ambitious dioceses of Chicago, Philadelphia (which had seemed too near Baltimore), and Boston (which had to compete with neighboring New York).

Going Big: O'Connell, Dougherty, Mundelein and the American Version of Romanità

The three "Romans" were Dennis Dougherty, William H. O'Connell, and George Mundelein. All three had completed their education in Rome and constantly emphasized their *Romanità*, which was the deciding factor both in their careers and in the way they saw things.

William H. O'Connell returned to the American College in Rome in 1895, a few years after he had finished his studies there, in order to replace—presumably on Satolli's recommendation—Dennis O'Connell, who held entirely different views. After six more years in Rome, he became bishop of Portland, Maine in 1901, archbishop of Boston in 1907, and finally a cardinal in 1911. He led the Boston diocese until 1944.

Dougherty's career included a detour caused by American colonial policy. In 1903 he was ordained bishop of a Philippine diocese, and in 1915 returned to America as bishop of Buffalo. But in 1918 he was appointed archbishop of Philadelphia, and in 1921 brought this city its first cardinal's hat. For thirty-three years he performed his duties with a particularly firm hand and generally acknowledged efficiency, accompanying and promoting a hitherto unimaginable degree of institutional growth, so that he became known above all through the many photos in the press showing him in the symbolic act of laying still another foundation stone. He described himself as "God's bricklayer," leading his generation of bishops later to be called the "brick and mortar generation."

Like other "Romans," Dougherty saw himself as marked by his special relationship to Rome, and in public he repeatedly stressed that "after God I owe what I am to the Holy See." If many members of the preceding generation of bishops had complained about Rome's failure to understand Americans, now the new kind of American princes of the church informed others, such as General Secretary Burke, that Americans who had not been in Rome or elsewhere abroad, understood nothing at all (Hennesey 1981, 240 ff.).

However, it was George Mundelein who came to symbolize this period. He is comparable to Dougherty and O'Connell in every way, and yet in his life their common tendencies appear in a grandiosely enhanced form. A German immigrant's son born on New York's Lower East Side, he grew up in very modest circumstances. He went to the parish elementary school and finally, with the financial support of a family friend, he also attended Manhattan College. After three years in a seminary, in 1892 he was admitted to the American College in Rome, and after another three years completed his education with a dissertation on Pius X and his critique of modernism. While he was in Rome he was ordained to the priesthood by Bishop Charles McDonnell. In the latter's Brooklyn diocese, Mundelein subsequently assumed a variety of tasks that would not usually have been assigned to a greenhorn, even if he were a Roman. In 1897 he was appointed chancellor of the diocese, and because he had advanced so quickly, he had to wait quite a while before his career moved forward again. From 1909 to 1915 he served as McDonnell's auxiliary bishop, until finally toward the end of 1915 he was appointed archbishop of Chicago. In 1924 he became the first American cardinal resident west of the Atlantic Coast. During his long reign, which lasted from World War I to the outbreak of World War II, a shift in power took place within American Catholicism. Chicago became the biggest and richest diocese, and in many respects Mundelein set the new standards. This was true for his style of leadership as well as for the way in which he represented the church to the outside world. Mundelein's style combined farseeing thoughtfulness, shown especially by his enthusiastic support of education, with a belief in centralized, top-down administration and a tendency to ostentation. The last two characteristics suggested that "the bigger, the better," a motto that the autocratic Mundelein not only subscribed to but occasionally expressed in public.

The kind of interest the archbishop took in education, and also what he understood by orderly administration, was quickly demonstrated when in his first year in office he set about standardizing Catholic schools. He found almost three hundred schools in his diocese, in which 2600 nuns were teaching. Apart from a few secondary schools mainly run by a religious order, these schools were without exception parish elementary schools. The pastor, who reported to the bishop, was responsible for taking care of the school building and hiring for his teaching staff nuns who were subject to their own religious orders and determined their own programs. There was communication and coordination within each of the religious orders, but not with other schools in the same diocese, and this was a nightmare for a man like Mundelein. He established a diocesan board of education and assumed responsibility for both curriculum and staffing. From 1920 on, the diocese had a unified school system. At that time there were 323 schools, with more than 3,000 teachers and 160,000 students. The backbone of this system was provided by the nuns who constituted more than 90 percent of the teaching staff. Since the beginning of the 1920–21 school year they had been paid $35 for ten months' instruction. This inexpensive teaching staff also explains why parishes, according to Edward Kantowicz's calculations, were obliged on average to devote only 10 percent of their annual budgets to schools (Kantowicz 1988b: 320). In addition, the various charities and welfare organizations were combined and placed directly under diocesan supervision. These early efforts to consolidate put an end to uncoordinated parallel activities and helped standardize the quality of education in the school system. However, they also discouraged many independent initiatives undertaken by religious communities and parishes, and as a result the size and power of the archbishop's staff increased. Religious orders in particular became mistrustful, and began to worry about their independence. Their initial experiences with Mundelein led them to conclude that in dealing with such a power-hungry man they should not give an inch.

Mundelein suffered the consequences of this when, counting on the support of certain religious orders, particularly the Jesuits and the Dominicans, he set about realizing his most ambitious goal. At the time, the archdiocese did not have a single seminary, a lack Mundelein wanted to repair, as he announced as soon as he arrived in Chicago. However, his plans went far beyond a mere seminary. He had in mind the eventual establishment of a Catholic University of the West, which was to develop out of a college with a curriculum in philosophy and theology sponsored by the archdiocese and various religious orders. He moved a step closer to this goal when Edward Hines, who owned a building supplies firm, gave him half a million dollars, stipulating only that the money was to be used to found a Catholic institution in memory of his son, who had been killed in the war, though this institution need not bear the family's name. Mundelein bought a large piece of land north of Chicago; it was located near what is now O'Hare airport and included a lake. At one end of this lake the buildings for the episcopal seminary and the academic departments were to be built, whereas the land at the other end of the lake was offered to the religious orders so that they could build housing for novitiates and professors belonging to their own communities. The religious orders did not accept Mundelein's offer, so that buildings were constructed at only one end of the lake, although they turned out to be quite large. In all, fourteen spacious structures were erected on the extensive grounds, including a church, a library, seminary buildings, residences, and a kind of summerhouse for the cardinal. The campus is remarkable not only for its architectural consistency, but also for its carefully thought-out symbolism. Buildings in the colonial style form a semicircle whose center is marked by the church and the library. Thus the massive arrangement reflects the American classic style. However, when one enters the library, one finds a faithful copy of the library in Rome's Barberini palace, the former seat of where *De Propaganda Fide* and its college are housed: "American on the outside—Roman on the inside," or "Roman to the core." These architectural allusions produce a grandiose statement: "American on the outside—Roman on the inside" does not mean that the American façade merely camouflages the Roman core, because both are put on display and claimed as part of the American church's heritage. The implication is rather that the Roman and American traditions are bound together in an imposing structure and yet remain distinct.

This optimistic statement arouses skepticism only because it is so massively presented, as if the builders did not yet fully believe it and were not yet completely sure of their newly won status in American society. There is something ostentatious about everything Mundelein did, whether he was clothing a hundred needy children at Christmastime, inviting to his birthday dinner all the seminarians who were also named George, or organizing in 1926 a Eucharistic World Congress to show off his diocese and the completed University of St. Mary of the Lake. The congress, whose official closing ceremony was staged on St. Mary's grounds, was by far the largest of its kind, attended by twelve cardinals, 373 bishops, 8,000 priests, and a million faithful.

"Going big," always choosing the larger number in order to prove to oneself and to others that one has made it, is typical of a way of behaving and thinking that these new princes of the church as well as the rest of the clergy, including the construction-happy pastors, shared with their flocks. They all behaved like parvenus, and thereby showed that they were not quite sure of themselves, but they also worked like parvenus—that is, like people who are conscious of their recent achievements but still have ambitions, especially for their children. Vivid memories of humble beginnings and an awareness that they were still far from being accepted by the old elites, not to mention being treated as peers, perhaps explain their characteristic mixture of conservatism in theology and ecclesiastical politics, on one hand, and their sociopolitical progressivism on the other.

Anyone with a career like Mundelein's not only felt an obligation to his own past but also believed in organization and centralized control. Like most American Catholics of his time, Mundelein combined moral and theological conservatism with a belief in the beneficial effects of government intervention. This led to an attitude that in Europe would have been described as social-democratic, but for which Franklin D. Roosevelt's New Deal liberalism provided the adequate concept in America. No wonder, then, that Mundelein and Roosevelt got along well, and that many authors describe them as personal friends (Koenig). Mundelein stood by Roosevelt when in the mid-1930s most Catholic reformers were disappointed with the New Deal and stopped supporting the president. In 1935, using more or less gentle pressure, he succeeded in getting Notre Dame to confer an honorary doctorate on the president in order to boost his position among Catholics.

This sociopolitical orientation formed a common bond between a large segment of the brick and mortar bishops and the new official elite. Since these expert activists were still recruited primarily from the clergy, they also had their early education in common. The bipartite nature of a bishop's career led some from the seminary to parish service and then back into the diocesan administration, whereas others, after further training in Rome, quickly gained management roles. As a result, two classes emerged: the line officers with a shorter, purely American education, and the graduates of the Roman service academy who were soon to advance to the rank of general staff officers.

Clerical Activists as New Actors on the National Scene

A third group now emerged, composed of a new kind of official and activist who did not enter parish service after completing his studies but rather was either assigned to a task in one of the central organizations—this was most likely to occur in the case of a priest belonging to a religious order—or continued his education. In the latter case, however, he did not go to Rome but rather went to Catholic University in Washington or to Notre Dame, and took a degree in sociology or social ethics. Afterward he was employed in a department of the NCWC, worked in one of the offices that bishops like Mundelein had created within their own enlarged staff operations, or remained at the university. Often in the course of his career he might move back and forth between these activities. In any case he filled the new professional positions that had developed in the larger dioceses and on the national level as a result of the centralization of American Catholicism. Through his own work he contributed to further centralization and professionalization.

A precursor and an example of this new type was the previously mentioned John Augustine Ryan. Having grown up on a family farm in Minnesota as the eleventh child of Irish immigrants, he graduated from the seminary in St. Paul and was ordained there in 1898 by John Ireland. After two years at Catholic University, he returned to the seminary in St. Paul to teach moral theology. While doing so, he wrote a dissertation in social ethics on the subject of fair wages, and was awarded a doctorate by Catholic University in 1906. In 1914 he was appointed Professor of Political Science at Catholic University, later becoming Professor of Moral Theology. During his first years on the faculty there he wrote his most ambitious book, *Distributive Justice,* which was published in 1916. The previously mentioned memorandum on social reconstruction, which became known as "the bishops' program of social reconstruction," followed. In it Ryan argued for a social security program patterned on the German model and for a legally guaranteed minimum wage. From 1920 on, Ryan led the NCWC's Social Action Department, remaining in this position until his death in 1945. An unshakable supporter of the New Deal, he took part in all four of Roosevelt's presidential campaigns, and this support was rewarded when he was repeatedly invited to give a benediction at the inaugurations. In the 1930s he acquired the nickname "The Right Reverend New Dealer," which also served as the title of his biography (Broderick 1963).

If Ryan stands for the significance of the organizational apparatus he knew how to exploit, another priest, who was much better known at the time, reminds us of the importance of radio as a new means of communication.

With the exception of the *New York Times*, which had a small number of readers scattered all over the country, American newspapers remained regional papers whose reporting seldom reached beyond their area of circulation. In contrast, in the 1920s countless local radio stations were associated with networks that produced and broadcast politics, sports, and entertainment programs and for the first time addressed millions of listeners as a national audience. Charles Edward Coughlin, a parish priest in Michigan, was discovered as a radio personality when he tried to make use of the local radio station to raise money for a new church building. Soon he had his own regular program, in which he at first limited himself to religious themes. Gradually nearby stations started picking up his program, and ultimately every weekend CBS broadcast throughout the United States an hourlong program in which Father Coughlin commented on the issues of the time. From 1930 on he reached an audience estimated at thirty to forty million listeners. In any case, he employed 150 secretaries to deal with correspondence and small donations.

Coughlin reacted to the economic crisis by popularizing the church's social encyclicals as an anti-capitalist program, and in 1932 he campaigned for Roosevelt. However, he soon became disappointed by the New Deal and founded his own National Union for Social Justice and a newspaper which was published under the title *Social Justice*. In time his criticism of Roosevelt became more pointed, and at the same time increasingly clear anti-English and anti-Semitic tendencies appeared in his commentaries. In 1942 his bishop finally told him to limit his future comments to religious themes, an order that Coughlin, who had just turned fifty, faithfully obeyed for the rest of his life (Tull 1965).

Social Movements

While activist priests such as Ryan and Coughlin attempted to derive a legislative program from the fundamental principles of Catholic social ethics and to propagate it through political activity and public commentary, a broad variety of lay activities sought to bring about social reforms they organized themselves. One example is the Rural Life Movement, which was particularly widespread in the Midwest, and which was also promoted by the Benedictines at St. John's Abbey in Collegeville, Minnesota. This rural movement's ideas combined criticism of urban life with Thomas Jefferson's democratic agrarianism, which posits that virtues such as thrift and a sense of community flourish only in the countryside, and that there democracy, private property, and freedom are ensured. Therefore Catholics, particularly those without jobs, should be encouraged to take over small farms. However, the Rural Life Movement was no more successful in this endeavor than John Ireland, who before the turn of the century had already tried to get Irish immigrants to settle in the Northwest in order to prevent them from becoming a proletariat.

The Catholic Worker Movement, on the other hand, vacillated between hoping that life in the countryside would have such wholesome effects and rejecting private ownership. The founders of this religio-socialist movement, the journalist Dorothy Day and Peter Maurin, an independent scholar who had immigrated from Belgium, had three goals. They experimented with new forms of life in rural communes for those who wanted to escape unemployment or sought an alternative to the monotony of industrial labor. In cities they set up "houses of hospitality" that were to offer not only shelter and food but also education. To promote the education of workers, Dorothy Day and Peter Maurin founded their own monthly, *The Catholic Worker*, and began to hold round table discussions in their own homes, hoping to develop a new form of adult education organized by the participants themselves. Most of the hopes were not fulfilled. Nonetheless, more than fifty hospitality houses remained, along with the monthly periodical, which is still sold for 25 cents and reminds us of Dorothy Day's hope that it is possible "to be a radical but not an atheist" (Segers 1988, 167 ff.).

The Catholic Worker Movement and its periodical always represented a rallying point for a small, decidedly pacifist, left-leaning minority within American Catholicism. Conversely, most of the large labor unions and their umbrella organization, the American Federation of Labor (AFL) were occasionally suspected of being Catholic organizations. Cited as proof was the large proportion of Catholics in their ranks (it is estimated that in the 1920s half the members of the AFL were Catholic) (Schatz 1988, 248) and the active involvement of many priests.

American communists blamed these priests for keeping them from gaining a foothold within labor unions, even during the economic crises of the time. In any event, American unions remained anticommunist and performed within American Catholicism the function prescribed for them by communist strategy. They served as recruiting grounds for Catholic politicians, and this helped further strengthen the ties between the Democratic party and the Catholic milieu, which were in any case very close in big city party machines.

Yet quite independently of these ties, the 1920s and 1930s repeatedly showed how much Catholics were involved in politics, whether they wanted to be or not. On one hand, collective interests and identities were still at stake, and on the other, political developments abroad had a polarizing effect on American Catholicism.

Politicizing Experiences: The Oregon Education Controversy, Al Smith's Presidential Candidacy, and the Spanish Civil War

Catholic interests were already more involved in politics because attacks on remaining peculiarities such as Catholic school systems seemed more promising than assaults on Catholics in general. Thus in 1922, with the support of some Masonic lodges, the Ku Klux Klan set itself up as the defender of public schools as the most important American institution. Together, they got a referendum on the ballot in Oregon, and by a small majority succeeded in making public school education compulsory. However, this success turned out to be a setback for the supporters of public school monopoly. A congregation of teaching nuns appealed to the Supreme Court, and in 1925 the court not only struck down the Oregon law but also questioned the legitimacy of a unified school system, holding that granting a state the right "to standardize its children" was incompatible with the freedom that must be respected by every government (Tyack 1988, 284).

Now as before it was a matter of defending interests and institutions peculiar to Catholics, and in other areas as well there was as yet no normalization. For example, a Catholic candidate for public office was still not just a politician who happened to be Catholic. At any rate, this was the conclusion most Catholics drew from the 1928 presidential election, which had long-lasting effects. The Democratic candidate, the popular New York politician Al Smith, who had already been four times elected governor of his home state, lost to the Republican incumbent, Herbert Hoover—and ever since it has been debated whether a Protestant candidate would have beaten Hoover. One thing is certain: Smith's religion and his criticism of Prohibition, which made his religious affiliation crystal clear, played an important role in the campaign.

If experiences of this kind produced a kind of solidarity from which Catholic candidates up to John F. Kennedy benefited, at the same time the polarizing effects of politics became discernible within American Catholicism. The Spanish Civil War in particular led to the formation of two camps, each represented by an influential periodical. When Franco rebelled in 1936, *America* began to describe the Spanish Popular Front government as communist and held it responsible for numerous crimes. In contrast, *Commonweal* recommended that one just as clearly distance oneself from Franco's royalists. In doing so *Commonweal* relied chiefly on the French commentator and philosopher Jacques Maritain, who exercised a long-term intellectual influence on American Catholicism by helping spread neo-Thomism. But at first he was best known for his tireless efforts to bring to public attention the atrocities committed by both sides in the Spanish Civil War.

America was at that time already an intellectually demanding publication put out by the Jesuits, who were then still rather conservative, whereas *Commonweal* was published by lay people and set the tone among people associated with Catholic New Deal progressivism. Its founder, Michael Williams, edited the periodical, and it was financed by John J. Raskob, a friend of Al Smith who later organized the latter's presidential campaign (Valaik 1988; Clements 1988).

3. When All Was Still Right in the World

Like World War I, World War II marked an important turning point for American Catholics. On one hand, military life showed how much more integrated they had become, and on the other, the post-war world offered them opportunities for social advancement of particular benefit to second and third generation immigrants.

The proportion of Catholics among the 5.2 million American soldiers and also among the 260,000 who died in the war was probably one-fourth to one-third. While in this case as in all others involving official American statistics we are dealing with estimates, for various reasons the religious affiliation of certain groups can be precisely determined. Among the 11,887 conscientious objectors there were 135 Catholics. In contrast, the numerous Catholic priests in uniform—3,306 in all—were particularly conspicuous because military pastoral care was centrally organized (Adams *et al.* 1992, 1: 150; Hennesey 1981, 278 ff.). It was said that a disproportionately high percentage of officers, and especially of career officers, were Catholic as well, and later this often was cited as proof that Catholics wanted to go beyond the call of duty in order to prove that they were good Americans. A more likely explanation is that for young men who came from poor families but had good educations, a career as a military officer was an attractive alternative to attending an expensive college.

The G.I. Bill of Rights

In any case, during World War II some ten million Protestants served alongside at least four million Catholics, including officers and chaplains, and this no doubt shook some of the prejudices. Catholics, however, not only had the most to gain socially and psychologically as a group, but also as individuals derived special benefits from the sociopolitical steps taken to help veterans. Under the Servicemen's Readjustment Act of 1944, which became known as the "G. I. Bill of Rights," the government paid all educational expenses for every veteran, including housing, and also provided a supplement to cover living costs. Those who did not want to attend college but returned instead to their jobs could obtain a loan to buy or build a home. The G. I. Bill thus paved the way to colleges and universities for those who had the required educational background and the desire to better themselves but lacked the necessary funds. Suddenly very many more young Catholics were going to college, and especially to Catholic colleges and universities, which had their hands full trying to respond to this demand for education. Many critics thought, however, that the unexpected boom contributed to the secularization of these institutions, that is, that it caused them to postpone the necessary discussion of their future mission and their Catholic character.

American Catholics were full of confidence after the war, and in this respect they were in harmony with the general mood. America had finally become the leading power in the world, and memories of inflation and unemployment faded when the restrictions of the war economy and their consequences had been overcome. At first, production was still not able to keep up with the newly unleashed demand, and this caused prices to shoot up. But 1947 already belonged to a new era, in which economists' dreams seemed to be coming true. Although the number of people seeking employment rose from 60 million to 80 million, a quarter century of prosperity had begun, marked by steady economic growth, a high rate of employment, and low inflation. By 1970 average real incomes had risen by 80 percent (Adams *et al.* 1992, 1: 159).

Even more important than this prosperity itself was the intangible effect of its being accessible to everyone. Anyone prepared to make an effort was rewarded with a higher standard of living and entry into the ranks of respectable citizens. Those who wanted to rise in society found it easier to do so than ever before. Economic optimism softened antipathy toward immigrants and people's gratitude toward veterans inclined them to make allowances for all groups, even if their behavior was not in accord with middle-class Protestant norms. Moreover, the enemy of the American way of life was now located outside America. Communism now represented everything un-American, and the struggle against this opposing power was played out in the form of the Korean War and the Cold War in Europe. This battle also affected internal politics and led to a notable change: this time the agents of an un-American power who had to be unmasked were not immigrants. Instead, they probably came from established families and had gone to Yale.

The Religious Boom of the 1950s

However, reconciliation and confidence marked the general mood, which was also reflected in the religious culture of the time. American statistics on religion, which rely not on the official census but on information supplied by the churches (see tables 1 and 6), show a steady growth from 1870 to 1967. For a century, the number of church members rose faster than the general population, beginning at 18 percent in 1870 and ending at 64 percent in 1967, with the clearest increases occurring in the decade preceding the turn of the century (from 22 percent to 36 percent) and in the 1940s and 1950s (from 49 percent to 64 percent). Therefore people refer to a religious revival in the 1950s or sometimes to an "Eisenhower Revival." The latter term is justified not only because Eisenhower was president from 1952 to 1960, but also because he and other politicians of the time laid particular emphasis on the social function of religion.

This appropriation of religion for civic purposes shows that the situation had changed greatly since the 1920s and 1930s, when politicians and social scientists influenced by contemporary theories of modernization and secularization assumed that religion was becoming increasingly meaningless in both individual and social life. In their famous book *Middletown* (1929), Robert and Helen Lynd sought to describe how life in a typical American county seat (Muncie, Indiana) had changed between 1890 and 1924. As students of the first generation of sociologists, the Lynds saw what they had been taught to expect: religion appeared as something left over from an earlier time. In the 1950s and 1960s, in contrast, it was clear that two out of every three Americans had freely chosen to affiliate themselves with a religious denomination. Thus in 1968 Rodney Stark and Charles Y. Glock revived interest in the almost-forgotten field of the sociology of religion when they published their book *American Piety,* and when Theodore Caplow and his collaborators revisited Middletown from 1976 to 1978, they observed particularly important changes in religious matters. In these publications three characteristics of the generalized religiousness are already discernible that appear even more clearly in later studies by George Gallup and Jim Castelli and by Andrew Greeley.

The first of these characteristics is that religious communities with rising membership rolls inevitably became more representative in terms of social statistics, and thus approached the American average. In contrast to Europe, older, female church members living in rural areas were not disproportionately represented, and the perceptible shifts were not downward but upward, so that the proportion of Catholics who were college graduates or had higher-than-average incomes was greater than in the population as a whole.

In addition, this middle-class religiousness indicates an increasingly pluralistic differentiation and organizational diversity that put increasing demands on church members' financial capabilities and willingness to make sacrifices. Within the broad framework that is more implied than defined by the concept of Protestantism, the discontented can change churches rather than abandoning religion altogether. Anyone who thinks his own denomination is too conservative, too progressive, or simply controlled by the wrong people, can usually find another Protestant denomination that suits him. With growing social mobility, this possibility of switching churches was taken advantage of with increasing frequency. Caplow and his colleagues have calculated that in Muncie, Indiana in 1925 there were 798 church members for every church, whereas in 1976, because the number of churches had grown, there were only 550 church members for every church, with the result that the financial burdens borne by each member grew heavier.

Thus the variety of choices in the religious marketplace resulted in migrations within Protestantism, which in turn produced a market for church real estate. Thus a congregation that was composed of the children and grandchildren of immigrants, and that had recently achieved social respectability, tended to trade its wooden church building for a more solid one in a better location. Often, these wooden churches were bought by reform-oriented younger families who had just split off from another congregation that had moved up the social ladder earlier. These new congregations went into debt to buy these buildings, and at first had to do without a minister, while the congregation they had left found that a smaller number of church members now had to bear the steadily increasing costs (Caplow 1983, 282).

At the beginning of the 1960s, Stark and Glock had already done surveys in an attempt to determine the direction of this migration. Their data can also be interpreted from the opposite point of view, that is, in terms of stability. A trend towards decreasing chances of survival for religious and cultural traditions emerges if we tabulate only the survey participants who say they still adhere to their parents' religion or who like their parents indicate no religious affiliation.

The leading groups in this index of cultural resistance are Jews and Catholics, the latter being in 1964 still strongly ethnic in character. Next come Baptists, Lutherans, and Methodists. This was a group composed of the frontier religions that spread through the Midwest in the middle of the nineteenth century, the Lutherans, as the religion of the German and Scandanavian Protestants who had settled in the northwestern states, still bearing a strong ethnic stamp as well. In contrast, the older, more established denominations such as the Americanized Anglicans and the New England Calvinists found it much harder to retain their membership. Being born into a religion other than Christianity and Judaism or without religion proved to be the most unstable situation in which parents could put their children. Only 18 percent of the adults surveyed had followed their elders in this regard. During the so-called revivals of the 1950s and 1960s American religious communities grew to such an extent, along with the middle class in a prospering society, that religion gained a new importance.

The third mark of the changed situation was thus a stronger social pressure to belong to a Judeo-Christian religion. The issue was religion as such and not any particular religion, and that seemed to go for both the public and the individual function of religion. Thus a privatist and individualistic conception of religion went hand in hand with a conception of religion in terms of its civic function. In both cases what mattered were effects that seemed to be independent of the concrete doctrines of the religions concerned, so that they could be expected from (almost) any religion. These tendencies did not remain unchallenged, however; in particular, there was increasing criticism of "liberal" Protestantism, which appeared to consist chiefly in appeals for humanitarian and social reform. Billy Graham, for example, emphasized that at most religion could lead to indirect reforms: "we must change men before we can change society" (Gaustad 1982, 2: 515). The revivalists of the 1950s followed their predecessors in stressing the central significance of individual conversion, and like their predecessors, they contributed thereby to the further relativization of dogmatic content and organizational form of particular religions. This was especially the case when, following the psychotherapeutic trend of the time, revivalists succumbed to the temptation to praise religion chiefly for its beneficial secondary effects, such as peace of mind or unshakable self-confidence.

Peace of Mind and "Positive Thinking"

Rabbi Joshua L. Liebman, in his 1946 book *Peace of Mind*, began the popularization of this therapeutic view of religion. He was followed by a Methodist preacher, Norman Vincent Peale, who published *A Guide to Confident Living* in 1948 and in 1952 a second book of the same kind that became a worldwide bestseller: *The Power of Positive Thinking*. Billy Graham tried to make peace of mind appear less of a goal in itself by entitling his book *Peace with God* (1953). The Catholic contribution to this therapeutic wave of "positive thinking" was Fulton J. Sheen's countless television programs and books. Ordained a priest in 1919 in St. Paul, he had an opportunity to continue his studies in Louvain and Rome, and, starting in 1926, he taught at Catholic University. During this time he began to make radio broadcasts that quickly made him well known. Unlike Father Coughlin, however, he avoided controversy and in his "Catholic Hour" program he dealt only with religious subjects. In other words, he was already promoting "positive thinking" before the expression came into vogue. Thus after the war, he did not find it difficult to satisfy people's desire for ideas about how to rebuild their lives. In 1949 he published two books whose titles, *The Way to Happiness* and *Peace of Soul* responded to the new mood, and from 1951 to 1955 he moderated a television series, *Life Is Worth Living*.

Religion's mission no longer seemed to consist in shaking up the deceptive certainties of this world and the middle class way of life; rather, its purpose was to demonstrate "how to get more out of life." "Positive thinking," and even the duty to be optimistic, was established as a cultural leitmotif determining not only evangelistic style but also political rhetoric. Thus the new religiousness appeared to support the republic and all its institutions, and to bind society together as well. In the 1950s the phrase "in God we trust" was added to the pledge of allegiance, and in the Capitol building a room was set aside for prayer. Yet this multi-purpose chapel reveals the dilemma. In

American culture, the emphasis on concrete religion continued to be seen as sectarian or divisive, and therefore out of place. Religion in general, on the other hand, seemed more and more necessary.

Eisenhower accordingly emphasized that he was religious but did not belong to any particular denomination: "I am the most intensely religious man I know . . . that does not mean that I adhere to any sect." Nonetheless, after his election as president in 1952, he declared that the American form of government "makes no sense unless it is founded in a deeply felt religious faith," adding, "and I don't care what it is" (Herberg 1972, 162).

What he was talking about was thus not a concrete social doctrine advanced by any concrete church, but rather what Rousseau called "civic religion." The goal is to bring society together, and thus dogmatic barriers are to be kept as low as possible. Rousseau recommended that the doctrines of such a civic religion should be "simple, few in number, and commonly understood," and Eisenhower agreed, explaining that every religion furthered social unity. This claim could not, of course, be taken literally, since the president would probably have been annoyed to see his home state of Kansas full of Hindu "sacred cows." What he had in mind was probably the triad of "Protestant, Catholic, Jew" that Will Herberg described in his famous book.

The inclusive mood as well as the equal status accorded Judeo-Christian religions as civic religions seemed to indicate that Catholics had completed their long march into the center of American society, and that Catholicism and America were no longer seen as opposites. In any case, that is how most Catholics and their contemporaries in America saw things at the beginning of the 1950s. Despite the advances in integration, however, there were still both old and new grounds for Catholics to carefully distance themselves.

The old ground consisted in the fact that although organized anti-Catholicism was hardly ever seen any more, the corresponding cultural propaganda still found an audience. Thus Paul Blanshard's 1949 book, *American Freedom and Catholic Power*, which dealt with the incompatibility of the two elements mentioned in its title, went through five reprintings in its first year. Blanshard had been involved since 1947 in efforts to revive the old anti-Catholic coalition. From these efforts resulted an organization whose name united old and new elements, *Protestants and Other Americans United for the Separation of Church and State.* Nothing much came of this organization, because neither Protestants nor "other Americans" showed much interest in it. Nonetheless, the name of this association contains two important hints. Cultural warfare aimed directly at Catholics had long ceased to be effective, but there was still the possibility of shifting its operations to another theater. To the extent that American Protestantism developed into a majority religion with a minority consciousness (Herberg 1955, 47), the subject of the separation of church and state came to the forefront. The "wall of separation" to which Thomas Jefferson had referred in a letter was raised to the status of a fundamental law, as if the constitutional ban had gone beyond forbidding the establishment of religion.

An additional argument for taking a careful distance was made by postwar Catholic intellectuals who were less concerned with constitutional law or the concrete separation of civil and ecclesiastical activities in educational and social policy than with the cultural distinction between religion and politics.

John Courtney Murray's Criticism of the Concept of Civic Religion: The Constitution As a Formula for Peace, Not a Religious Creed

In reaction to the inclusive mood of the time and to civic religion's concept of integration, the theologian John Courtney Murray was one of those who sought to describe the proper relationship of distance and proximity between church and state. On one hand, he emphasized the compatibility of American political culture and the Catholic tradition; on the other, he tried to protect this tradition against a monopolizing embrace.

After taking a degree at the Jesuits' Boston College, Murray joined the order. He studied at Woodstock College and in Rome, where he received a doctorate from the Gregorian University in 1936. Later he taught dogmatics at Woodstock College, remaining a member of its faculty until his death in 1967. In the articles he published from 1943 on in *Theological Studies,* of which he was co-editor, he was increasingly concerned with the relation between Catholicism and American culture. From these articles gradually emerged a Catholic reformulation of the liberal-democratic conviction that religion and politics were useful to each other, so long as they retained their own identities. Starting out from this position, Murray eventually returned to the battle between the Americanists and the defenders of an intra-Catholic pluralism. The American Bill of Rights, he wrote, is not a bit of Enlightenment philosophy, but rather emerges directly from the history of Christian culture. The ethical and political principles at the foundation of the American Constitution derive from the natural law tradition, and hence Catholics can unconditionally subscribe to these American convictions. America's principles "approve themselves to the Catholic intelligence and conscience." To this tradition also belong the self-imposed limitations of the political order. If Americans have taken "e pluribus unum" as their motto, that is because they are as much concerned with plurality as with unity. Above all, it is important that "the two orders, the religious and the civil, remain distinct." Catholics can therefore not only accept American political culture, but also heartily support it, because it clearly separates politics from religion. From both history and present-day social reality only one tenable conclusion can be drawn: the Constitution offers "not articles of faith but articles of peace" (Murray 1960, 41–56).

Thus Murray provided a formula that could serve as a guide within American Catholicism as well, for it showed how one could in good conscience become an American while remaining a Catholic. Murray, who later served as one of Vatican II's *Periti,* was given the assignment of revising the declaration on religious freedom. But when he first dealt with these subjects he seemed to be ahead of his time and of his superiors. In 1954 he was ordered to make no further statements on this subject. Thereupon this last of the obedient Jesuits withdrew from a book contract and for the next decade he abstained from discussing religious and political subjects.

4. "Well-off and Boring"?

Unlike Murray, most American Catholics were hardly affected by the Aristotelian idea that there could be too much of a good thing, and that integration into American society could ultimately become excessive. If they were troubled at all, that was not the source of their concern, and who could have blamed them?

The Catholic "Empire"

The combined effects of the baby boom and immigration, which was slowly increasing again, were more noticeable in the pews of Catholic churches than in the population as a whole. The number of Catholics doubled in the two decades following 1940, rising from 21 million to 42 million, and this unusual rate of growth might already lead us to expect an increase in church-building. However, this period, which more or less corresponds to the pontificate of Pius XII, was also characterized by a certain drifting away from the church that reflected Catholics' rise in social status.

While black agricultural workers no longer found work on the increasingly mechanized farms in the South and thronged to urban centers in the North, many Catholics followed the path laid out for them in the G.I. Bill. They used free college education as a way of entering white-collar jobs, and veterans took advantage of low-interest construction loans to join middle-class white-collar workers in sprawling suburbs. Even during this move up into the middle class, however, the history of the immigration of various groups remains discernible. Andrew Greeley suggests that a group can be said to have joined the middle class when a higher than average proportion of its members are college graduates or hold "prestigious" jobs. These criteria were met at long intervals first by Irish Catholics, then by Italian, and last by Polish, yet in the 1960s most Polish Catholics were also working at desks during the day and mowing their lawns in the evening (Greeley 1979, 93).

Compared with preceding generations, twice as many Catholics now regularly took part in the life of the church, and an increasingly large percentage of these more demanding churchgoers lived in quite different neighborhoods. All this led to a wave of church construction, and the names of the new buildings betray the period in which they were constructed. For the first time, buildings were not named primarily after European national saints, and thus, for example, the Pacelli Elementary School went up alongside a church named after St. Thomas Aquinas.

At the beginning of the 1960s some 42 million American Catholics were served by 35,000 diocesan priests in 17,000 parishes belonging to

120 different dioceses. There were in addition 22,000 regular clergy working in various areas. Dioceses and parishes maintained 950 hospitals and sanatoriums, 350 retirement homes, and above all a far-flung educational system. In more than 12,000 elementary and secondary schools at least 5.5 million students were taught by over 100,000 nuns and about 80,000 other teachers. 350,000 students attended 280 Catholic colleges (see statistical table in appendix).

Spellman, the "American Pope"

This Catholic empire had already become visible during World War II, not only in America but throughout the world, and Pius XII acknowledged the significance of American Catholicism as soon as a consistory could be convened after the war. In 1946 the archbishops of New York (Spellman), Detroit (Mooney), Chicago (Stritch), and St. Louis (Glennon) were elevated to cardinals, alongside Dennis Dougherty of Philadelphia. John J. Glennon, the eldest of these new cardinals, had been born in Ireland in 1862. He had been archbishop of St. Louis since 1903, and died in the same year he was made a cardinal. Spellman, in contrast, was still a student in 1903, but during World War II he became the most prominent American bishop, and after the war his fame and influence grew so much that until his death in 1967 he represented American Catholicism as only Gibbons had before him. The "American pope," as he was often called, had grown up in a small town in Massachusetts, and after attending seminary he had had an opportunity to complete his training in Rome, where he took a doctorate and was ordained to the priesthood in 1916. Afterward he returned to Massachusetts, and worked in a parish for two years before becoming editor of the diocese's newspaper. In 1925 he went back to Rome, this time for seven years, so that he had ample time to learn how the Vatican worked. Above all, he made the acquaintance of Eugenio Pacelli, who upon returning from Berlin had become the Vatican's secretary of state. In 1932, Spellman left Rome to serve as auxiliary bishop in Boston, and at first seemed to have arrived at the end of his career. But in 1936 Cardinal secretary of state Pacelli visited the United States, and was accompanied by Spellman everywhere he went, including the White House. Afterward, Spellman was regarded as an intermediary between Rome and Washington, even though he was far down in the church hierarchy. This changed, however, when Pacelli became pope in 1939 and in the same year appointed Spellman archbishop of New York.

Thus the long series of in-house appointments in New York was broken. In the capital of radio and newspaper journalism a bishop now presided who was not hesitant to make use of the media. Moreover, his fame significantly increased when he also became military vicar, supervising military chaplains. He traveled tirelessly to all the theaters of war, celebrated Christmas with the troops, and became a great favorite with the press and the president, though not with the president's wife.

After the war the cardinal, who was always willing to express his opinion, represented the patriotism of American Catholics, and early on he took a stand against illusions concerning the One World Order and Uncle Joe Stalin. At that time no one found surprising the assertion that communism and Catholicism were incompatible, but Spellman's insistence that communism was "un-American" and that he would participate in "no conspiracy of silence" in this regard was also warmly received (Gannon 1962, 336).

All this is worth noting only because the archbishop of New York, that is, John Hughes's successor, could now publicly define what was American. That Spellman was in danger of turning America into an object of religious veneration and that his power eventually became almost unlimited is no secret, either within the church or outside it. Nevertheless, the cardinal enjoyed affection and respect not only because of his winning ways but also because in his optimism, his unshakable faith in America's leadership role in the world, and even his insistence that his voice should now be heard, he could credibly represent the majority of American Catholics. Thus even a rather progressive author such as John Cogley sees him as a benevolent if autocratic patriarch who worked hard (Cogley 1986, 186). In the 1960s developments within the church occurred that were not to Spellman's liking. However, unlike his friend James F. McIntyre, for example, who had first been his auxiliary bishop in New York and now resided as archbishop and cardinal in Los Angeles, Spellman accepted with equanimity these disturbances within the church. He remained in the background during the Council, and afterward asked to be relieved of his duties on account of his health. However, at the pope's wish, he stayed in office until his death in 1967.

In the interim the great majority of Catholics had moved out of the urban ghettos and become part of suburbia, that is, they had joined the uniform middle class whose endless and monotonously similar single-family subdivisions were spreading like algae around the edges of the cities. The political thinking of these Catholics was however in no way correspondingly individualized, but remained determined by a collective memory and by old solidarities. Similarly, a Catholic politician was still identified as such both by Catholics and non-Catholics, regardless of whether he tried to take advantage of this fact or wanted to be considered a candidate like any other.

The Catholic Hope for Normality: McCarthy and Kennedy

At the beginning and at the end of the 1950s, two Catholic politicians seldom compared to each other made this claim to normality and ended up involuntarily demonstrating that religious denomination still played an important role. One, Joseph R. McCarthy, mobilized Catholic newcomers' populist feeling against the old, primarily Protestant elites. The other, John F. Kennedy, did not want to be considered a Catholic candidate, but was elected president, by a very slim majority, only because Catholics voted for him almost as a bloc.

In 1950, McCarthy, a graduate of Marquette University and U.S. senator from Wisconsin since 1946, took advantage of the already very pronounced anticommunist mood to give a new twist to an American weapon that was as old as it was dangerous. He did not question the loyalty of immigrants or minorities, but rather that of the establishment. Just as in the case of Prohibition, although with a different target, it mattered that regardless of the issues involved, many Americans thought the victims "had it coming."

In January 1950, a former State Department employee, Alger Hiss, was found guilty of giving secret documents to a communist agent. In February, McCarthy gave a speech before the Republican Women's Club in Wheeling, West Virginia that later became known as the "Wheeling speech." In this speech McCarthy asserted that it was not the underprivileged who had betrayed the nation and sold secrets, but rather those who had taken advantage of all that the richest country in the world had to offer, the most expensive education and the most interesting government jobs. And the worst of them were the smart young men who had been "born with silver spoons in their mouths" (Hofstadter 1962, 13).

McCarthy won support particularly among farmers in the Midwest and industrial workers in the Northeast, in part because Catholics who had not yet quite "made it" were susceptible to populist rhetoric directed against the elites. Conversely, and to some extent as the mirror image of this Catholic memory of collective disadvantage, the rest of the population was still affected by anti-Catholic prejudices. This became evident toward the end of the 1950s, when the Democrats, three decades after the defeat of Al Smith, again nominated a Catholic for president. Kennedy's religion immediately became a dominant issue in the campaign, and he was ultimately able to win only because Catholics demonstrated a solidarity that was no longer in accord with their pluralistic social structure and their behavior in previous elections.

The issue is very clearly reflected in a speech that Kennedy, after a long telephone conversation with John Courtney Murray, delivered before the Baptist preachers of Houston and the surrounding area. He said that he was not the Catholic presidential candidate they had read about in the newspapers, but rather the candidate of the Democratic party. In public situations he did not speak for his church, and it did not speak for him. The point of the campaign was not what church he belonged to, since that concerned him alone, but rather what kind of America he believed in (*Webster's* 1971, 569). Kennedy ultimately defeated Richard Nixon by a razor-thin margin of two-tenths of a percent. Among Catholics, however, a majority of whom had earlier voted for Eisenhower, and who did not habitually vote Democratic anymore the picture was very different: Kennedy led Nixon by 56 percent.

The young, forward-looking Kennedy and the jovial Pope John XXIII seemed to ensure that the 1960s would begin as the 1950s had ended. Thus one of the baby boomers wrote, in retrospect, that as a ten-year-old he had experienced pangs of conscience because he found the new pope more likable than the old one after whom his school was named. Pius had reminded him of Woodrow Wilson, whereas to him and his friends John XXIII seemed like a grandfather. Vatican II could

Table 3
1960 Presidential Election

	Kennedy	Nixon
All voters	50.1 percent	49.9 percent
Protestants	38 percent	62 percent
Catholics	78 percent	22 percent

Source: Zöller 1985, 391.

not lead to a break with tradition because the pope who had convened it ultimately *was* the past (Goeghegan 1988, 351).

The Change in Mood

However, the mood quickly changed, and the confidence of the immediate postwar period was replaced by a phase of uncertainty. Every evening people saw on television America's humiliation in Vietnam and student radicals' attacks on a culture they despised all the more because they were unable to offer an alternative to it.

Religious culture also changed profoundly, and this was particularly evident within the Catholic Church. When Catholics departed from their accustomed ways, these changes were in fact more dramatic, because up to that point Catholicism had better withstood the spirit of the time and thus had farther to fall, but they also seemed more dramatic because demonstrating nuns were then still a novelty and offered material for news stories no television editor could resist.

Two tendencies are immediately apparent in this changed religious scene. First, the social pressure that had earlier influenced the climate of opinion in favor of religion now diminished. Second, Catholicism was particularly hard hit by this development.

In 1967, the small proportion of persons without religious affiliation grew from 2 to 3 percent, and by 1976 it had risen to 6 percent. Among the great majority who still considered religious affiliation important, there was a decrease in religious fervor.

In 1962, 46 percent of the people polled said they had attended church or synagogue during the preceding week, but in 1972 only 40 percent made this claim. In 1958 three out of four Catholics (74 per-

Table 4
Church Attendance (during the week before polling)

Year	Percentage of People Polled
1937	41
1940	37
1950	39
1954	46
1958	49
1962	46
1967	43
1972	40
1978	41
1980	40
1984	40
1988	42

Source: Gallup and Castelli 1989, 31.

cent) had met their Sunday obligation. In 1968, this had dropped to 65 percent and a decade later only every other Catholic (52 percent) had gone to church on a normal Sunday. During the same period, the corresponding figures among Protestants dropped only from 44 to 40 percent. The difference between the regularity of Catholics' attendance and that of Protestants thus diminished from 30 percent (74 percent to 44 percent) to 12 percent (52 percent to 40 percent).

Since the end of the 1960s, stability and change thus seem very unequally distributed between Protestants and Catholics. Nonetheless, this is deceptive, because within Protestantism significant changes took place that would soon become important for the development of Catholicism. Once again, these have to do with internal shifts, that is, with church-switching. At the beginning of the 1970s, 62 percent of Americans still identified themselves as Protestants, but an increasing proportion of them no longer belonged to their parents' church. The proportion that had consciously made a different choice rose from 4 percent (1955) to 18 percent (1964), and finally 33 percent (1985) (Gallup and Castelli 1989, 21).

American religious culture bears the stamp of the principle of free will, and with the increasing mobility (which can also be described as decreasing social control), it became easier to exercise the basic right of freedom of choice. Considering the pronounced internal pluralism of American Protestantism and its socioeconomic advantage, it is hardly surprising that the consequences first appeared there. It was foreseeable, however, that American Catholics would hesitantly follow. The only remaining question was what forms voluntaristic religiousness could assume within the different structure and tradition of the Catholic Church.

In any case, migrations within American Protestantism increased during the 1960s, but contrary to what Stark and Glock had expected, they did not strengthen the hand of the "liberals" but instead clearly worked to the advantage of the "conservatives" (Greeley 1989b, 34). Despite their ambiguities, the labels "liberal" and "conservative" are still more appropriate for describing these developments than are other current terms. For example, the distinction between "main-line" and "non-main-line" attempts to classify religious groups as majority or minority, as central or marginal, and thus depends on power relationships that no longer exist because of the migrations from one denomination to another. Neither is it justified to speak of fundamentalism or anti-fundamentalism in this situation, because the groups that gained in membership did not all adhere to a literal interpretation of the Bible, and therefore cannot be considered fundamentalist in the theological sense of the word.

To describe these groups as liberal or conservative is not only the least inaccurate way of characterizing them, but also reflects the fact that the common denominator of both camps is primarily political. They gravitate toward forms of social and cultural politics that are liberal or conservative in the American sense of these terms.

Ultimately, the chief losers were the Calvinistic churches of New England, such as the Disciples of Christ and the United Church of Christ. By the middle of the 1980s, they had lost 15 to 30 percent of their members. But the Episcopalians, and also the Methodists, who once almost amounted to an established church in the Midwest, suffered losses of about 15 percent (Greeley 1989b, 39) as well. This trend becomes still clearer if one follows Greeley in listing the younger age groups separately. Then we see that the Methodists, who in 1950 still represented almost one fourth of all American Protestants, by the

1980s account for only 11 percent of Protestant church members aged between twenty and thirty. The winners were conservative groups such as the already large Southern Baptist Convention, which grew from eleven million members in 1965 to more than fifteen million by the end of the 1980s, and charismatic groups such as the Disciples of God, who doubled their membership to more than a million.

It is therefore not surprising to find juxtaposed a so-called "private Protestantism" concentrating on conversion and salvation, on one hand, and on the other, a "public Protestantism" that is chiefly concerned with social relationships, favors a "liberal" theology, and at many points in American history assumes the character of a social movement (Hoge 1976). However, what is new and significant over and beyond Protestantism itself is the fact that such distinctions now become a measuring rod for participants as well.

Thus the changes that have taken place in American Protestantism since 1965 have resulted in two far-reaching new developments. Protestantism has become religiously and politically more conservative, and in many respects it has assumed the role that used to be ascribed to Catholics. This is true not only for the fervor and regularity of religious practice, but also for the degree of conviction with which social and political positions are maintained. In addition, since the end of the 1960s it has become increasingly clear that in American Protestantism denominationalism has decreased in importance as a principle of organization and orientation and has been replaced by a conflict in worldviews that extends through all the individual religious communities. Denominations, with their own doctrinal traditions and social histories, serve less and less as a basis for self-definition and affiliation; instead, this function is increasingly fulfilled by the opposition between two social-moral and cultural-political milieus whose contours are sharpened still further by the contrasts the media draws between them. This opposition of two camps and their battle for cultural influence finally became so dominant that when the sociologist James Davison Hunter, looking back on the 1970s and 1980s, described the changed political landscape and the relationship between politics and religion, he gave his book a title that ensured its success: *The Culture War* (Hunter 1991).

5

A WORLD WITHOUT NUNS
1963–1986

FOR CATHOLICS IN particular, the changes were so massive and so surprising that observers both inside and outside the church saw them as a kind of cataclysm. Priests leaving the priesthood, Catholics ignoring certain church doctrines without fearing for the salvation of their souls, theologians getting into trouble with the magisterium—all that was not surprising. Many priests still left the priesthood quietly, many preachers and professors obediently avoided certain subjects, and many lay people worked out by themselves or with the help of their confessors the contradictions between church doctrines and their conduct of their own lives.

What was new was the scale of these deviations and their relationship to the public sphere. Whereas lay people generally continued to regard problems with their consciences as just that, many priests and nuns no longer seemed to interpret a change in their way of life and retreat from commitments they had made as an individual crisis; instead, they wanted to be recognized as representing a common concern. For example, when at the end of the 1960s the theologian Charles E. Curran decided that he could no longer represent the church's views in every respect, he did not see this as a reason for resigning his position at Catholic University. On the contrary, henceforth he represented the view that theology was not limited to interpreting church doctrine and carrying out historical research, but could also claim to have its own, independent teaching function.

1. The Earthquake

This kind of opposition suddenly became the order of the day, not only being put forth in apparent good faith, but also demanding institutional guarantees within the church. As just noted, many observers found this so surprising that they experienced it as a kind of upheaval in nature. Martin Marty was clearly thinking of a lightning bolt when he wrote that after Vatican II Catholicism had been suddenly struck by voluntarism (Marty; qtd. from Kress 1986, 73), and the Catholic Church historian Philip Gleason refers to a "spiritual earthquake." Gleason also reminds us, however, that this earthquake upset American Catholicism so much because Catholics had previously lived in their own cultural milieu. They were accustomed to stressing the unity, exclusiveness, and difference of their own Catholic culture and contrasting it with American culture, so that the impression of disintegration now was all the more disturbing (Gleason 1979, 185). Many people therefore also tended to trace the new situation back to a single decisive event, as if Pope John XXIII, having tried, as he said, to open a window, had conjured up a storm, or as if *Humanae Vitae* had changed good Catholics into rebels. The first of these interpretations is the more common, and both progressives and conservatives endorse it indirectly when the former see themselves as guardians of the Vatican II's achievements and the other side as trying to reverse these achievements, while the conservatives argue that the Fathers of the Council could not have meant what they said.

Fish on Friday or *Humanae Vitae*: The Discussion of the Causes

Meanwhile, this explanation was also given a more subtle sociopsychological interpretation that became known as the "Fish-on-Friday syndrome" (Hudson 1981, 380). It resembles Tocqueville's theory in explaining revolution as resulting not from a crisis coming to a head but rather from reforms that demonstrate that a situation can be changed. Fish-on-Friday stands for the assumption that if elements that are in themselves minor but have symbolic value are abandoned, then it is realistic to fear or to hope that other elements that are supposed to be unalterable may soon be open to change as well.

The competing interpretation sees not Vatican II but rather the encyclical *Humanae Vitae* (in which Pope Paul VI reaffirmed the condemnation of artificial birth control) as the source of the disturbances. Greeley in particular finds it striking that church attendance first decreases significantly and then slowly begins increasing again. In his view, after an initial shock Catholics became selectively obedient.

Table 5

Papal Authority

Percentage of people agreeing with the statements that it
is certainly true that God vested Peter and his successors
the popes with authority over the church and that the pope
is infallible in certain cases.

	Apostolic Succession	Infallibility
1963	70	68
1974	42	32

Source: Greeley 1989/1992, 20.

They had resolved to let the pope be the pope, to ignore his teachings
on birth control, and to resume attending mass on Sundays—that is,
to be Catholics on their own terms. Greeley sees the consequences of
Humanae Vitae as explaining the fact that a comparison of the National Opinion Research Center's polling data in 1963 and 1974 reveals
a significant decline in the pope's authority. In 1963 only 10 percent
of American Catholics doubted the divine origin of papal power. Ten
years later, the proportions were reversed: only four out of ten Catholics polled still believed in the mission given to Peter.

The shift is still clearer in the case of papal infallibility: in 1963,
more than two-thirds of Catholics polled still supported this claim,
whereas ten years later hardly a third did.

Other opinion polls also point to *Humanae Vitae* as the source of
the problem. For example, the so-called Notre Dame Study recorded
the authority American Catholics accorded to particular levels of the
church hierarchy on various matters. These assessments are quite so-
bering so far as political attitudes are concerned. Yet an echo of the
birth control issue is heard in the fact that in matters of sexual ethics Catholics accord the least weight to the judgment of the pope, bishops, and priests, the greatest to their own private opinions (Leege 1987,
no. 11).

In any event, despite these plausible findings it may be doubted
whether selective obedience first appeared in 1968. The tendency not
to consider doctrines and ethical commandments as inherently binding or as binding because of the authority of their source, but rather

to evaluate them in relation to their subjectively experienced usefulness for the conduct of life, already had its own tradition in America. It is obvious that neither the Fish-on-Friday thesis nor reference to *Humanae Vitae* offers a sufficient explanation. This is so for two reasons. First, both explanations presuppose that a single causative event should be sought in the 1960s. Such a view is suggested when statistics or surveys from the 1950s are compared with the situation at the end of the 1960s and a dramatic upheaval is noted. Even if comparisons are made over a longer period, the changes at the end of the 1960s remain striking enough, but it is clear that the various indicators fall to "only" the level already recorded in the 1940s. Then it is the particularly religion-friendly climate of the 1950s that appears as an exception requiring explanation.

Secondly, however, the explanations mentioned above not only target too limited a period but also concentrate too much on the reactions of lay people as reflected in opinion surveys. Thus we should be able to advance further by bringing in "hard" data and especially by paying attention to developments among priests and members of religious orders. Once again our only source of information is the official yearbook. However, these few statistics are extremely fertile if we note that the individual groups of persons vary according to their proximity to the developments. Thus it might be expected that the numbers of students in various seminaries most immediately reflect the situation, because they deal with only a few age groups, whereas other categories include all persons above a certain age. The age threshold, which is itself related to the length of training required in each case, explains why groups that theoretically span all generations react to developments with differing degrees of rapidity. For example, the statistical table in the appendix tabulates under the rubric "nuns" the respective age groups from eighteen to twenty-five, which are lacking in the case of priests. This table also shows during the thirteen years preceding the opening of Vatican II, the number of Catholics in the general population rose by sixteen million, thus increasing by more than half. However, this augmented the proportion of Catholics in the general population by only 3.5 percent, though one could also point out that Catholic participation in the exceptional population growth was still slightly above average. The proportion of Catholics in the general population subsequently remained the same; henceforth, official church

A World without Nuns

Table 6
Percentage of People Identifying Themselves with a Religious Denomination

	Protestant	Catholic	Jew	Other	None
1947	69	20	5	1	6
1962	70	23	3	2	2
1976	61	27	2	4	6
1987	57	28	2	4	9

Source: Gallup and Castelli 1989, 120.

figures—drawn from records of registered and tithing members—reflect general population growth fairly closely. The proportion of Catholics oscillates between 23 and 24 percent. In Gallup polls, which of course did not entail any demand for tithes, 28 percent of the people surveyed identified themselves as Catholics.

The figures provided for priests should be viewed with caution, because diocesan priests and regular clergy (priets in religious orders) were not listed separately in the years immediately following the war, so that it is difficult to compare the figures for 1950 with those for 1963. The 1950 yearbook gives the total number of priests as 43,000, but it remains unclear whether all the regular clergy were included in this number or only those who were serving in a diocese as pastors or teachers. However, whether or not this figure is too high, a comparison with the total of 56,000 priests in 1963 shows that seminaries had also received a share of the large numbers of veterans pursuing higher education.

There was population growth in the second half of the 1960s as well. However, this after-effect of the baby boom affected only the number of diocesan priests, which grew by 10 percent, while the number of regular clergy was already declining.

The corresponding figures for nuns and brothers are even more striking. Seminaries are clearly the most strongly affected by the various developments. Here, too, we must interpret the figures carefully, because some of these institutions concentrate on the last three years of training, whereas others offer the whole range of college education. Taken together, however, the figures reveal some fairly clear trends. In seminaries run by the dioceses as well as in those run by religious orders, the number of students doubled in the 1950s, and then fell by half up to 1970. In the following decade this decline was repeated, and then the numbers stabilized at this low level, at least in the diocesan seminaries. The corresponding institutions operated by religious orders suffered at this time not only from a greater decline in the number of applicants, but also from demands for more uniform programs of study in theology, which forced them to make crucial structural changes and often even to close. Once again the figures are not entirely comparable. Nonetheless, the development in diocesan seminaries corresponds more or less to the general tendency, that is, a greater increase followed by a still greater decrease and a gradual leveling-off. Religious orders offer a different picture. Both the number of seminary students and the general development of the membership figures show that for young Americans, becoming a diocesan priest had lost less of its attractiveness than becoming a priest in a religious order.

Why did large numbers of young women enter convents in the 1950s and later leave in large numbers, while the number of diocesan priests has remained relatively stable since the 1960s? Why is the decrease in the number of regular clergy greater than among diocesan priests, and why is the decline in general membership in religious orders greater than that in the regular clergy? In such questions, relationships clearly emerge that go beyond the Fish-on-Friday syndrome and beyond the effects of *Humanae Vitae*. We can discern in them the unequal possibilities of choice and the dissimilar prospects for the future that were connected with entry into the various spiritual professions at various times.

Possibilities of Choice, Future Prospects, and Planning One's Life: An Attempt at an Explanation

After 1945, many young men chose to enter the priesthood, a decision they had often made during the war. They came mainly from lower middle class white ethnic groups in the Northeast, and most of them were the first members of their families to attend college. In some cases, relatives may have had doubts about a young man's vocation, but they respected his decision, supported him, and proudly told others about him. Nevertheless, the G. I. Bill and an expanding economy also offered him other careers, and thus for many the first year of study in one of the three hundred or so seminaries run by religious orders was a backdoor way into a college and then into a law or medical school. This detour left many a later attorney or physician with a bad conscience and the seminary with a yearly donation.

The sisters of these young men found themselves in an entirely different situation. A few had acquired medical skills and other experience while serving in medical corps during the war, and long before women's liberation, they became a new kind of female doctor capable of handling anything. However, this route was not open to most young women. The labor market, which was determined by heavy industry and agriculture, offered them few opportunities, particularly since they had to compete against males with better training.

That is not to say that young women who entered a convent in those days viewed their choice as the least of two evils. On the contrary, those who were interested in such a way of life found their decision made easier by the fact that their sociocultural environment offered women hardly any more prestigious profession. The teaching profession perhaps offered comparable social recognition and presumably satisfaction. However, two out of three nuns were teachers anyway— though not in public schools but in traditional Catholic milieus, and often as members of the same order to which their own teachers had belonged. In any case, these young women remained close to their own ethnic groups and not only had the feeling that they were giving back what they had received, but also that they were helping "their own people" to amount to something. Once again: religious motivation was no doubt the presupposition for interest in convent life, but the social environment of the time not only contributed to this choice but also subsequently honored and supported it.

Fifteen years later, this support had virtually disappeared, along with the milieu itself. The families of the brothers and cousins of the young women who had become nuns in 1950 now lived in the suburbs and shared the standard of living and habits of the prosperous white middle class. Catholic schools and the nuns who kept them afloat seemed a symbol of the ethnic ghetto that had been left behind, and many a pastor saw these schools only as burdensome and expensive relics of the past. At the same time, the double disadvantage for women that at the end of the 1940s was still produced by social conventions and by the economic structure had begun to fall away. Although during the war women had worked in shipyards and munitions factories, these lines of work were afterwards closed to them again, and this was regarded as a return to normal life. On the other hand, about all that was required of a man in Detroit or Pittsburgh who wanted his family to share in the economic miracle was that he be willing and able to work hard.

In the meantime, however, ideas of what was normal were not the only things that had changed. In the emerging service economy, women who knew how to express themselves and could spell were now more in demand than were uneducated men. In any case, the situation had changed for women in two respects, for the activities of many nuns seem to have declined in prestige while other new possibilities were opening up.

In contrast, a young man who was thinking of becoming a priest did not have to reckon with such pronounced opposites in making his decision. His position also had to be seen in relation to the collective social advancement of Catholics. A young priest was no longer so likely to be the only college graduate in his family, and his brothers and sisters could generally count on having higher incomes. It was definitely no longer certain that he would be the only one in his parish who had pursued his education somewhat further; he was more likely to have trouble keeping up with his parishioners in this respect. Nonetheless, he could still expect to be the boss in his parish, and with the increasing perception of a shortage of priests, to be better paid and treated, and generally called upon and respected. Thus, for example, young priests surveyed in 1989, five years after they were ordained, reported a high level of satisfaction with their profession (Hemrick and Hoge 1991, 27).

Individualism and Voluntarism, Catholic Style

American Catholicism was thus not suddenly overwhelmed by the spirit of modernism. The characteristics of American religious culture, and especially the structural principle of voluntarism, were from the outset present in American Catholicism as well. Their consequences did not fully develop, however, so long as American Catholicism still existed under special conditions. In the 1960s it became clear that American Catholics, including lay people as well as priests and members of religious orders, no longer belonged to a minority seeking to rise in society, and that they had abandoned the modes of behavior corresponding to their earlier situation. "Father knows best" had described the proverbial reaction to both convincing and not-so-convincing instructions offered by priests in a situation where unity seemed more important than anything else. However, these Catholics became just as individualistic and voluntaristic as other Americans as soon as they believed they could allow themselves such luxuries. Once they had established a place for themselves at the center of American society, they insisted on adopting the corresponding values and ways of life. Therefore the more people saw service to the church as compatible with such values and ways of life, the more willing they were to enter it.

Americanized Catholics no longer wanted to be represented politically by their priests and bishops, and in any case they insisted on being convinced before allowing themselves to be led. Thus in elections Catholics could no longer be counted on to provide the "Catholic vote." Like the overwhelming majority of other voters, most Catholics gravitated toward the center, and thus reacted negatively when a party or candidate took clear positions. When Goldwater adopted a distinctly right-wing stance or McGovern a distinctly left-wing stance, most Catholics joined the majority in voting for Johnson and Nixon. In any case, the signs of their already not very clear party preference no longer pointed in the traditional—that is Democratic—direction. Connections between higher socioeconomic status and voting behavior had emerged that once again confirmed how much Catholics had established themselves at the center of American society. Most of the ethnic groups to which the great majority of Catholics belong voted for Ronald Reagan in 1980, and the earlier the bulk of the group immigrated, the more heavily it voted for Reagan. The more these voters felt assimilated and successful, the more prepared they were to elect a Republican (Zöller 1985, 399).

From the middle 1970s onward, figures on religious behavior stabilize at a clearly lower level. Ninety-five to 96 percent of those born Catholics still consider themselves Catholics. Of these, at least half (50–55 percent) regularly participate in the life of the church, while another fourth do so only sporadically. Andrew Greeley points out that these varying degrees of fervor are clearly connected with specific stages in life. Unmarried young men, for example, participate much less, but when they have families they return to the pews.

The baby boomers, a particularly large age group that on average married later because more of them went to college and because of the general change in lifestyle, substantially contributed to the impression that overall church attendance declined dramatically in the second half of the 1960s and then unexpectedly recovered. About half of this statistical change can be explained by the baby boomers' tendency to remain single longer, and this also somewhat qualifies Greeley's references to the consequences of *Humanae Vitae* (Greeley 1982, 20 ff., 46).

In any event, religious attitudes and behavior resemble political attitudes and behavior. American Catholics are fundamentally loyal and opposed to all extreme positions. Anyone who tries to show that in matters of social ethics or the conduct of life, including sexual habits, certain ideas and practices are the only ones acceptable to Catholics has to offer a persuasive argument. Moreover, he must first be certain that the subject chosen is one on which traditional Catholic doctrine and logic allows unequivocal statements to be made. Otherwise he would do better to refrain from attempts to mobilize people, since the foreseeable failure of such attempts can only harm the authority of the church's teaching function.

From the answers to a very unspecific Gallup poll as well as from individual results of the broadly based Notre Dame Study we can conclude that the debates in the 1970s and 1980s had an effect on churchgoers. In both cases we find a marked skepticism with regard to political statements, regardless of the fact that the Gallup poll's question as to whether the church should keep out of politics might be considered as suggesting a positive reply, whereas by favoring certain subjects the Notre Dame Study suggested the opposite.

The Notre Dame Study is interesting above all because it allows various differentiations to be made. First, in giving their opinions on seven prominent public issues, the respondents were permitted to emphasize the responsibility of specific ecclesiastical authorities or their individual consciences. Regarding aid to developing countries, 83 percent of those surveyed consider this the hierarchy's responsibility, and 70 percent considered the pope responsible. On the other end of the scale is the subject of birth control, which 47 percent of those surveyed saw as the individual's responsibility alone, with 45 percent disagreeing, although only Catholics close to the church were included in this poll.

These active Catholics were also asked to rank according to their importance thirteen issues in internal church politics and ethical teaching. The emphasis on individual spirituality came out on top, and the church's opposition to abortion was ranked second. In contrast, birth control was ranked next to last. Only the ordination of women seemed less important to those surveyed.

A similar picture emerged if Catholics were asked about their wishes in relation to the work carried out in their own parish, and about ten other activities. Regular churchgoers ranked the religious education of teenagers and children first and second, naming as third most important aid to needy members of the parish. On the other hand, "work to change unjust socioeconomic relationships" seemed to them the least important kind of activity. When the Notre Dame Study was made public, its scholarly directors lamented the fact that American Catholics were tending toward individualism and privatism (Leege 1987, no. 11, p. 4; Leege and Trozzolo 1985, 8).

2. "Churchmice": The Sociology of Activism

If American Catholics are as loyal, temperate, and apolitical as they appear in such opinion polls, then one wonders how the controversies of the 1970s and 1980s came about—controversies that involved two feuding ideological camps that apparently permeated all parts of the church and each had their own infrastructure.

Another peculiarity of the Notre Dame Study points to the sociology of activism and to the answer to the question just formulated. This investigation was supposed to provide a picture of actual relationships in parishes and thus could not be satisfied with determining general trends in opinion alone. Hence four groups were distinguished, namely regular Sunday churchgoers, parish volunteers, parish employees, and priests. Two principles of the distribution of opinions become evident. First, proximity to a given problem, that is, the probability of being involved oneself, plays a decisive role. Second, the issues of divorce and birth control reveal a clear difference between priests on one hand and all three of the lay groups on the other.

Aside from that, the two groups working for the parish are opinion leaders within the church and clearly tend to interpret the parish's mission and their own work pragmatically. They see Vatican II as a general program of reform that has not yet been realized in practice. Thus when participants in the Notre Dame Study were asked whether the church should "follow through more on changes and guidelines that resulted from Vatican II," the unusually large degree of agreement among full-time parish employees (3.18 on a scale from 1 to 4) shows how much it reflects the way this group views itself (ibid.).

Although these full-time parish employees represent an important new factor in the life of the church, no reliable figures are available because church yearbooks list only priests and members of religious orders. However, even if such employees were included in church statistics, the latter would still be misleading, because not all those whom Germans refer to as "churchmice" appear on parish or diocesan payrolls. Regular church employees in this sense include deacons, whose professional career usually began with theological study but intentionally or unintentionally ended one step short of the priesthood. Recently, we also find in this group many people who, after long careers in other fields, have completed the required additional training. Then there are non-ordained employees, whose functions in parish administration and organization often go far beyond secretarial work. Such staff employees initially made it easier to deal with growth by enlarging existing parishes rather than establishing new ones, and thereby to mitigate the problems caused by the shortage of priests.

However, "churchmice," who have been described more ambitiously in sociological terms as "the new educated class" (Varacalli 1983, 10), also include other people who may or may not be considered church employees in the legal sense of the term, depending on the locality. First, there are teachers in Catholic schools (a group in which the number of members of religious orders is steadily decreasing), whose employer may be the parish, a religious order, or a group of supporters. The same is true of employees of hospitals, retirement homes, and social services. Such employees still see themselves and are seen by others as obligated to participate actively in the life of the parish. Whether they are counted for statistical purposes as members of the church staff or as volunteers depends on the previously mentioned variables. In any case, the total number of active participants has sharply risen at the parish level, and volunteer groups are composed not only of housewives and white collar workers who donate their free time, but also of professionals, with the result that the staff and volunteer groups have increasingly similar status.

Yet even this is only part of the new sociology of the church. The altered nature of the average parish includes two additional developments that mutually determine and reinforce each other, namely the growth of structures operating above the local level and the emergence of a Catholic professional intelligentsia resulting from the combination of educational expansion and changes in the life of religious orders.

Further Organization of the Church on the National Level

The most striking institutional growth occurs in the number of dioceses, which increased from 23 archdioceses and 102 dioceses in 1950 to 36 archdioceses and 162 dioceses in 1993. This increase by more than half is significantly greater than the increase in the number of parishes, which grew from 15,000 to 20,000 over the same period. The changes in the organizational structure of individual dioceses, that is, the establishment of new diocesan institutions and new departments within the diocesan administration, might be considered equally important.

However, the greatest effects on the structure of individual dioceses were produced by the expansion of the national level, which can in fact be described as a direct result of Vatican II. In the nineteenth century, the three plenary councils held in Baltimore were instrumental in unifying the American church. Meetings of the archbishops also became an important if unofficial institution, and after World War I negotiations finally led to the foundation, not of a National Catholic Welfare Council, but of a National Catholic Welfare Conference. Just as when "War" was replaced by "Welfare," the commonly used abbreviation NCWC was retained, but the Vatican had made it clear that this was to be an advisory committee and that the jurisdiction of individual bishops was to remain intact.

Conferences of bishops, which were not even mentioned in the *Codex Juris Canonici* of 1918, were first recognized in canon law as a result of Vatican II, which produced the decretal *Christus Dominus* (on the pastoral office of bishops). Paul VI ultimately ordered that conferences of bishops be established everywhere, an opportunity American bishops immediately seized (Dulles 1989, 207). In 1966 the NCWC was replaced by two new organizations, the National Conference of Catholic Bishops (NCCB) and the United States Catholic Conference (USCC). Thus the NCCB was established as a decision-making body to which only bishops and their auxiliary bishops and coadjutors belonged, whereas lay people, priests, and members of religious orders could participate in the deliberations and activities of the USCC, although the latter remained under the bishops' control.

Members of the NCCB—currently numbering more than three hundred—are supposed to take part in the annual meetings that take place in November. These meetings provide an opportunity to appoint people to many posts. Among these are the fifty members of the Administrative Committee, which can make decisions regarding urgent issues that arise between plenary meetings. A representative for each of the twenty-seven committees of the NCCB is elected, and one bishop is assigned to act as representative and another as a member of each of the five USCC committees (Communications, Education, Human Development, Domestic Policy, International Policy). The assembly also elects the general secretary and the treasurer.

There is a special procedure for electing the president and vice-president. Before the meeting in November, each of the approximately three hundred bishops who are eligible to vote submits in writing a list of five candidates. The ten candidates most often nominated are put on the ballot presented to the assembled bishops, who elect first the president and then choose the vice-president from the remaining nine candidates. According to Thomas Reese's analysis of these elections (Reese 1989, 290), with only two exceptions candidates have appeared on the ballot several times before being elected vice-president. Once elected vice-president, however, they were always subsequently elected president if they ran again.

The Episcopal Three-Class Society

As a result of these regulations, the approximately three hundred bishops are now divided into three groups that are incorporated into the national organization and representation of the church in wholly different ways. Two out of three bishops are called upon to exercise their voting rights only once a year, and most of these two hundred bishops are presumably glad to be able to return to their dioceses once they have voted. The remaining third is then divided into two clearly distinguishable groups. The fifty members of the Administrative Committee and the thirty-seven bishops who are responsible for the various committees are generally reelected several times and thus have an opportunity to become familiar with an area. However, this also means that they have to explain and represent to the other bishops the views of staff members and expert consultants. If instead of following the latter they wish to advocate a position of their own, then they have to legitimate themselves in another way, namely by seeking to represent the bishops as their president or vice-president. From this annual ranking, in which all three hundred bishops participate actively and passively by nominating five of their colleagues, there in fact emerges an elite group whose members have enough support to control the organization and to represent the bishops publicly. However, precisely because this elite position imparts real power, this privilege has been restricted to a small group that constantly changes because the terms of office are limited. By interpreting collegiality in an egalitarian manner, the bishops thus prevented any of their number from becoming too powerful, but they also unintentionally further increased the power of the national organization.

The latter's growth and significance is already discernible in the fact that a remodeled school building that had served as the NCWC's headquarters since 1919 was replaced first by a much larger building and then in 1989 by a separate office complex. It is in this complex, which is across the street from Catholic University, that the NCCB's and USCC's four hundred employees now work.

Whether a secretariat of this size is justified depends on the tasks the church's national organization is supposed to assume. In its discussion of the liturgy as well as in its decretal on the status of bishops, Vatican II assigned a unifying role to the conferences of bishops. Together they were responsible for dealing with methods of promulgating the faith as well as with institutions that prepared young men for the priesthood, and this is in fact what some of the NCCB's committees do. Also in accord with the prescriptions of Vatican II, some committees deal with the situation of individual groups such as Hispanics, African-Americans, or women. In addition, there are tasks that can be described as representation or lobbying: a secretariat in the capital is needed to represent the church on occasions such as the inauguration of a new president and to point out that certain legislative proposals will have specific consequences for Catholic schools or Catholic hospitals.

An organization of this kind and size comes into being only when people see the church as having a comprehensive mission to shape political opinion both inside and outside the church. Then the issue is not only "Catholic interests" or supporting moral demands that cannot be abandoned, as in the case of the debates concerning abortion. Rather, the church is expected to supply a consistent moral judgment on politics as a whole and to exercise a moral influence on the political process.

This was precisely the way things were seen by the new kind of church activists, whose self-concept was quite distinct from that of the Catholic socialists of the 1920s. In their view, the national Catholic organization should become a comprehensive lobbying organization that would formulate a "Catholic" position on all political issues, not only in congressional hearings but also in the public sphere in general, while at the same time continuously lobbying within the church as well. In the course of the 1970s and 1980s, the NCCB and the USCC came ever nearer to realizing this ideal, even though the majority of bishops presumably did not support it. However, it is irrelevant whether individual bishops became involved in political activities as a result of personal commitment, or hoped thereby to improve their images, or believed that discussion of political programs that were said to concern only politicians and the public were harmless or perhaps even distracted attention from conflicts within the church (Varacalli 1983, 74).

Multiple Reproductions of the Structures

Wholly independently of the various motives involved, one can indicate two grounds for the national organization's growth. First, every conceivable reaction of the conference of bishops or individual bishops led to the national organization's being further expanded and imitated at other organizational levels. Secondly, for the first time there was within Catholicism a social group that had an interest in becoming active within this organizational structure and in using the latter's expansion to validate its own social position.

The organizational structure at the top was thus increasingly reproduced at lower levels. When a committee, taskforce or office with a specific assignment was established in Washington, sooner or later some counterpart had to be set up in the dioceses, with its own staff—

whether because otherwise the central institution was left high and dry, or because this was the only way one could have a say or express opposition in Washington, or because individual dioceses came under pressure to deal with some subject in order not to seem backward. In any case, over time the NCCB set up thirteen regional offices to reflect the country's diversity, while the dioceses adopted in varying degrees the NCCB's committees and administrative structure. As already mentioned, it mattered little whether those involved argued progressively—that is, wanted to create a basis for a given measure proposed by the central committees—or were interested chiefly in keeping the pressure on "those people in Washington" and ensuring that official statements were "more balanced."

By demanding representativeness, this conservative reaction to campaigns on social and moral issues, namely their effort to "prevent worse things from happening," or to "denounce one-sidedness," paradoxically led to a second principle of reproduction: if the organizational structure was to be reproduced from the top down, the social structure should also be reproduced from the bottom up. So that ordinary churchgoers could identify with the positions and actions taken, the focus must not be exclusively on the poor of the world and minorities in America, but also include those whom politicians remember mainly just before elections. As Bill Clinton put it, these are the people who play by the rules, pay their taxes, and raise their kids.

It was precisely these "ordinary Americans" who were strongly represented at the lower levels, because parishes depended on their participation, their contributions, and their volunteer work. Things looked very different in diocesan committees and especially in national committees, where professional activists set the tone. Nonetheless, the issue was not a numerically appropriate representation of the majority, but rather an intellectually adequate defense of their ways of life and values. Thus a gap appeared that was soon filled by a few neoconservative Catholic intellectuals who specialized in providing a counterweight to the Catholic "new left" and its social and moral activism.

The Formation of Two Camps within Catholicism

Comparing these groups with Catholic social activism in the 1920s and 1930s and with traditional American "right-wingers" inside and outside the church demonstrates that we are justified in speaking here of a new-left activism and a neo-conservatism. The older progressives had worked for concrete social and political measures, emphasizing in particular the connection between education and social advancement. Like the labor unions with which they were associated, they believed in an America that they thought needed to be reformed in various ways. Thus they were resolutely anticommunist and a Marxist-inspired theology would have struck them as a contradiction in terms.

The new activists are not, however, primarily interested in social politics, which they often contemptuously describe as reformism but still consider appropriate where minorities are concerned. In their view, America is beyond renewal; it has to be condemned, because it stands for exploitation, oppression, and male sexist domination. Individual emancipation begins with the moral emancipation of America, but the latter appears as a positive concept in these activists' rhetoric only when it is a matter of emphasizing the necessity of establishing an independent church distanced from Rome. In other contexts, these activists see the enemy in America as well as in Rome, an enemy that is doing its best to reverse the emancipation that is symbolized within the church by Vatican II. The counterparts of this new activism, if they are not its most important opponents, are therefore the groups that do all they can to make such fears appear justified. They have formed an "unholy alliance," as Margaret O'Brian Steinfels, a left-leaning liberal and editor of *Commonweal* points out in agreeing with a book by the neo-conservative George Weigel (O'Brian Steinfels 1992, 377 ff.; Weigel 1989, 702 ff.). The radical organizations on one side, which nowadays seldom still describe themselves as leftist, see themselves instead as fighting for specific rights (as does the Association for Rights of Catholics in the Church, the ARCC), and they are opposed by the radicals on the other side, which are for the most part less organized and associated with periodicals such as the *Wanderer* or *The Catholic Eye*.

Each group wants to define the other out of the church, each sees Vatican II as the turning point that first put the church on the right or wrong path, and each considers American culture fundamentally corrupt and beyond redemption (Greeley 1986, 205 ff.). The traditionalist right is insignificant, organizationally and intellectually; Opus Dei, which the progressives constantly present as a danger, has hardly any intellectual influence on the public and produces neither meetings nor publications.

Instead, the so-called neo-conservative intellectuals have assumed the role of providing the inarticulate majority with arguments and criticizing the progressives who dominate the national organization and the theology departments. Because of the previously described institutional growth, they find so many fields of activity and opportunities that they can hardly deal with them all.

From the 1970s on, the concept of neo-conservatism was used to describe those who opposed, in an unorganized way, the so-called cultural revolution and its slogans. Although it lumped together very different kinds of people and positions, there were some common denominators. Many of these intellectuals were social scientists, most had earlier considered themselves "leftists," and they included a surprising number of Jews and Catholics.

These former progressives had no connections with traditional American right-wingers. They were the sons and grandsons of European immigrants, and they therefore did not understand the traditional right's political isolationism, and did not have access to its social circles. Instead, like the older progressives, they maintained that America had an indispensable role to play in the world. They even clung to the old reformism, even though most of them had gradually ceased to believe that government intervention was beneficial in all contexts. Whether or not they remained New Dealers, they were far less prepared to engage in a general moralistic critique of America than were the descendants of the New England cultural establishment. An initial rallying point was provided by *Commentary,* a periodical published by the American Jewish Committee and edited by Irving Kristol and Norman Podhoretz. Catholic writers such as Michael Novak and George Weigel published their work in *Commentary* and periodicals such as the *New Republic* even before, reacting to the pastoral letters of the 1980s, they began to see themselves as a Catholic group and founded their own periodicals such as *Crisis* and *First Things.*

Their position seemed to be determined above all by their adherence to the Catholic optimism of the "Tocqueville-Acton tradition," that is, by their refusal to believe that America is corrupt and irredeemable. As contemporary conservatives, they were the heirs of the progressive Americanists of the nineteenth century. By associating themselves with the older Catholic liberal-conservative tradition while at the same time appealing to a Catholic Whig tradition, they tried to escape the opposition of two oversimplified traditional concepts and the corresponding positions taken by Vatican II. That is, they tried to distance themselves from a traditionalism without development as well as from a modernism that lacks continuity and is open to all positions except arguments drawn from Catholic tradition. Michael Novak and George Weigel gained fame as the neo-conservatives' public spokesmen, while Avery Dulles achieved a similar position in academic theology, though he long stood alone.

The Catholic Cultural Principle and the Sociology of Activism

The politicization of religion with which the Protestant churches had long been familiar overtook American Catholicism as well during the 1960s. Catholics and Protestants now lived in the same world and were therefore subject to the same developments. An ineradicable distinction remained, however. Catholicism's and Protestantism's conceptions of their churches were expressed through differing organizational structures, and these were anything but secondary, since they embodied presuppositions regarding how one could try to cope with social and cultural change. As a cultural principle, Protestantism amounts to the attempt to confront continually changing relationships through individual learning and the corresponding choices made by individuals, and the lack of a nationwide church constitution leads to the organizational duplication seen in American Protestantism. Thus in religious history there are also winners and losers, because as we have seen, one can switch denominations rather than giving up religion altogether.

This kind of internal competition is not possible for Catholicism, because its cultural principle is institutional learning, and therefore it reacts to change through institutional differentiation. It seeks to channel the spirit of the age, to assign it a precisely circumscribed place within the church, and in this way both reduce its effects and transform its energy into a positive force. This seems to be an attempt to square the circle, but the church succeeded so long as it was able to transform social movements into religious orders, to make them into a rule of life.

Thus while the Protestant cultural principle can be summed up in the formula "diversity in equality," the Catholic cultural principle amounts to the opposite, namely "unity in inequality." For Reformation thinkers, what was scandalous about Catholicism was that it recognized varying degrees of religious vocation corresponding to different demands, so that the majority of one group could rely on the representative achievements of the other.

The Catholic principle stands or falls with its ability to transform social movements into regulated ways of life, that is, to give them an institutional shape; conversely, such a movement's ability to maintain itself becomes the measure of its power and substance. Both presuppose that all those concerned are willing to accept the resulting inequalities of the ways of life, and that the church hierarchy is willing and able to determine and maintain the relevant institutional boundaries.

However, American Catholicism was now immersed in a culture so clearly marked by the Protestant principle that people are inclined to see everything as resulting from individual choice and to distrust hierarchies as much as they distrust the discriminating division of labor into various religious vocations and ways of life.

Sharing, joining, belonging, and getting things done: these are American mottoes, and they suggest that a separate, special existence is highly undesirable. This is particularly true when giving up the active life also means giving up the good life. The growing affluence of others matters not only because it promises access to consumer goods, but even more because it offers an opportunity for social mobility and communication. In any case, it is not surprising that the crisis of the 1960s appeared chiefly in the form of a crisis in the life of religious orders. Hecker had translated his goal of reconciling Catholicism and American culture into the rules of a new religious community from which the Paulists, the so-called American order, emerged. This may have been the last time that such a group established itself in such a way, since religious orders no longer provide the only organizational form for the intelligentsia within the church. Anyone who wants to belong to a party concerned with church politics or with social and moral issues now finds it easier to do so. Because American Catholicism has developed its own national public sphere, one can pursue such interests professionally without having to subordinate one's whole life to the dictates of a religious order's rule.

This began with the life work of another Paulist, Father John Burke, who founded the NCWC and by clever maneuvering made it into a permanent institution. His work was continued in the previously described twofold reproduction of the structures, with the result that there emerged an institutional tangle of action groups, periodicals, educational establishments, foundations, and so on that provided a field of action for the new Catholic intelligentsia. This new class of highly qualified "churchmice" not only took over a classical function of the religious orders, namely the representation of Christian consciousness (but without being obliged to live their position, that is, to set an example of asceticism), but became the religious orders' heir in two senses, even sociologically. First, they were recruited chiefly from the children of middle class Catholic families who had taken advantage of the educational expansion of the postwar years, and were sufficiently influenced by the Catholic milieu to want to work within the church, but did not want to assume an unlimited obligation. This holds for those who are from the outset determined to keep their jobs and their lives separate, who like the rest of society claim their right to a private life, but it also holds for those who begin to doubt their vocation even before they are ordained or enter an order.

However, the members of religious orders who are released for activities within the national organization, or those who have left their orders but are not disqualified for service to the church in other ways, must deal with this new class of "churchmice." The latter specialize in leading intellectual discussions about the consequences of change. Some of them claim to represent progress, others stability, and they organize these two poles of the Judeo-Christian interpretation of history independently of each other.

Both parties are only partially integrated into the division of labor within the church, and thus can fulfill the role of religious orders only very incompletely. When they concentrate on debates internal to the church, they take on a traditionally rich and necessary task, but unlike their clerical predecessors, they cannot combine it with pastoral care for specific groups. On one hand they can perform only a single task; on the other, they are not subject to any rule or institutional entity that would express their role's special and limited character.

Finally, this new class of people has changed the institutional division of labor insofar as through its own functional one-sidedness it contributes to making other "classes" equally one-sided. It transfers the logic of its own ideological duality to comparable groups such as professors of theology and intellectually-oriented religious orders, which it incorporates, and by claiming intellectual monopoly it consigns preachers even more to a pastoral role and bishops to an administrative one.

The rise of this new class thus represents above all a challenge to the church's organizational structure. Its goal is to reorganize the collaboration of different functional groups and thereby to define an institutional place for each of them. Ultimately this results in the paradox that only bishops can channel development in an orderly way, even though these same developments have largely deprived them of the means of doing so.

3. Unsuccessful Mobilization

After the elation of the 1950s and the subsequent deep uncertainty, by the end of the 1970s the outlook was for calmer conditions and recovery. The general climate was determined by an apolitical exhaustion as well as by confidence, and church statistics indicated an end or at least a slowing of the downward trend. Yet just at this time, namely in the years between 1976 and 1986, American Catholicism was kept busy by an unprecedented series of campaigns for political mobilization. The draft documents, positions pro and con taken in hearings, reworked texts and updated statements made on both sides by speakers who had recently become well-known, all included elements of a media-savvy strategy, and in fact the public image of the church was for many years defined by controversies over planned political statements.

Nonetheless, it was not primarily a matter of representing the Catholic Church in the public sphere, and for this reason it was not only the top-level organizations in Washington and the media that were involved. On the contrary, at enormous expense efforts were made to involve all levels of the church organization. Of course, active and passive roles have to be distinguished, and it is therefore justified to speak of a mobilization campaign within the church. The national organization not only provided documentation of all kinds, but also organized large meetings, prepared delegates in special workshops, and even participated in choosing the right delegates. The whole thing quickly came to look much more like a "revolution from above" run by bureaucrats than an American grass-roots movement.

The Detroit Peace and Justice Conference

This impetus from above began with the so-called Bicentennial Program of 1975–1976, which culminated in a final three-day event, the Peace and Justice Conference. The Catholic contribution to the bicentennial celebration of the American declaration of independence was thus supposed to consist in a discussion of the deplorable condition of America and indeed of the rest of the world. Many bishops were not happy with this plan, but the archbishop of Detroit, Cardinal John F. Dearden, supported it. Since it was apparently no longer possible to debate the plan itself, its opponents concentrated instead on the assignment of responsibilities, that is, on who should be authorized to approve the program of events and later to evaluate it. Joseph L. Bernardin, who was then bishop of Cincinnati and president of the NCCB, and who had been general secretary from 1968 to 1972, suggested not appointing an independent committee, but rather letting the standing committee and the chair make the decisions. The so-called left wing, under the leadership of the archbishop of Newark, Peter Gerety, wanted to establish an ad hoc committee to which employees and lay people could also belong. The compromise consisted in creating such a committee but not making Gerety its chair; instead, Archbishop John R. Roach of Minneapolis, who was then vice-president, was made chair and given the task of maintaining balance.

The later developments leading up to the meeting in Detroit are interesting only because they indicate how the professional activists worked and thought. All across the country seminars were set up to prepare interested people for Detroit and to get them to engage in similar activities in their own areas. However, this way of selecting volunteers in advance did not meet with the organizers' approval. In the discussion groups that met in many parishes, following a program worked out in Washington, and even in the preparatory seminars it became clear that most of the participants were white middle-class Americans—and the only thing surprising about this is that the professionals found it surprising.

The organizers drafted a memorandum on the selection of delegates and sent it to every diocese in an effort to achieve "somewhat of a balance" at the Peace and Justice Conference. This did not mean that the delegates were to reflect American Catholicism's social structure or the current spectrum of opinion. The memorandum allowed each diocese to send nine participants, who were to be more or less equally distributed among three groups. At the top level of the diocese, the bishop himself, the diocesan coordinator for the bicentennial program, and the director of adult education or the head of the social justice office were to be chosen. Three other participants who had participated in earlier activities were to be selected from different parishes. Finally, the third group was to be composed of actual "victims of injustice." In addition, approximately a hundred Catholic organizations were given the right to send representatives. The national organization itself was among these, as well as representatives of minorities (Varacalli 1983, 149).

The three-day conference in Detroit, in which more than a thousand persons ultimately took part, evolved into a chaotic "happening" that reminded many observers of the notorious 1968 Democratic party convention in Chicago, which gave the public and the traditional white labor vote the impression that the party had been taken over by radical minorities.

Thus Polish ethnic organizations complained that they had found all sorts of groups in Detroit, but no representative of "working class European ethnic Catholics." Cardinal John Krol of Philadelphia, who had been unable to prevail over a majority of feminists in a workshop on ordaining women, complained that the whole conference was dominated by such groups (Varacalli 1983, 102 ff.).

Within the church, the chief result of the unfortunate experiment in Detroit was that many people who had previously been considered left-liberals now distanced themselves from the activists. For instance, Andrew Greeley, one of the exponents of the earlier progressivism focusing on social reforms, characterized those who participated in the spectacle in Detroit as "A ragtag assembly of kooks, crazies, flakes, militants, lesbians, homosexuals, ex-priests, incompetents, castrating witches, would-be messiahs, sickies and other assorted malcontents" (ibid.).

The Political Pastoral Letters of the 1980s

Like Greeley, the bishops seem to have seen the problem as resulting from the selection of "assorted malcontents." Their reaction did not consist in self-criticism but in a call for more control. They did not ask themselves whether in politicizing the church they were on the right track; instead, they decided that the Peace and Justice Conference had merely slipped out of the organizers' control, and they now took the themes of peace and justice into their own hands. The bishops drew up a timetable coordinated with both their own plenary assembly in the second half of November and the political calendar. In order to avoid the appearance of partisanship, nothing was to happen in presidential election years. Thus the time between the conference of bishops in November 1979 and the presidential election in November 1980 was out, and three years remained before the 1983 conference of bishops, which would once again take place close to a presidential campaign. In November 1980, the bishops therefore established an ad hoc committee of the NCCB and simultaneously named a corresponding USCC committee, so that staff members of the conference of bishops and other experts could participate in the preparations.

The first workgroup was called the "Ad Hoc Committee on War and Peace in the Nuclear Age," and was to be led by Bernardin. The second was called the "Ad Hoc Committee on Catholic Social Teaching and the U.S. Economy," and the archbishop of Milwaukee, Rembert G. Weakland was appointed chair. The bishops planned to issue the pastoral letter on war and peace promptly, whereas that on the economic order was to be issued only after a relatively lengthy period of preparation. This made it possible for leading bureaucrats to participate in both groups; otherwise, the widespread belief that J. Bryan Hehir, the director of the USCC's Department of Social Development and World Peace was the author of both texts could not have arisen.

The Committee on War and Peace submitted a draft in summer 1982, to allow time for comments. One of the reactions was a full-fledged counter-draft by Michael Novak, which he titled, playing off the committee's name, "Moral Clarity in the Nuclear Age." Subsequently, a second, revised version was submitted, which the bishops used as a prototype for their pastoral letter, and which they approved in 1983 at an extraordinary session in Chicago, where Bernardin had

in the meantime taken over as archbishop. The pastoral letter was titled "The Challenge of Peace: God's Promise and Our Response."

This wide-ranging document sets forth principles that can be described as elements of the "just war" doctrine, and then concentrates
on the problem of nuclear war. The so-called "first strike" or the threat
thereof is condemned without qualification and under all conditions.
By proceeding in this way, the bishops opened themselves to two objections that were raised both before and after the pastoral letter was
approved, and which the bishops did not answer. First, the text makes
it appear that the moral judgments formulated are a direct and necessary consequence of the previously stated doctrines, even though
Novak, for one, had shown that these same principles can lead to the
opposite conclusion. Second, the supposed clarity of the pastoral letter is achieved only at the price of a corresponding simplification: the
bishops concentrate on nuclear weapons and ignore the fluid boundary
between conventional and non-conventional weapons, as well as the
possibility of exploiting a superiority in conventional weapons.

Finally, the bishops argue completely naively and without much
originality when, at the end of their long document, they assert that
there is a substitute for war, namely, "negotiations under the supervision of a global body." On one hand, this international arbitration
board is to be "so constituted as to pose no threat to any nation's sovereignty," yet on the other "it must be realistically fashioned to do its
job" and "given the equipment to keep constant surveillance on the
entire earth." This new "international authority" can thus fulfill its
task only if it has the will and the means to meet threats backed by all
sorts of weapons with credible deterrent threats—that is, if it can do
what the bishops have already condemned (Ellis 1967, 2: 886).

The bishops' first power play thus did not produce anything new,
for everything in the pastoral letter can be described as deriving from
what Catholics regard as indisputable moral doctrine. Before the second attempt could be carried out against still greater objections, the
interlude required by the 1984 presidential election occurred. However, after Ronald Reagan had been reelected and won a majority of
Catholic votes, it seemed all the more necessary to connect the two
concepts contained in the second committee's name: Catholic social
teaching and the United States economy.

The NCCB committee, enlarged by the addition of seven "advisors" and four top staffers from the USCC, had been working on a first draft since the beginning of 1981, and between November 1981 and July 1984 it had conducted fifteen hearings, most of them lasting two days, at which 113 experts spoke. These experts included staff members of ecclesiastical organizations, former politicians and officials, a few business executives, foundation employees, and finally, scholars, more of whom were theologians than economists. The list of invited speakers, which was published along with the first draft of the text, is noteworthy in several regards. Two of the experts were apparently considered indispensable. Michael Novak was called in three times to defend a position that would otherwise have been too weakly represented. On the other hand, David Hollenbach, a well-known leftist social ethicist, appeared twice as an expert, even though he was also one of the committee's permanent advisors. In addition, a certain one-sidedness in the selection of experts is evident. For instance, Richard McBrien and Charles E. Curran were invited to testify as representatives of progressive theology, but Avery Dulles is absent from the list. Moreover, certain schools of economics and social sciences, for example the so-called Chicago school, were not represented.

All this is instructive but not significant, because a more "balanced" list of speakers would not have changed the result. The selection of expert witnesses, which was already somewhat problematic, necessarily led to a very inconsistent view of the situation, not to mention the suggested solutions. Thus in the introduction to its first draft, the committee noted that in the course of the hearings one thing had become evident: there was no clear consensus regarding either the kind of problems confronting the country or what the best way of dealing with them was. Shortly afterward it was said that the authors were aware of the difficulties encountered when trying to bring religious and moral values to bear on economic life (*Origins*, 15 November 1984, 337 ff.).

Even the committee's chair, Archbishop Weakland, reported meeting with such difficulties. In an article written for the periodical *America*, he pointed out that when the bishops issued a pastoral letter, one could not expect from them the kind of economic analysis that one would expect from a research institute specializing in the same area. The bishops should seek primarily "to articulate moral objectives" (Weakland 1985, 131).

This insight came to nothing, however, for Weakland and the members of his committee saw neither the distinction between the formulation of principles and concrete proposals nor the reference to the greater professional competence of others as a reason for limiting their own scope. Thus we find in the text indisputable if often banally formulated principles juxtaposed but not logically connected with concrete recommendations regarding labor policy and the assertion that Catholic social teaching requires general economic planning (*Origins,* 15 November 1984, 337 ff.).

The committee chair was well aware that in this respect criticism was to be expected. Thus in the previously mentioned article he reported that during the internal deliberations two objections in particular were raised. First, the recommendations were too reminiscent of both the Democrats' unsuccessful New Deal program and the corresponding problems in many European countries. Second, in every area government was accorded too large a role. Weakland's reply was both correct and incomplete: according to Catholic social teaching, he wrote, government had a positive and indispensable role to play in efforts toward social justice (Weakland 1985, 131). Hence the voluminous text included no attempt to define and limit the role of government more precisely, and the whole debate concerning the modern, service-oriented state was completely ignored.

The first draft was presented to the bishops at their November 1984 meeting, and subsequently published along with an invitation to comment on it in writing. According to Weakland, more than 10,000 pages of the most diverse comments were submitted. The bishops received a selection of these and at a special session held in Collegeville, Minnesota in June 1985, they discussed the text and the responses to it. Finally a second draft was written, which the bishops discussed at their November meeting. Afterward the committee returned to work and in the summer of 1986 presented a third version of the pastoral letter, which after a few revisions was finally approved and issued under the title "Economic Justice for All: Social Teaching and the U.S. Economy."

What did this decade of top-down politicization and mobilization of American Catholicism produce? No one would suggest that it improved the understanding of international politics or economic processes, and proponents of these pastoral letters probably did not wish to make such claims. But neither was Catholic social teaching further developed or plausibly applied to new and different conditions. The bishops' demands are close to the tradition of Catholic social teaching and to what Weakland called moral goals, but one does not follow from the other. By trying to do more than remind people of the principles of the "just war" doctrine or social teachings, they ignored Vatican II's admonition that Christians "might in equally good conscience come to different conclusions regarding the same issue" (Qtd. in Novak 1985, 17). It does not help to take every point of view into account, for example J. Bryan Hehir's version of the Democratic party program as well as Michael Novak's version of the Republican program. What will help is not making statements more "balanced" but avoiding this kind of slippery terrain in the first place.

That is why people suspected that the whole thing was a mere subterfuge. *Newsweek* said that the church apparently found it easier to criticize the government than to confront its own problems (Varacalli 1983, 74). To be sure, no such conscious effort to distract attention can be attributed to most of the bishops, and in fact other, less-noticed pastoral letters were issued at this time, for example the one on the condition of Hispanics. Nonetheless, it is correct to say that many subjects that challenged the bishops themselves were pushed into the background or even completely abandoned as a result of activities associated with the Peace and Justice conference.

This became obvious when, shortly after the publication of the pastoral letter on economics, the media turned their attention to other topics and the politicization campaign within the church came to an abrupt end. It was clear that many bishops were not very interested in the pastoral, and some openly admitted that they had not understood all the implications of the text that was approved (Dulles 1988, 177).

In any case, this belated Catholic epilogue to the 1970s was now exhausted, so that church officials could finally turn their attention to the new situation in which the rest of the society, including Catholics, had been living since the beginning of the 1980s.

6

ON BEING CATHOLIC IN AMERICA

T HE OUTLINES OF this new situation emerged from a general mood that was once again very confident and from the everyday problems of a Catholicism that had so firmly established itself at the center of society that its problems no longer reflected its marginalization, that is, its excessive distance from the center, but rather its assimilation, that is, its excessive proximity. On one hand, the more Catholics from other cultural traditions were helped to reduce their distance from the center of society, the more successfully they could be brought into the church. On the other hand, the remaining problems came down to the question: how can a Catholicism so comfortably established in society still create enough distance to ensure its separate identity? This kind of distance was no longer produced by the marginal position of Catholics, but rather at best by conscious fashioning and cultivation of its own institutions. This held for all institutions concerned with religious careers, but in particular for Catholic schools and colleges, which were now gradually being recognized to be American Catholicism's greatest asset.

1. The End of the Downhill Trend

Statistical Recovery

According to church statistics, by 1980 the number of Catholics had grown to fifty million, thus remaining at 23 percent of the total population. Gallup poll statistics nevertheless indicate a significant number of borderline Catholics: in the 1970s 28 percent and in the 1980s 29 percent of those surveyed identified themselves as Catholics, but one out of five said that he was not a member of the church, and this explains the difference between "hard" statistics and "soft" self-identifications (Gallup and Castelli 1989, viii).

209

The Average Catholic Compared Demographically

Gallup poll figures also offer an interesting opportunity to compare personal data on Catholics and average Americans, and thus to define the position of Catholics in society. Such a comparison indicates that Catholics are over-represented in the 18–29 year-old age group, and under-represented in the over 50 year-old age group, that is, on average they are younger.

The proportion of Catholics identifying themselves as "white" is clearly above average, 96 percent to 87 percent. "Non-whites" include not only African-Americans, but also Asians and even some Hispanics, so that the 4 percent of "non-white" Catholics reminds us that the Catholic Church has not had much success among African-Americans. On the other hand, contrary to widespread assumptions, Hispanics by no means flock to the church by themselves. Otherwise, by the 1980s the 7 percent of Americans who identify themselves as Hispanics would have composed 20 to 22 percent of Catholics. In fact, they composed only 17 percent.

With regard to graduation rates, despite the relatively high proportion of first- and second-generation immigrants, particularly Hispanics, Catholics deviate from the average by only plus or minus 2 percent. Comparative data do not go back far enough to allow us to specify what changes are reflected in this figure. However, the extent of this development can be glimpsed when we read that in 1947 the archbishop of Boston stated with pride that he did not know a single bishop, archbishop, or cardinal in the whole American hierarchy whose father or mother had graduated from college. Every one of them, he said, was "the son of a working man and working man's wife" (Hennesey 1981, 284).

Catholics' income also rose above the average. In the two upper income groups they were 2 percent over the average, and in the lowest they were 4 percent under the average.

The collective history of American Catholics emerges most clearly in their regional distribution and in their political preferences. They were particularly numerous in the East; in the Midwest and West, which they had settled along with other groups, the proportion of Catholics was exactly average; in the South they were clearly in the minority. Their tendency to vote Republican was still 3 percent below

Table 7
Catholics Compared to the Average American

	Average American	Catholic American
Men	48 percent	49 percent
Women	52	51
18–29	27	30
30–49	37	38
50+	36	31
White	87	96
Non-white	11	4
Hispanic	7	17
College graduate	19	17
Some college	25	27
High School graduate	33	34
Less than High School	23	22
$40,000+ per year	21	23
$25,000–40,000	23	25
$15,000–25,000	22	21
Less than $15,000	29	25
East	25	38
Midwest	25	25
South	31	19
West	19	18
Republican	29	26
Democrat	39	42
Married	63	62
Single	20	23
Divorced/separated	8	7
Widowed	8	7

Source: Gallup and Castelli 1989, 101.

the general average, and their tendency to vote Democratic about as much above. Nonetheless, such a small gap between the two parties already involves a fundamental change. It also reveals that a third of all those surveyed and a third of the Catholics surveyed (32 percent) were not prepared to commit themselves to a party, and that in their political tendencies younger Catholics no longer differed from the general population (Gallup and Castelli 1989, 132 ff.).

In both groups, the proportion of married couples remains slightly over 60 percent, but the various alternatives are somewhat differently distributed. Eight percent of the general population and 7 percent of the Catholics said they were divorced or separated, hardly a significant difference and in any case no indication that Catholics still have a stronger commitment to marriage. The explanation of this fact, along with the slightly smaller proportion of widows and the substantially greater number of single people, is probably to be found in the number of Catholics in the different age groups. The proportion of Catholics in the younger age groups is significantly higher than in the general population, and they marry later than did earlier generations.

The Notre Dame Study also reveals what these Catholics of the 1980s expected from their church and what they politely ignored. Churchgoers from two thousand parishes were asked to rank a list of ten parish activities according to their importance. Here is the result:

1. Religious education for teenagers.
2. Religious education for children.
3. Helping the poor in the parish.
4. Efforts on behalf of people interested in the church and Catholics who have become estranged from the church.
5. Religious education for adults.
6. Improving the liturgy.
7. Increasing participation in the parish's social life.
8. Improving contacts with non-Catholic congregations in the neighborhood.
9. Helping the poor outside the parish.
10. Working to change unjust socioeconomic conditions.

The responses given by these practicing Catholics are clearly marked by a conception of subsidiarity of which there is scarcely a trace in the pastoral letter issued by their bishops. To put it in more American terms, people are responsible first of all for themselves and their immediate surroundings. In these churchgoers' opinion, the parish should concentrate on what individuals and other institutions cannot do effectively, and the ranking of the tasks involved also corresponds to their social proximity. At the top of the list is what concerns the family; then comes the parish, with the religious and social life inside the parish ranked over its relations with the outside, and efforts with regard to the rest of the world deemed least important. The authors of this part of the Notre Dame Study discern here the sin of individualism and are astonished that there is so little interest in activism on behalf of social justice (Leege and Trozzolo 1987, 6 ff.). However, we need not see these answers as an expression of a religion reduced to private concerns. The people surveyed are well aware of the importance of the church community, and they are not oblivious of their neighbors. They take the word "neighbor" literally, however, and think first about the needy in their own parish. The latter should be helped, but not by a committee chiefly concerned with discussing the causes of injustice.

2. The New Ethnics

American Catholicism grew up along with the European immigrants, and these so-called "ethnics" have now adapted to the lifestyle of the white middle class. However, the less the majority of Catholics are differentiated from the surrounding society, the more noticeable become the minorities within the church that have been called "the new ethnics." This general term includes very different groups: on one hand, Native Americans and African-Americans, who have experienced and suffered from modern American history from the outset, and on the other, Asian immigrants and Hispanics from Central and South America. All together, they prevent the church from settling down too comfortably at the center of American society.

The old pattern of incorporation is most closely followed by the few Catholics of Asian ancestry, most of them refugees from Vietnam. They show a pronounced readiness to adapt and attach particular value to educating their children. Like the Jewish immigrants that preceded them, the second generation tends to gain access to colleges and the corresponding jobs. They count not on their status as minorities but rather on their own efforts, and they also resemble their Jewish predecessors in never doubting that they have made the right choice in coming to America.

The situation and behavior of Native Americans and African-Americans are quite different. They are, in a manner of speaking, "born minorities," and they have remained largely determined by their collective fate. For this reason, independently of failings on the part of the church, they have found the path to Catholicism only when, as a result of geographical separation or social advancement, their connection with their heritage has been lost.

Hispanics are located between these extremes of an unconditional willingness to adapt as an orientation towards an individual future and its opposite, the continuing burden of a collective heritage. Their situation differs from that of earlier immigrant groups chiefly in that it is easier for them to evade the pressure to adapt. This is partly the result of the fact that in the contemporary cultural climate ethnic difference is no longer seen as an absolute defect, that is, as insufficient Americanization; on the contrary, it is often valued as contributing to the richness of a multicultural society. In addition, Hispanics, who settled chiefly in New York, Florida, and the Southwest, found a network of their own organizations and media already established in these places, and were therefore able to make use of modern transportation and communication technology to maintain their connection with their native culture.

Native Americans and the White Man's Religion

To the extent that Native Americans live on reservations, it continues to be the tribe as a whole that adopts a given religion, so that there emerge mixtures of Christian and indigenous religious forms such as the Native American church, to which some Navajo tribes belong. The use of the hallucinatory drug *peyote* (mescaline), which is part of their worship services, is supposed to bring the believer into contact with the Holy Spirit. This church and its traditional Native American practices became known to the general public when three Navajos objected to being found guilty of violating California drug laws. The Supreme Court ultimately reversed the verdict, noting that religious freedom takes precedence over mere laws (Gaustad 1982, 2: 554).

The religious practices of Native Americans who no longer live in constant contact with their tribes are correspondingly individualized, and thus they join various denominations, if any at all. Statistical data are lacking, but very few Native Americans seem to be involved, and the few separate "ethnic parishes" that have been established for them are exclusively in cities which, because of their proximity to reserva-

Table 8
Black Americans' Religious Self-Identification

1991		1993	
Fundamentalist Protestant	66.5%	Evangelical	73%
Liberal Protestant	17.7	Mainline	10
Catholic	7.4	Catholic	6
None	5.0		
Jewish	0.2		
Other	1.8	Unaffiliated	11

Sources: Feigelman *et al.* 1991, 137; Leege 1993, 6.

tions, have become transitional points. Thus the *Catholic Almanac* for 1991 reports that in Milwaukee the "Congregation of the Great Spirit" was consecrated, and that it was the third such parish alongside the earlier ones in Tucson and Rapid City (*Catholic Almanac* 1991, 72). Thus among Native Americans the white man's religion continues to be relatively unsuccessful in both its Protestant and Catholic forms; they seem to have a difficult time with Christianity.

African-American Catholics: Missed Opportunities and New Hopes

In contrast, 90 percent of African-Americans identify themselves as Christians. They are distinguished from the general population chiefly in that among them the proportion of Catholics and Jews is significantly smaller.

Comparable figures are found in an article by Feigelman, Goreman, and Varacalli published in 1991 and in a lecture given by Leege at the National Opinion Research Center in 1993. Feigelman and his colleagues base their work on the National Opinion Research Center's data for 1982 through 1987, while Leege uses the most recent National Election Survey (NES). The latter avoids the controversial concepts of fundamentalist and liberal Protestantism, but under the rubric "unaffiliated" it lumps together those with no religious affiliation, Jews, and members of other non-Christian religions.

Two important clues can be derived from a comparison of these two surveys. First, African-American Catholics now represent a minority of 6 to 7 percent. Second, toward the end of the 1980s African-

American Protestants, who already had strong evangelical tendencies, moved even further in this direction.

It may at first seem surprising that African-Americans find Catholicism so unattractive, since the Catholic conception of the church precluded a division into segregated and unsegregated congregations. Nonetheless, the Catholic Church has clearly not succeeded in credibly presenting its universalism as anti-racism. This is connected first of all with the fact that the crucial developments were not contemporaneous. By the time American Catholicism had grown to a significant magnitude as a result of immigration—and in the process had become a white church—African-Americans had long since found a place of worship, or been assigned one. The racism and sectionalism resulting from the separate evolution of the North and the South unintentionally allowed a free space to emerge in which African-Americans could develop their own church and their own religious style within Protestant pluralism. In contrast, Catholicism offered no such niche. Only in a few places that had a significant proportion of African-American Catholics, such as Baltimore or New Orleans, could parishes emerge that were de facto African-American congregations and that developed their own liturgy.

These structures were already in place before Catholics began to play a role. However, the Catholic Church was not free of slavery and racial discrimination. Like other property owners, the Catholic planters of Maryland had black slaves, and even the Jesuits made use of slaves in providing for themselves. Before the Civil War, the church avoided taking a position with regard to freeing the slaves, and afterward, although segregated congregations were not established, the races were separated in other Catholic institutions in the South. Black students were denied admission to the existing Catholic schools, and neither the number of students nor the available financial means were sufficient to allow separate black schools to be established. As a result, the church found it very difficult to recruit African-American priests, and this further increased the importance of the religious orders that had early on admitted black students to their boarding schools or, like the so-called Josephites (members of Saint Joseph's Society of the Sacred Heart, SSJ), focused on pastoral care for black Catholics. When after 1970 it became common to appoint an African-American auxiliary bishop in dioceses with a large African-American population, most of the candidates were found in these orders.

Since the beginning of the century, African-Americans had been leaving the South because of the increasing mechanization of agriculture. They settled in the cities of the North, moving into neighborhoods where white ethnics had lived, and where the immigrant church was still present in the form of its schools and hospitals. Many African-Americans concerned about their children's future first encounter Catholicism through parochial schools, which have advantages over public schools in problematic inner-city neighborhoods. In this way, the church attracts African-American families that are prepared to participate actively in the life of a congregation as well as in education. An example is the Holy Angels Church in Chicago, which proudly claims to be "the largest black Catholic school in the United States." With fifteen hundred pupils and over a thousand applicants on its waiting list, this school can select not only its pupils but also its parents, and demand a great deal from them. Parents are expected to attend mass on Sundays and to participate in regular parents' night activities; they are also expected to vote and to prove that they have done so by presenting their stamped voter registration cards at the school. Such a rigorous policy can be enforced only when a black priest and a black principal can self-confidently refer to "the majestic Catholic faith and the African-American experience" (Braxton 1987).

The available statistics and demographic data concerning the approximately two million black American Catholics point in the direction of the Holy Angels Church. Compared with other African-Americans, black Catholics are more likely to live in cities and to have completed their education, and they also earn more (Feigelman 1991, 134). They are distinguished above all by their educational behavior. Thus a large-scale study conducted in 1990 concluded that black Catholics only rarely left school before graduating (18 percent vs. 31 percent of other blacks and 21 percent of all whites), and that one out of four black Catholics was a college graduate (26 percent vs. 25 percent of white Catholics, 24 percent of all whites, and 15 percent of all blacks) (Lachman and Kosmin 1991).

In 1947—that is, long before the Supreme Court decision of 1954 and the civil rights movement of the 1960s—Archbishop Josef E. Ritter of St. Louis and a few bishops who followed his example made a lasting contribution by abolishing segregated parochial schools in their dioceses. They had thereby finally given a signal that the Catholic conception of the church precluded segregation, and by emphasizing education they had also charted an important new goal.

With 10 percent of the total population, African-Americans today constitute an important minority. However, in the Catholic Church they are still clearly underrepresented. Moreover, they are concentrated chiefly in the South and in the Northeast, as is shown by the assignment of African-American bishops. In 1990 there were thirteen black bishops, including the archbishop of Atlanta, who resigned in the course of the year as a result of an affair. The 1991 *Almanac* still lists the bishop of Biloxi and eleven auxiliary bishops. One of the thirteen original bishops, the auxiliary bishop of New Orleans, had been in office since 1966, four had been appointed after 1970, and eight after 1980. Three auxiliary bishops served in southern dioceses (New Orleans, Galveston-Houston, and St. Louis), seven in the Northeast (Baltimore, Washington, New York, Newark, Detroit, Cleveland, and Chicago) and one in Los Angeles (*Catholic Almanac* 1991, 480 ff.).

Hispanics on the Road to Americanization

The future of American Catholicism will be much more strongly affected by so-called Hispanics than by other minorities. Hispanics differ from the early European immigrants as well as from Native Americans and African-Americans in that they have not been part of American history from the beginning but for the most part immigrated after World War II. Moreover, unlike earlier immigrants, it was easy for them—and made easier for them—to remain in contact with their heritage.

According to U.S. Bureau of Census figures, the Hispanic population, which in 1950 was four million, or about 2.5 percent of the total population, had grown to 22.5 million by 1990, or 9 percent of the total population (1990 Census, table 1).

Very different groups of Spanish-speaking immigrants from Central and South America and the Caribbean are lumped together under the rubric "Hispanics," and for this reason they themselves tend to avoid the term. They prefer more specific terms (Gallup and Castelli 1989, 140), not only because their heritage is more precisely indicated

by these terms, but also because they have already very strongly identified with their new country (Duignan and Gann 1986), and now see
America as a political rather than geographical entity.

According to the 1990 census, more than half (14 million out of the
official tally of 22.5 million) of these Hispano-Americans come from
Mexico. Four million more come from other Latin American countries. Almost as many, over three million, come from relatively small
Puerto Rico, but they are not legally immigrants, whether or not
Puerto Rico gains U.S. statehood in the near future. Finally, the one
million Cubans represent the smallest but so far most well-off and
politically influential Hispanic group.

The Mexican, Puerto Rican, and Cuban immigrant groups, which
are particularly homogeneous, are concentrated primarily in regional
centers. Thus in New York Puerto Ricans constitute 10 percent of
the population, in California one out of three residents comes from
Mexico, and two-thirds of the people living in Miami are Cubans.

Contrary to widespread assumptions, not all of these Spanish-
speaking immigrants bring with them a strong Catholic heritage. First
of all, among these immigrants, as in their homelands, the proportion
of Protestants is growing (Martin 1990). Reliable figures are lacking,
but with increasing frequency it has been reported that Baptists and
similar denominations are having considerable success among these
immigrants. Gallup and Castelli conclude from a survey conducted
in the archdiocese of New York in the early 1980s that 70 percent of
Hispanics identify themselves as Catholics, while another 18 percent
identify themselves as Protestants (Gallup and Castelli 1989, 140). In
1988 Greeley drew a similar conclusion from the National Opinion
Research Center's figures: between 1977 and 1987 the proportion of
Catholics among Hispanics sank from 77 percent to 71 percent while
the proportion of Protestants grew by the same amount. Greeley con-
firms that this shift was almost exclusively to the conservative Protestant denominations, and he offers a profile of these newly converted
Protestants. Compared to the average Hispanic, they are more educated, more likely to be white collar workers, and earn at least 25 percent more (Greeley 1988, 61 ff.), though it is not clear whether their
adoption of Protestantism is the cause or the result of their rise into
the lower middle class.

Thus a significant number of Spanish Americans are not even nominally Catholic. Moreover, with regard to the still overwhelming majority who belong to the Catholic Church, calling their native countries "Catholic" is as simplistic as in the case of nineteenth-century immigrants. This is particularly clear in the case of the largest group, Mexican-Americans, because for a long time Mexico's revolutionary-progressive conception of the state drew its sustenance almost entirely from a residual aggressive hostility to religion. Caught between official anti-clericalism and syncretistic popular piety, the church's institutional structure remained rather weak. In any case, only the Cubans brought their own clergy with them, since Mexico and Puerto Rico, unlike Ireland, were not able to export priests. In fact, to train priests for Puerto Rico, Spellman founded a seminary there that is still supported by the archdiocese of New York. Thus pastoral care for the various groups of Hispanics is provided by priests who are either second-generation immigrants or did not even grow up in Spanish-speaking families. However, for such groups this is no more cause for concern than other signs of increasing assimilation.

The resulting picture is confusing. On one hand, it is made especially easy for Mexican-Americans to retain their distinctive identity. Like earlier immigrants, they can immerse this identity in a complex separate milieu, and this leads many Hispanics to conclude that they can get along without knowing English. Unlike their predecessors, however, present-day immigrants are not confronted by a society that puts strong pressure on them to adapt and forces them to abandon any foreign characteristics. On the contrary, the cultural elite encourages newcomers to define themselves ethnically, and politicians intimate that special characteristics will be respected if they are presented as the interests of an organized group. On the other hand, however, these new Americans do not look nostalgically back toward their native lands, which have little to offer in comparison with their new home. Thus, while intellectuals may complain that so-called "Tex-Mex" is not an innovative combination of cultures, but merely the American lifestyle with a whiff of Spanish, most Mexican-Americans have clearly chosen it.

In surveys taken in the 1970s Mexican-Americans were already emphasizing that they were Americans first, and Mexicans second. A comprehensive study of *The Changing Demography of Spanish Americans* concludes that they were becoming increasingly similar to aver-

age Americans, and that in another generation or two there would be
hardly any difference between the two groups (Jaffe *et al.* 1980, 22 ff.).
This does not prevent the increasingly self-confident Hispanics from
stressing their Spanish and Native American heritage, not in opposition to the religious and political culture of the United States, but as
an increasingly powerful element that was always already present in
that culture, at least in the Southwest. Hence they tend to react negatively to trends in cultural politics that still assign them only the role
of victims in the history of Christianity on the North American continent and in the history of the United States. When in 1991 the National Council of Churches urged its members not to take part in the
anniversary activities that were to take place the following year, on the
ground that Columbus's arrival and the beginning of the Christianization of the Americas were no cause for celebration, the executive board
of the Northeast Hispanic Catholic Center in New York approved a
counter-resolution characterizing the Council's statement as a racist
depreciation of many people's history (*Catholic Almanac* 1991, 100).
Most Hispanics thus saw their pronounced willingness to integrate
and adapt as absolutely compatible with demanding that their special
characteristics be respected, and the same attitude obviously deter-
mines their religious behavior as well.

Like African-Americans, Hispanics now represent all over the country, but particularly in cities, a minority of at least 10 percent, and in
the Southwest they are often in the majority. Unlike African-Americans, they are clearly over-represented in the Catholic Church.

Spanish-speaking bishops were first appointed after 1970, and by
1991 there were twenty-one of them. If we consider first the thirteen
auxiliary bishops and their regional distribution, the older structure
of the American church is still discernible. About half the Spanish-
speaking auxiliary bishops are in the old Northern dioceses and only
the other half in the Southwest. The Spanish-speaking bishops and archbishops reside exclusively in the Southwest, namely in the archdioceses
of Santa Fe and San Antonio and in the dioceses of El Paso, Las Cruces,
Corpus Christi, Fresno, Pueblo, and Tucson (*Catholic Almanac* 1991,
480 ff.). All these bishops have Spanish names, but almost all were
born in the United States and have had a normal North American education. Apart from the fact that they themselves are "educated" Americans, they see assimilation moving forward without their having done

anything to advance it. Therefore they know that the special characteristics of Spanish-American religiousness have a future only if they
can gradually be made independent of the Spanish language and preserved as stylistic elements within an English-speaking church.

However, this presumably temporary Spanish-speaking ministry is
constantly prolonged by the continuing influx of immigrants. Therefore the bishops and the Conference of Bishops have sought to avoid
making a decision in favor of either pastoral care exclusively in the
native language or compulsory integration. Instead, in their 1983 pastoral letter "The Hispanic Presence: Challenge and Commitment" and
in their 1985 "National Pastoral Plan for Hispanic Ministry," they re-
asserted in rather vague terms the value of cultural pluralism. In practice, this has been seen as encouraging bilingualism, and thus institutions such as PADRES (Padres Associados para Derechos Religiosos,
Educativos, y Sociales) in Los Angeles and the National Resource Center for Hispanic Ministry in San Antonio distribute materials in English and Spanish for working with Hispanics.

It can be predicted that as large numbers of Hispanics are assimilated, the focus will shift from language to the liturgy and preaching.
What this means becomes clear if we ask why the religious style of
conservative Protestant denominations like the Baptists is so attractive to newly arrived Hispanics. According to David Martin, the explanation for recent Protestant successes in Latin America can be perceived in Hispanic immigrants. Being accepted into a congregation
that makes rigorous demands regarding their lifestyle and conduct can
be seen as confirming that they have attained middle-class prosperity
and seem American. In addition, there is the attraction, which is apparently felt throughout the hemisphere, of a mixture of unambiguous
Protestant ethics (industry, thrift, reliability) and spontaneous, emotional forms of worship.

3. Priests, Clerical Training, and Theology

The Development of Seminaries

For a long time, American bishops' concerns about the priests in
their charge were focused more on discipline than on recruiting a sufficient number of new priests or providing adequate training for them.
In this, the bishops were in accord with the priests themselves. The

rebellious priests who had joined forces with the trustees as well as the later New York radicals had sought above all to strengthen their own positions, and counted more on Rome and canon law than on the understanding of their immediate superiors. The latter sponsored a few young priests, for example by making it possible for them to study in Europe, yet as soon as institutions for training priests were proposed, the problem of how power was to be divided arose. As a result, from the middle of the nineteenth century on, many bishops founded their own seminaries, because the religious orders seemed to them too independent and too European, and the "progressive" wing hoped that their own Catholic University of America would provide an alternative to studying in Rome, that is, an elite education uninfluenced by *Romanità*. Conservatives like McQuaid and Mundelein adopted a strategy of improving the quality of their own seminaries, even with the help of religious orders, while sending as many young priests as they could to study in Europe.

Nonetheless, the history of the priesthood and clerical training in America had begun with the activities of the religious orders. Under the Jesuit John Carroll, almost all the priests in the diocese of Baltimore, which at first included the whole of the republic, were Jesuits, and from 1791 on the Sulpicians long monopolized clerical training. Decades later, other orders began to establish novitiates and some dioceses founded their own seminaries. Many bishoprics entrusted religious orders with clerical training, while others insisted that teaching staffs consist solely of priests from their own diocese. Toward the end of the century two seminaries of a special type finally emerged. In this period, when the subject of ethnic-oriented ministry was still in the forefront, two priests who were both said to have particularly strong personalities succeeded in establishing seminaries for their own immigrant groups. In 1885, Joseph Dabrowski, a Polish immigrant, founded the SS. Cyril and Methodius Seminary in Detroit, and in 1892 Joseph Jessing, who came from Münster, Germany, opened his Josephinum in Columbus, Ohio. *De Propaganda Fide* recognized both institutions as papal colleges.

However, the leaders were still the Sulpicians, who not only continued to operate St. Mary's in Baltimore but also had established, at the respective bishops' request, seminaries in Boston, New York, and San Francisco. Joseph M. White, who has written the sole comprehensive study of American diocesan seminaries, reports that St. Mary's did not begin to flourish until 1860. This resulted not only from the effort to train new priests made by Sulpicians, who were now able to recruit faculty for these seminaries largely from American members of their order, but also from the fact that toward the end of the nineteenth century St. Mary's had an unusually influential and active rector. Alphonse Magnien, who had begun his career in France as an assistant to the "liberal" Bishop Dupanloup, became one of Cardinal Gibbons' intimates and a personal friend of John Ireland. During his rectorship, which lasted from 1878 to 1902, enrollment rose from 90 to 250 (White 1989, 165 ff.).

At this time, not only the Sulpician seminaries but also other American seminaries followed the French model. A distinction must be drawn between the four years of the minor and the six years of the major seminary, although both courses of study were usually offered at the same place. This division was retained even after the third plenary council of bishops held in 1884 had established a committee under the leadership of Archbishop Michael Heiss of Milwaukee that was supposed to standardize what was taught. The major seminary was given a clearer structure by dividing it into a two-year program of philosophical study followed by four years of theological study. By 1890 this kind of seminary had become the rule everywhere.

No extensive changes were made until after World War II, when Catholic institutions were caught up in the wave of government support for education. In order to be able to apply the G.I. Bill (officially, the Servicemen's Readjustment Act) to returning theology students, the government needed a list of church-approved seminaries and theology departments in universities. Thus the conference of bishops was forced to set up an office to make a comparative evaluation of such institutions, and in time this resulted in a standardizing process dictated from above, which in turn set in motion a process of concentration. Increasingly, dioceses made recognition of a seminary's degrees dependent on its adherence to a prescribed curriculum and on the qualifications of its faculty. The result was that many of the so-called minor seminaries were closed, followed by the less effective major seminaries. The novitiates of many religious orders, in which two or three instructors sometimes taught twenty students, were particularly hard hit. Later on, many dioceses also found themselves unable to maintain their own seminaries because the combination of increasing requirements and declining enrollments raised average expenses to unjustifiable levels.

Prognoses regarding the Shortage of Priests

The foreseeable shortage of priests finally led to a plethora of studies, particularly in the 1970s and 1980s, that were funded partly by the bishops and partly by the Lilly Foundation. Yet even in the reforming mood after Vatican II, when enrollments in seminaries rose higher than ever, a few surveys were made.

In 1966, Joseph Fichter published the results of a survey of young priests, noting two common complaints. Chaplains did not like living in parish houses, and they thought their seminary training had given them an intellectual foundation but no preparation for dealing with lay people or with administrative tasks (Fichter 1968). In 1969, Potvin and Suziedelis reacted to this widespread criticism with their recommendations for reforming seminary training (Potvin and Suziedelis 1969), and in the following years curricula were changed to more strongly emphasize the professional needs of future priests. This attempt to incorporate practical considerations into theoretical training often led only to a psychologizing of pastoral theology.

At about the same time, the conference of bishops asked the National Opinion Research Center (NORC) to survey bishops, diocesan priests, and regular clergy. The resulting data were published in 1971 and analyzed the following year in Andrew Greeley's book *Priests in the United States* (Greeley 1972). At the end of the 1970s and at the beginning of the 1980s, attention was focused on predictions regarding the shortage of priests and on the reasons for interest or lack of interest in a clerical career. Thus in 1971 the so-called Knights of Columbus Study—named after the lay association that funded it—surveyed young Catholics. Approximately 2 percent of those surveyed indicated interest in a clerical career, and their answers to subsequent questions showed that they had grown up in an environment that encouraged this interest (Fee 1981).

Finally, Schoenherr and Sorensen tried to determine more precisely the foreseeable decline in the number of priests by projecting various current trends as far as the year 2000. They calculated a best-case scenario (projection A) that predicted a decline to about 22,000 and a worst-case scenario (projection C) that predicted a decline to about 13,000. It seemed to them realistic to expect that by the end of the century the number of American priests would be cut in half, to about 16,000 (projection B) (Schoenherr and Sorensen 1982). In every case, these estimates concerned the number of active diocesan priests, and this makes it difficult to check these predictions against the generally available data in the *Directory* (see the statistical table in the appendix), because the latter does not distinguish between active and retired priests. Still, we can see that the decline was significantly smaller than predicted even in the optimistic projection. Instead of a sharp downward curve we find a much slower but continual decrease, and this corresponds to the "recovery" that can be discerned in other indicators of religious life in the 1980s. Even in this case, however, a certain stability appears only if one compares the actual development with the earlier, generally too pessimistic expectations.

Young Priests' Attitudes and Their Self-Evaluations

In subsequent investigations the questions were more specific and precise. For example, in 1990 Potvin and Muncada attempted to determine why some students successfully completed their studies while others broke them off prematurely (Potvin and Muncada 1990). In 1991, Hemrick and Hoge published a study, *A Survey of Priests Ordained Five to Nine Years*, that is even more instructive. They surveyed a relatively large group of 1,518 priests who had completed their educations between 1980 and 1984 (Hemrick and Hoge 1991), so that a comparison of diocesan and regular clergy could be based on meaningful figures.

Among young diocesan priests, 24 percent had already been assigned to parishes as pastors, 47 percent were chaplains or associate pastors, 7 percent were teachers, and 6 percent had career-track positions in diocesan administration. 2 percent were providing pastoral care in hospitals and 1 percent were doing missionary work. The remaining undifferentiated group of 13 percent was apparently larger than had been anticipated when the questionnaire was drawn up, and was involved in a wide range of activities, including campus ministry, service in retreat houses, and graduate study.

Among the regular clergy, 29 percent were providing pastoral care in parishes. As might be expected, in this group the proportion of mis-

Table 9
Priests' Ethnic Self-Identification

| | NORC 1971 | | Hemrick and Hoge 1991 | |
	Diocesan	Regular	Diocesan	Regular
Anglo-Saxon				
English, Scottish, Welsh,				
Anglo-Canadian)	7	7	8	10
Irish	39	34	26	24
German/Scandinavian				
(German, Austrian,				
Dutch, Swiss)	25	25	19	20
French	7	9	8	6
Italian	5	5	10	10
Polish	6	7	—	—
Latin				
(Spanish background)	2	2	4	5
Non-White				
(Black American)	1	1	1	1
Asian, e.g. Vietnamese	—	—	—	1
Filipino	—	—	1	—

Source: Greeley 1972, 32; Hemrick and Hoge 1991, 6.

sionaries (7 percent) and especially teachers (27 percent) was significantly higher (Hemrick and Hoge 1991, 6).

As the NORC had done twenty years earlier, Hemrick and Hoge asked priests which ethnic group they belonged to. Unfortunately, these two surveys were differently formulated, so that possibilities for comparing them are limited. The NORC study related the responses given by bishops and other priests to their ethnic group's percentage of the total population, so that any ethnic imbalances in the composition of the clergy would become visible. Such quantitative relationships are lacking in Hemrick and Hoge's investigation. Moreover, the two studies use different terms to designate groups, and the latter are also sometimes differently composed. Whereas the NORC study refers to Anglo-Saxons, Hemrick and Hoge distinguish between clergy of English, Scottish, Welsh, and Anglo-Canadian descent. Both studies count Austrian, Dutch, and Swiss clergy as German, but the NORC also includes Scandinavians in this category, although given the small number of Scandinavian Catholics, this has little effect. On the other hand, Poles disappear into the category of East Europeans. Finally, the changed conditions are also reflected in the fact that certain concepts are replaced by others. People who twenty years earlier were called "Latin" now appear under the rubric "Spanish background," and "non-whites" have become "black Americans." But in spite of all these differences it is worthwhile to set the data published by the NORC in 1971 alongside those in Hemrick and Hoge's 1991 study.

This table shows that the proportion of the long-dominant Irish and also of the Germans, who are the second largest group, has diminished considerably. In addition, it is clear that the number of Italians, who entered the American middle class later, has doubled, and that Hispanics have begun to move in the same direction.

Hemrick and Hoge's survey also offers a certain amount of information that cannot be compared because pertinent questions were not or could not be asked earlier. Thus in the 1980s priests were asked which authors were important to them. In this way a theological hit parade emerges that allows us to make many conclusions, some of them curious. The respondents listed fifty-one authors. Karl Rahner was far in the lead, with 278 respondents mentioning him. Avery Dulles was mentioned fifty-five times, as much as Leonado Boff and Gustavo Gutierrez put together. The great majority of authors were mentioned by no more than twenty respondents, a fate that Charles Curran, Hans Küng, and Joseph Ratzinger shared with Thomas Aquinas (Hemrick and Hoge 1991, 11). More significant is that what respondents said about their own professions reflects a high degree of satisfaction. The latter is shown by the fact that 88 percent of the diocesan priests and 91 percent of the regular clergy agreed with the view that their profession was "highly respected" (Hemrick and Hoge 1991, 27). The picture is complemented by another study, also done under Hoge's direction, on priests' changing theological and political attitudes. This study shows that Catholic priests have on the whole become more conservative, but this does not result from the higher average age. The older age groups have retained their tendency toward New Deal liberalism and the Democratic party, whereas the younger priests have been influenced by the "neo-conservatism" of the 1980s (Hoge, Shields, and

Verdieck 1988, 142). In this respect they resemble other people of the same age, since a majority of younger Catholics close to the church now describe themselves as Republicans, which is truly a new development in the history of American Catholicism (Leege 1993, 29).

The attitudes of young regular clergy do not differ from those of other priests of their generation. They set even greater store by their own reputation, but this self-assessment may be the flipside of their awareness that they are bucking the trend. The development that had been feared for the clergy in general seems to have befallen the regular clergy. According to calculations made by David Nygren and Miriam Ukeritis, between 1963 and 1990 the number of regular clergy fell by 27 percent, and the number of brothers and nuns fell by 45 percent— almost the 50 percent decrease Schoenherr and Sorensen had projected. The consequences were especially devastating for female orders, for their average age rose above sixty (Nygren and Ukeritis 1992, 257 ff.). For young women interested in joining a convent, this meant that they would be spending their lives in the company of older women and in caring for elderly women.

The development of religious vocations thus presents a divided image. Religious orders were most strongly affected by the shock of the 1970s, and their recovery during the 1980s was minimal. Here we have to note that this is the case far more for female orders than for male orders, and that in both cases the active orders were affected more than the contemplative orders. In any event, American Catholicism had become accustomed to a world without nuns to the extent that ecclesiastical institutions could no longer rely on nuns to do the work. Whereas earlier a school's whole teaching staff belonged to the order concerned, today a few nuns work with a larger number of salaried teachers, though in most cases the school belongs to the order and is administered by one of its members. This suggests that the future of active female orders will depend on whether the area of Catholic education and social work remains open to them and whether they develop new and different forms of membership, for example, by accepting unmarried lay people.

Such structural changes are unlikely to occur in the male orders, because they possess a stabilizing element in the priesthood. They have never been involved in caring for the sick or in social work, and the significance of missionary work will continue to decline, so that the financial security and reputation of these orders will henceforth be connected even more exclusively with their schools and universities.

The situation among diocesan priests is much less threatening. Toward the end of the 1960s, their numbers rose from 34,000 to 37,000, but by 1993 had declined to 33,000 (see the statistical table in the appendix). Depending on whether one chooses 1963, 1970, or 1990 as the point of reference, this means that there was a decline of from 3 to 7 percent. The number of priests leaving the priesthood was twelve per thousand in 1974, and ten years later it was only four per thousand.

The comparatively small decline in the number of priests can be put into perspective only if one takes into account the fact that the number of Catholics rose substantially during the same period. The ratio of priests to Catholics went from about 1:1200 to 1:1700.

Thus here as well the development is in the direction of concentration and differentiation. A smaller number of priests, who cannot count on being relieved by younger priests and have to remain in office longer, will be serving larger parishes. They will therefore have to rely on an increasing number of formally qualified assistants, who will themselves demand a greater voice. Bishops will be wise to see to it that these even more indispensable future priests are trained as well as possible, so that in this respect the educational system is also of particular importance. This involves not only the development of academic theology, the relation between seminaries and university departments of theology, and the balance of power between theologians and bishops, but also the bishops' responsibility for the Catholic educational system as a whole.

Professional Theology and Its Interests

During the nineteenth and twentieth centuries, the relationships between the American church and universities went through a shifting series of separations and associations that affected the training of clergy of all faiths. American institutions of higher education had all been founded by religious communities. Harvard, Yale, Princeton, and Georgetown were established and supported by different denominations, and even at the time of the Civil War university presidents were still usually clergymen. Subsequently, a first wave of secularization brought about a transition from the denominational college to the Christian college. Cornell University, founded in 1869, described it-

self as "non-sectarian" (Burtchaell 1991, 23). The German-style research university, hardly compatible with the Christian college, did
not emerge until later. Thus the education of Protestant ministers was
moved out of the universities and organized in countless institutions
operated by the various denominations. On the other hand, Catholic
priests continued to be trained in seminaries and novitiates, while in
the few Catholic universities, which had by this time gained in stature,
theology did not develop into a professional discipline but was taught
within the general liberal arts curriculum. Anyone who wanted or had
to take a degree in theology went to Europe, or later on, to Catholic
University in Washington. Toward the end of the 1940s and at the beginning of the 1950s, seminaries and universities could recruit their
new faculty members only from Catholic University, because during
the war it was impossible to study in Europe.

Afterward, the emphasis shifted from the seminaries to the universities, and an organized, professionally self-confident academic theology developed. In the meantime, in addition to Catholic University seven other universities (Boston College, Duquesne, Fordham,
Marquette, Notre Dame, Loyola-Chicago, and St. Louis) were granted
the right to offer doctorates, and by 1993 the Catholic Theological Society of America (CTSA) already had fifteen hundred members (Egan
1992, 13). By no means all these theologians are priests or teach in
seminaries. Moreover, the number of female members is increasing.

In the 1970s and 1980s the center of Catholic theology thus shifted
from the seminaries to the universities, and simultaneously new fields
of endeavor were opened to theologians as a result of the continuing
expansion of the educational system and the ecclesiastical organization. Therefore attempts were made to ensure the profession's future.
First, the CTSA sought to influence the employment practices of the
dioceses and of the two hundred thirty Catholic colleges and universities in a way favorable to its members, and to establish corresponding
regulations. Then a power struggle between bishops and professional
theologians developed. The controversy was initiated by theologians
who argued in semantic terms that their academic teaching was equivalent to the magisterium, or at least tried to enhance the status of their
activity. This became particularly apparent in the decade-long debate
regarding the document *Doctrinal Responsibilities.*

In the beginning, the intention was undoubtedly to defuse inevitable conflicts. In 1979, the CTSA teamed up with professors of canon law, who were reputed to be generally conservative and inclined to insist on precise terminology. Thus a clear distinction was still drawn between the magisterium and theology in the initial statement of the common goal. The theologians' association invited the canon lawyers' association, the Canon Law Society of America (CLSA) to draft a "set of norms to guide the resolution of the difficulties which may arise between theologians and the magisterium." However, on its long journey through the committee the text tended more and more to adopt the notion of a "doctrinal complementarity" between bishops and theologians, and this was echoed in the plural of its title, *Doctrinal Responsibilities.* The draft completed in 1983 occupied the conference of bishops and various Vatican offices for more than six years, chiefly because the Vatican insisted that the bishops' magisterium be clearly emphasized (Reese 1989, 4).

Meanwhile, the conflict between Charles E. Curran and the executive committees of Catholic University was evolving into an illustration of these debates, because Curran tried to make his case exemplary: "from my first public comments I insisted on the goal of making the whole affair a teaching moment" (Curran 1987, 336). Finally, Richard P. McBrien, another representative of the "progressive wing," came to his aid, thereby making the real issue even clearer. What was at stake, McBrien said, was not only the extent of a theologian's academic freedom, but also the role of theology in the church. Granted, theologians' freedom to teach is in principle limited by Revelation and the didactic authority of the church, but only in principle. What Revelation truly entails, and what is actually part of the tradition of church teaching, are not questions that McBrien wants to be decided by bishops whose understanding of Catholic tradition is based on courses they took thirty or forty years ago. Despite the fact that a few bishops earned doctorates years ago, they all share an essential defect: "bishops are not professionally trained and professionally active theologians." Ultimately, then, theologians determine the content that delineates their role, and therefore they cannot be satisfied with making a discursive contribution to the further development of the understanding of the faith and the tradition of teaching through historical research or theoretical systematic speculation alone. Here McBrien is contradicting Archbishop Pilarczyk, who as a member of the board of trustees of

Catholic University had said that theologians engage in "speculation," and that "a Catholic university is a kind of speculative think-tank" (McBrien 1988, 454 ff.).

Curran's lawsuit against Catholic University ended in 1988 with the court's decision that there was no right to teach in a Catholic university a Catholic theology unacceptable to the Catholic Church. Curran's case attracted a great deal of attention, but it remained the only one of its kind, because this kind of conflict can arise only when the bishop involved is both the owner and the employer. This is the exception, because almost all American Catholic universities are maintained by religious orders or private organizations. For example, McBrien teaches at the University of Notre Dame, but the bishop responsible for this area, who resides in Fort Wayne, had nothing to do with hiring him or renewing his contract. The bishop is not forced to step in if McBrien or one of his colleagues expresses a view that appears to contradict church doctrine. Even the president of Notre Dame is not obligated to intervene, though he has to take various long-term effects into account. He has to determine whether bishops will hire theologians trained at Notre Dame if they regard the theology department as too progressive or too reactionary, as well as what effects its reputation may have on the opinions of parents and graduates and on their willingness to make donations.

This indirect influence is gradually dwindling, however, because the center of theological training has once again shifted. Universities like Harvard and Chicago have reincorporated theology into their structures, and that means that now theology is also becoming nonsectarian. The majority of the students in Harvard's and Chicago's divinity schools are now Catholic, and in the theology departments of Catholic universities the opposite trend has set in. The development of unified theological curricula also strengthens the tendency to standardize many requirements at a lower level. Thus Matthew L. Lamb of Boston College points out that one can earn a doctorate in theology without knowing Latin (Lamb 1990, 5), while Jude P. Dougherty complains that at Catholic University theology students no longer receive any fundamental training in philosophy, with the result that they can no longer understand the modes of thought and argument characteristic of traditional Catholic theology (Dougherty 1992, 4).

The structure of the American university system and the lack of

legal agreements between church and state put the bishops in a power-
less position they presumably see as beneficial. It prevents them from
being confronted with too many repetitions of the Curran case, that is,
from having to exercise their teaching function negatively. However,
this puts even greater demands on them, for the more diverse institutions that train theologians become, the more precisely bishops have
to define the requirements that must be met by future priests—and the
same goes for the whole Catholic educational system.

4. Schools and Universities:
The Social Capital of American Catholicism

American Catholicism's success story is most clearly mirrored in
its schools and universities, and therefore they also serve as a show-
piece of the American church. However, this educational system's history was so closely connected with the arduous rise of the Catholic
Church in America that for a long time the memory of its humble beginnings clung to it. The nineteenth-century Americanists considered
Catholic schools the last bastion of a bankrupt conception of pastoral care and a hindrance to integration. Later on, many bishops saw
them as an expensive relic of the Catholic subculture that could be
abandoned on leaving the ghetto. They made people think of nuns in
starched wimples and the smell of floor polish, but not of the knowledge of natural sciences a pupil needed to pass the tests required to
get into a good college. In any case, statistics regarding the Catholic
educational system reflect both the waves of population growth and
changes in the climate of opinion.

From the Baby Boom to the Education Boom

From the beginning of the 1950s to the middle of the 1960s, the baby
boom produced a spurt in population growth. The number of Catholic
schools rose from 10,800 to 13,200, and their enrollments rose from
3 million to 5.6 million. The necessary teachers could no longer be
found in the religious orders alone. While the number of religious
teaching in the schools also rose from 80,000 to 100,000, their role
grew proportionately smaller as the number of lay teachers had to be
increased, so that the latter now composed 40 percent of the teaching
staffs.

Table 10
The Development of Catholic Schools (1950–1993)

	1950	1963	1980	1990	1993
Elementary schools	8,502	10,776	8,149	7,544	7,346
Number of pupils	2,560,626	4,609,029	2,317,200	1,985,930	2,007,299
Secondary schools	2,382	2,432	1,527	1,379	1,413
Number of pupils	419,878	1,004,927	846,559	630,667	635,740
Teachers	106,777	183,336	167,713	156,082	161,635
Teachers in religious orders	82,048	102,343	41,135	19,012	15,866

Excerpted from the statistical table in the appendix.

In the 1970s enrollments declined substantially, but the various kinds of schools were differently affected. Elementary schools experienced a decrease from 4.6 million to 2.3 million, that is, their enrollments were cut nearly in half, and of the almost 11,000 elementary schools in 1963, only slightly more than 8,000 were still in operation by 1980. During the same period, enrollments in secondary schools declined by only about 15 percent, because the fading of the baby boom did not affect them until later. Nonetheless, 40 percent of the high schools were closed in a process of concentration that reminds us once again of the urban character of American Catholicism. The number of teachers decreased by only about 10 percent, so that more teachers were employed per student than before. The scope of the financial consequences first becomes visible, however, when one examines the changes in the composition of the faculty. Of the 100,000 members of religious orders, only 40,000 remained. Fifteen years earlier, there were ten religious for every eight other teachers, the latter being comparatively expensive and having taken vows neither of obedience nor of poverty. By 1980 there were twelve lay teachers for every four religious.

During the 1980s, there were further declines in all these categories. A few more schools were closed, the decrease in enrollments was now more substantial in secondary than in elementary schools, and the number of religious serving in the schools again fell by half. At the beginning of the 1990s, on the other hand, although a handful of

Table 11

Catholic Students in Public Schools and in Catholic Schools (1991)

Catholic Elementary School	1,962,387
Public Elementary School	3,089,547
Catholic High School	621,425
Public High School	727,453

Source: *Catholic Almanac* 1991, 528.

elementary schools were closed, except for the number of religious on teaching staffs the figures are rising again.

Here we must finally compare the attractiveness of Catholic schools with that of their public competitors, that is, see how Catholic pupils are distributed between the two systems. Since the public schools are now forbidden to ask about their students' religious affiliation, we must resort to examining the religious instruction parishes offer students in public schools. Since children who register for first communion or confirmation must have previously attended such classes, these figures are as reliable as other church statistics, that is, they hold for all officially registered members.

If we now compare the data regarding religious instruction published in 1991 with the figures provided by the Catholic school system, we see that Catholics' preference for their own educational system increases as one moves toward the upper levels. In the first eight years three out of five Catholic children still attend a public school, and this shows that there is a connection between high property taxes (the main source of income for local authorities in America) and the quality of the public schools. The suburban communities in which most middle-class Catholic Americans now live levy high taxes and therefore offer good public schools. In old inner-city neighborhoods, on the other hand, it is advisable to spend on a private school the money saved by having lower taxes. In choosing a high school, a larger number of Catholic parents decide on a private school, with the result that the ratio of students in Catholic high schools to those in public school is almost 1:1. It may be wondered what leads many parents to finance two education systems, namely a public system to which they contribute by paying taxes, but do not take advantage of, and a private system that charges them tuition fees that cover nearly all its costs.

Two explanations can be gleaned from various studies published during the 1980s. First, people's views of the Catholic school system and its chances of improving have fundamentally changed. Now it serves as a model for the public schools. Second, colleges are considered as providing the most important support for the church in the long term, because they alone can still be seen as shaping a Catholic milieu.

Community As a Recipe for Success: The Example of Chicago

The changed status of the Catholic educational system is reflected in the results of the pertinent research as well as in individual bits of information. The archdiocese of Chicago offers a particularly instructive example, even though Los Angeles is now the largest diocese, and Chicago only the second largest. All the same, the currently decisive developmental trends are more visible in this diocese than in any other. Chicago grew along with the great nineteenth-century wave of immigration, and the social structures characteristic of Catholicism are found there in exaggerated form.

The diocese includes all of Greater Chicago, about half of whose residents now live in the city and half in the surrounding suburbs (Cook County, Lake County). Thus in the inner city we find neighborhoods in which immigrants from southern and southeastern Europe have left unmistakable ecclesiastical structures, while farther out the postwar single-family housing developments have proliferated. The significance of white ethnics is also revealed by the fact that 40 percent of the population of these suburbs is Catholic. Finally, the diocese of Chicago has reliable school statistics because its school system was already unified in Mundelein's time.

In 1991, the 2,350,000 Catholics in the Chicago diocese supported through direct and indirect contributions 376 schools, including 325 elementary schools and 51 secondary schools. 150,000 pupils were taught in these schools and the diocese employed 6,500 teachers, or one teacher for every twenty-three pupils. In addition there were 550 school principals and assistants in the central administration, and a relatively large proportion of these positions, 223, were occupied by members of religious orders.

Table 12
Catholic Schools in the Archdiocese of Chicago, 1991

Catholics		2,350,000
Schools	376	
Elementary schools	325	
Secondary schools	51	
Students		149,548
Teachers		6,435
Elementary schools	4,583	(including 442 religious)
Secondary schools	1,852	(including 234 religious)
Administrators		542
Cost per student		
Elementary schools		$1,350
Secondary schools		$2,400
Tuition fees per student		
Elementary schools		$1,170
Secondary schools		$1,680

Source: Data provided by the diocesan administration.

The administration calculated the cost per pupil in 1991 to be $1,350 in the elementary schools and $2,400 in the secondary schools. Tuition fees were $1,170 and $1,680, and covered 80 percent and 75 percent of the costs at each of the two levels.

The diocese's statistics offer no further information, so we are forced to complete the picture by means of isolated individual analyses and surveys. Chicago receives special attention in these studies because several important research institutions are located there, such as the National Opinion Research Center, in which Andrew Greeley is involved. James Coleman, whose work on educational sociology has been influential, taught at the University of Chicago, and the popular magazine *U.S. Catholic*, which continually emphasizes the importance of the Catholic school system, is also published in Chicago.

An initial surprise was produced by the discovery that non-Catholic parents, pimarily in the inner city, were sending their children to Catholic schools. What attracted them was that in these schools there was a discipline that protected pupils from one another, and they could count on a climate that encouraged achievement. Reports that only 60 percent of the pupils in inner-city Catholic schools in Chicago were Catholic were first published in magazines like *U.S. Catholic,* and then found their way into the *New York Times.*

Studies by Coleman, Coleman and Hoffer, and Sebring and Camburn made it clear that discipline was merely a means to an end and that Catholic schools performed better in all areas and succeeded in keeping considerably more students in school until they graduated (see especially Coleman and Hoffman 1987, 132 ff.).

Coleman was also able to show that this success was not achieved by "creaming," that is, by skimming off the better pupils; instead, weaker students were encouraged more effectively than in the public schools. Cardinal Bernardin therefore joined some business people in founding a group that donates money for Catholic schools in inner-city areas where the proportion of Catholics is decreasing while the interest of African-American parents in Catholic schools is increasing.

The keyword that plausibly explains the success of Catholic students and has become established in the literature and even in the title of Coleman and Hoffer's book is "community." As the previously mentioned example of the Holy Angels School shows, Catholic schools are recruiting not the best students, but the best parents. They attract parents who are prepared to work with the schools and create overlapping, mutually reinforcing relationships among schools, families, and church congregations.

The College as a New Milieu

This interplay of differing social forms is even more discernible in Catholic colleges and universities, because in their case it is especially manifold and enduring, which is why strong interactions among students, the college, parents, and alumni associations develop. This means first of all that the choice of the college establishes a bond between the students and their parents that is otherwise no longer usual at this stage of life.

To pay for a college or university education, most middle-class families have to restrict their expenses for years. However, the more Catholic universities, by making a substantial investment in the quality of their faculties, gain in stature and become correspondingly more expensive, the more clearly the conscious choice of a school becomes a matter of one's worldview, and both considerations are often discussed among students or between students and their parents. If it now costs as much to go to Notre Dame as to Harvard, Stanford, or the University of Chicago, then what students and parents expect from a Catholic university has to tip the balance in favor of Notre Dame.

Thus Notre Dame or Georgetown are confronted with two opposite obligations. On one hand, rising academic standards require that the selection of personnel be more academic, and this strengthens the tendency to secularization. On the other hand, parents expect that the institution will provide a first-class education and at the same time preserve its Catholic character, while the university administration knows that without this additional selling point the school would lose its market share. Thus there are also strong non-religious motives leading Catholic universities to continue the discussion of their Catholic identity.

College creates a social network not only by deepening the bond between students and their parents but also by maintaining ties with and among alumni. The organizational form of this relationship is provided chiefly by alumni associations, which seek to keep former students in contact with each other. Thus in 1991, for example, a Notre Dame Alumni Club was founded in Moscow. Unlike the corresponding German groups, however, they also maintain relations with the university or college itself, to which Americans even today refer, without any ironic undertone, as their alma mater. This enduring relationship usually leads to the wish to interest sons and daughters in going to the same college, so that several kinds of communities interlace and mutually support and reinforce each other. This unplanned repetition and reinforcement of social ties explains why Catholic colleges and universities have survived predictions of their demise and even continued to grow as the Catholic middle class has approached the American average in the number of its children.

Initially, the baby boom had an impact on higher education as well. Before Vatican II more than fifty new institutions had been founded, and the number of students rose by around 100,000 or 30 percent. However, the subsequent decline that was visible everywhere else did not occur. The number of colleges and universities did gradually decrease to the original levels, but the remaining 230 institutions did not lack students, and over the following three decades they were even able to continue to increase their enrollments by about 20 percent. An increase in enrollment of 7 percent between 1990 and 1993 suggests that this trend is continuing.

From this constant development we can conclude neither that the potential for growth has been exhausted nor that the constant rise in tuition fees has had no deterrent effect. The fact that many students try to enter colleges later on tends to prove the opposite. People first study for two years at the nearest public university or college, where state residents pay tuition fees of only about $3,000 to $5,000 per year, and then apply to the private university where they would like to take their degrees. Thus the relationship between the state and the private school systems has once again become a political issue.

The legitimacy of private schools and private higher education has been unchallenged since the Supreme Court's 1925 ruling against the Ku Klux Klan's claim that public schools should have a monopoly on education (see above). However, direct or indirect public support for religious educational institutions is still considered incompatible with the first amendment to the Constitution, which is interpreted as requiring a strict separation of church and state. In the 1980s there was a decisive change in attitude. Whereas Catholic schools and universities were earlier dismissed as "sectarian," the public is now convinced that many problems would be solved if African-Americans and Hispanics seeking to improve their situation were able to send their children to Catholic schools. In addition, there is a general belief that the middle class, to which everyone claims to belong, can no longer afford the superior education offered by private universities.

Republicans, who do not believe in the beneficial effects of government intervention anyway, have thus discovered a new issue on which they can offer something to precisely the groups they will have to court in the long run, namely Catholic ethnics who have become crossover voters, the black middle class, which is still too small, and the already more numerous, upwardly mobile Hispanics. Proposals for financial aid to families rather than direct aid to institutions are more and more frequently discussed. The white middle class would be helped by tax credits for education, while new schools like Holy Angels are likely to be established only if parents have vouchers that they can use at either public or private schools.

In any event, Catholic schools and universities have now become a recognized part of the American educational system. The more one examines the causes of their success, the clearer it becomes that their achievements cannot be separated from their denominational uniqueness and proceed from the combined effect of several complementary communities.

That is why Andrew Greeley has tirelessly argued that the Catholic educational system is a good investment from a religious point of view as well. Like other Catholics, its graduates tend to drift away from the church while they are young and single, but they return to it more often than others, and then they participate so actively and make such generous financial donations that the money the church spends on education can be rightly seen not as a subsidy but as an income-producing investment. Here, too, this is not a matter of "creaming" but rather of a sort of religious surplus value, because only a few of the graduates Greeley described were themselves children of former students, and most of them did not come from strongly religious families (Greeley 1989b, 14).

In addition, during the 1970s the Catholic educational system offered many religious orders their last chance for survival, since without its financial support the cost of caring for their aging communities could not have been met. However, the decisive factor is still the fact that the Catholic school system provides American Catholicism with social capital. It produces a network of social relationships that in turn produces a community in which individuals can immerse themselves with differing degrees of intensity, depending on their situations in life. This makes it possible to experience one's own educational history as part of a family history and a history of institutions, that is, it demonstrates the relationship between the present and the past. One could also say that it functions as a milieu and provides a glimpse of what the church is all about.

Afterword

RELIGIOUS INDIVIDUALISM AND THE CHURCH AS A CULTURAL PRINCIPLE
The American Road to Rome

In the final analysis, the results seem contradictory. On one hand, Catholics have worked their way into the center of American society—they have "made it." Just as Tocqueville predicted, they see themselves as both Catholics and Americans, and thus controvert two opposed but nonetheless mutually confirming doctrines of incompatibility: that Catholicism is un-American, a view held by nationalists who consider themselves liberals, and that the church and the modern world will always be enemies, a view that makes traditionalists out of many conservatives.

Catholics have proven to be thoroughly loyal citizens of the republic. In fact, nothing supports the principles embodied in the Constitution of the United States more reliably than Catholic ways of thinking. Consider, for instance, the Founding Fathers' conviction that humans are capable of making rational decisions and therefore of governing themselves, but cannot be wholly trusted, so that it is appropriate to take institutional precautions to preserve the republic from self-destruction. It is hardly surprising that many people are expecting a "Catholic moment" (Neuhaus 1987) in American cultural history.

The document the rather anti-Catholic authors of the Constitution produced has been good for the Catholic Church, despite all the discrimination against it. The church has prospered more in the climate of a religiously neutral republic that is friendly to religion than in so-called Catholic countries where it has been both privileged and persecuted.

On the other hand, the more Americanized it became, the more

243

American Catholicism was subject to criticism directed against its culture and its conception of religion. In America, religion in general was held in high regard, but not any given religion as such or its concrete doctrines and institutions.

In actuality, the anti-institutional attitude had struck particularly deep roots in the New World. A voluntaristic conception of faith, which saw the intellect as the devil's whore, expressed itself as a general distrust of intellectuals and as a concrete distrust of an educated, professional clergy (Hofstadter 1962, 47). As this anti-intellectual and anti-elitist culture became democratized, individualism and populism (that is, the belief in the individual and the glorification of his dignity and understanding) became the positive expression of a common conviction.

The result was the emergence of a religious culture in which doctrine and theology were relegated to a secondary role. Religion's appeal was based on the services it provided rather than on the teachings it promoted. Many people have pointed out the danger that religion will be concerned only with ethics, or be conceived only as therapy, and in fact one might say that while Americans consider religion indispensable, they are not at all sure that this also holds true for the church.

Catholics, of course, long lived in their own world and were immune to this culture, and that is why traditional ecclesiastical structures were not challenged. The nostalgic attachment to the old country had a conservative effect, just as did the anti-Catholic pressure from outside. Later on, when the Catholic subculture had dissolved, the only peculiarities that remained were those that followed directly from the ecclesiastical structure. Thus among Catholics, religious voluntarism, for instance, led to an internal pluralization of opinions and modes of conduct, but not to a proliferation of denominations.

Today, Catholicism has found its place in American culture and American Catholics tend to underestimate the institutional character of the church or even to see it as a relic of earlier, authoritarian times (for example, see E. Kennedy 1988). At the same time, however, American Catholicism is confronted by a series of developmental challenges that demand that it be able to channel change through a division of labor, that is, by reacting like an effective institution.

Whether it is a matter of incorporating Hispanics without allowing a separate Spanish-speaking church to develop, giving theology an independent role without putting the church's magisterium in question, making room for different groups within the church without giving them a mandate, or determining the position of Catholic universities and schools as both different from and close to the church, it always comes down to the church's specific institutional function of defining the role of specific groups and organizing their cooperation. This balancing act has become more difficult under the conditions of individualization, but it is by no means impossible. It is precisely American individualists who treasure leadership in religion as well as in politics.

Thus it depends chiefly on the skill of the shepherds whether or not they will have followers and whether the church will be strengthened or weakened. Up to this point lay people are obedient when the bishops take a clearly Catholic position—as in the case of the abortion debate—and when this is not the case they lose interest.

Yet, independently of the importance of skillful leadership, the much feared religious individualism has not become a scapegoat because, first of all, it is ultimately inevitable, and secondly, it in no way prevents the development of universal perspectives. One might also say: because the opposition between individualism and so-called communitarianism is not a real opposition at all.

First, we must remember the commonplace that individual decisions to adhere to a given faith are based on a religious milieu, and conversely, an inherited belief eventually has to be adopted consciously if it is to endure. In any case, this individual inclination becomes unfavorable to the extent that it excludes the individual from established social structures. Thus in relatively unstructured societies, religious culture necessarily becomes more individualistic, and the chances that any given religion will survive increase or decrease in proportion to its ability to adapt to this individualism. In this respect Roman roads also lead to America—and European bishops would be delighted to have the American problem of religious individualism.

However, despite this unquestionable and inevitable tendency, current criticism depends on false assumptions, because social and religious individualization furthers rather than hinders the development of comprehensive perspectives. Thus American Catholics have made their self-conception manifest in increasingly larger and more abstract entities. They have expanded their loyalty beyond the extended family, first to the ethnic group and its religion, and then to the nation and their own denomination. At the same time, their concrete conduct of their lives outside their jobs has been oriented toward ever-smaller communities that they have themselves chosen. In this respect, Catholics do not differ from other Americans, and like the latter, they sometimes consider their current way of life as representing the highest level of consciousness.

However, their advantage over other Americans and especially Europeans is that in taking the next step, they can rely on the concept of the church to bring together their abstract self-identification and the concrete communities in which they live. American religious culture and its own institutions make it easier for them to follow this American road to Rome.

APPENDIX

Statistical Data for the Period
1950–1993

1. Explanatory Notes

The only generally available source of statistical information about the entire Catholic Church in the United States is the annual *Official Catholic Directory*. Its data are derived from reports submitted by parishes and religious orders. The *Directory* serves in turn as the basis for other Catholic and interdenominational yearbooks such as the *Catholic Almanac* and the *Yearbook of American and Canadian Churches*.

In many cases the possibility of comparing the data is diminished because over time what is included in a given category has varied, because in response to changed conditions new organizational forms have been introduced, and because alterations in the intellectual climate have required new modes of description.

The first problem arises with regard to data concerning the training of new priests by religious orders, since for a long time not only novitiates but also preparatory boarding schools ("petits séminaires") were included under the rubric "religious seminaries."

A second kind of discontinuity results from the fact that agencies providing social services are currently turning themselves into social relief offices and other forms of outpatient care in order to replace residential institutions as much as possible.

Finally, political considerations sometimes require that the same thing be given another name or appear under another rubric. Thus starting in 1990, "Homes for the Aged" became "Homes for Special Care."

Otherwise, however, the following statistical table provides a reliable picture of the development of postwar American Catholicism, from the baby boom through the crisis of the 1960s and 1970s up to the recovery in the 1980s and 1990s.

2. Table 13: General Statistics about American Catholicism (1950–1993)

	1950	1963	1970	1980	1990	1993
1. Catholics (mil.)	27.8	43.8	48.2	49.8	57.0	59.2
2. % of population	20.3	23.9	23.8	22.8	23.1	23.1
3. Parishes	15,292	17,298	18,244	18,794	19,860	19,863
4. Diocesan priests	42,910	34,465	37,020	35,418	34,553	33,476
5. Dioceses	157	120	130	138	155	162
(archdioceses, archbishops)	(21)	(28)	(31)	(32)	(33)	(36)
6. Cardinals	—	5	8	10	7	9
7. Regular clergy	—	22,075	21,141	23,203	18,559	17,576
8. Friars	7,377	11,968	10,156	7,941	6,743	6,260
9. Nuns	147,310	177,154	153,645	126,517	103,269	99,402
Seminaries						
10. Diocesan	72	107	110	92	74	75
11. Religious orders	316	554	340	252	159	138
Number of students						
12. Diocesan sem.	8,200	16,356	9,672	4,928	4,447	4,335
13. Religious orders sem.	17,422	33,218	16,038	8,298	1,786	1,556
No. ordained	—	—	—	—	641	605
14. Hospitals	739	811	737	633	641	624
15. Outpatient clinics	—	—	—	—	—	247
16. Social services	—	—	—	—	1,771	1,945

General Statistics (1950–1993) *Continued*

	1950	1963	1970	1980	1990	1993
17. Retirement homes	—	357	420	497	—	—
18. Orphanages	129	—	221	207	—	—
19. Sanatoriums	110	135	134	87	—	—
20. Elementary schools	8,502	10,776	9,606	8,149	7,544	7,346
Enrollment	2,560,626	4,609,029	3,413,610	2,317,200	1,985,930	2,007,290
21. Secondary schools	2,382	2,432	1,944	1,527	1,379	1,413
Enrollment	419,878	1,004,927	1,015,713	846,559	630,667	635,740
22. Teachers	106,777	138,336	200,438	167,713	156,082	161,635
Religious	82,048	102,343	78,371	41,135	19,012	15,866
23. Colleges and univs.	225	282	283	239	232	231
Enrollment	252,727	357,764	426,207	505,076	620,772	660,787

3. List of American Dioceses

(Listed alphabetically by state. An asterisk indicates an archdiocese.)

Alabama
*Mobile
Birmingham

Alaska
*Anchorage
Fairbanks
Juneau

Arkansas
Little Rock

Arizona
Phoenix
Tucson

California
*Los Angeles
*San Francisco
Fresno
Monterey
Oakland
Orange
Sacramento
San Bernardino
San Diego
San Jose
Santa Rosa
Stockton
Van Nuys-Byzantine

Colorado
*Denver
Colorado Springs
Pueblo

Connecticut
*Hartford
Bridgeport
Norwich
Stamford-Ukrainian

Delaware
Wilmington

District of Columbia
*Washington
* Military services, USA

Florida
*Miami
Palm Beach
Orlando
Pensacola-Tallahassee
St. Augustine
St. Petersburg
Venice

Georgia
*Atlanta
Savannah

Hawaii
Honolulu

Idaho
Boise

Illinois
*Chicago
Belleville
Joliet
Peoria
Rockford
St. Nicholas-Ukrainian
Springfield

Indiana
*Indianapolis
Evansville
Ft. Wayne-South Bend
Gary
Lafayette

Iowa
*Dubuque
Davenport
Des Moines
Sioux City

Kansas
*Kansas City
Dodge City
Salina
Wichita

Kentucky
*Louisville
Covington
Lexington
Owensboro

Louisiana
*New Orleans
Alexandria
Baton Rouge
Houma-Thibodaux
Lafayette
Lake Charles
Shreveport

Maine
Portland

Maryland
*Baltimore

Massachusetts
*Boston
Fall River
Newton Eparchy
Springfield
Worcester

Michigan
*Detroit
Gaylord
Grand Rapids
Kalamazoo

Lansing
Marquette
Saginaw
St. Thomas the Apostle

Minnesota
*St. Paul-Minneapolis
Crookstone
Duluth
New Ulm
St. Cloud
Winona

Mississippi
Biloxi
Jackson

Missouri
*St. Louis
Jefferson City
Kansas City-St. Joseph
Springfield-Cape Girardeau

Montana
Great Falls
Helena

Nebraska
*Omaha
Grand Island
Lincoln

Nevada
Reno-Las Vegas

New Hampshire
Manchester

New Jersey
*Newark
Camden
Metuchen
Passaic-Byzantine Eparchy
Paterson
Trenton

New Mexico
*Santa Fe
Gallup
Las Cruces

New York
*New York
Albany
Brooklyn
Buffalo
Apostolate to Lithuanians
Ogdensburg
Rochester
Rockville Center
St. Maron
Syracuse

North Carolina
Charlotte
Raleigh

North Dakota
Bismarck
Fargo

Ohio
*Cincinnati
Cleveland
Columbus
Parma-Byzantine
Romanian Exarchate
St. Josaphat in Parma
Steubenville
Toledo
Youngstown

Oklahoma
*Oklahoma City
Tulsa

Oregon
*Portland
Baker

Pennsylvania
*Pittsburgh-Byzantine
*Philadelphia
*Philadelphia-Ukrainian
Allentown
Altoona-Johnston
Armenian
Erie
Greensburg
Harrisburg
Pittsburgh
Scranton

Rhode Island
Providence

South Carolina
Charleston

South Dakota
Rapid City
Sioux Falls

Tennessee
Knoxville
Memphis
Nashville

Texas
*San Antonio
Amarillo
Austin
Beaumont
Brownsville
Corpus Christi
Dallas
El Paso
Ft. Worth
Galveston-Houston
Lubbock
San Angelo
Tyler
Victoria

Utah
Salt Lake City

Vermont
Burlington

Virginia
Arlington
Apostolate to Hungarians
Richmond

Washington
*Seattle
Spokane

Yakima

West Virginia
Wheeling-Charleston

Wisconsin
*Milwaukee
Green Bay
La Crosse
Madison
Superior

Wyoming
Cheyenne

BIBLIOGRAPHY

1. Annotated Bibliography

While working on this book I was able to make use of an almost inexhaustible multitude of American studies on my subject, which I consulted at Stanford, Notre Dame, and Catholic University—without once encountering a grumpy librarian. I found some books, collections of sources, and periodicals particularly useful, and this is reflected in my footnotes. The following references are therefore also intended as recommendations addressed to readers who would like to deepen their knowledge of the subject.

1. For a general overview of American religious history, consult first the studies by Martin E. Marty, whom one reviewer has called "near omniscient." His *Pilgrims in Their Own Land* (1981) can serve as an introduction and reference book.

In *Religion in America* (1981), Winthrop Hudson is less interested in narrative than in emphasizing the development of social forms and pointing out the parallels between intellectual trends in the various religious communities. The most logically consistent example of a description that combines religious history and religious sociology is nonetheless Nathan O. Hatch's *The Democratization of American Christianity* (1989), a book that explains why the peculiarities of American political culture were anticipated in the Americanization of Christianity.

2. If one wants to follow such references further, Edwin Scott Gaustad's two-volume study, *A Documentary History of Religion in America* (1984), which provides both a comprehensive selection of documents and a precise commentary on them, is indispensable. Equally indispensable, because it has no competitors, is the collection of documents assembled by John Tracy Ellis (*Documents of American Catholic History*, 2 vols., 1967). However, Ellis makes little attempt to make the conflicts within the church comprehensible; instead, his selection of sources and his commentary tend to harmonize matters from the point of view of a mild progressivism.

3. More precise information can therefore be found in general presentations such as Thomas T. McAvoy's *History of the Catholic Church* (1969), Jay P. Dolan's *The American Catholic Experience* (1985), which approaches its subject from the point of view of social history, and James

Hennesey's *American Catholics* (1981). Hennesey in particular offers comprehensive and reliable information.

The only previous history of American Catholicism to appear in German deserves mention because of its balanced and readable presentations, although it does not go beyond the middle of the twentieth century. This *Geschichte der Katholischen Kirche in den Vereinigten Staaten von Amerika* (1954) was written by Ludwig Hertling, a Jesuit who for many years taught at Georgetown University.

4. Three exceptional books must be consulted to understand important aspects of the history of American Catholicism and the phases through which it has passed. Ray Allen Billington's *The Protestant Crusade 1800–1860* (1958) describes the role of anti-Catholicism in American culture. Gerald P. Fogarty's *The Americanist Crisis* (1974) offers an account of a controversy that took place toward the end of the nineteenth century and that could be described as a cultural war within American Catholicism. Finally, Joseph A. Varacalli's *The Establishment of Liberal Catholicism in America* (1983), a sociological study of activism inside the church, offers a starting point for explaining the formation of the political and ideological camps that have been a problem since the 1960s.

5. If one is looking for typical theological expressions of American characteristics in relation to the World Church, that is, for a theology that is both American and Catholic, John Courtney Murray's groundbreaking essay "We Hold These Truths" (1960) and Avery Dulles's *The Reshaping of Catholicism* (1988) may be mentioned.

6. In looking for information proceeding from empirical social research, one comes across Andrew Greeley again and again. *Religious Change in America* (1989) can serve as an introduction to his many publications.

7. Finally, anyone who wants to keep up with current developments should consult periodicals such as *Origins*, which publishes important texts and documents, and the Jesuits' cultural magazine *America*, which reports on intellectual debates.

2. References

Abalos, David T. 1987. *Latinos in the United States.* Notre Dame, Ind.

Abell, Aaron. 1960. *American Catholicism and Social Action: A Search for Social Justice 1865–1950.* Garden City, N.Y.

Adams, Raymond W. 1932. "Isaac Theodor Hecker." *Dictionary of American Biography*, vol. 8. New York.

Adams, Willi Paul, *et al.*, eds. 1992. *The United States of America.* 2d ed. 2 vols. New York.

Ahern, Patrick H. 1954. *The Life of John J. Keane, Educator and Archbishop, 1839–1918.* Milwaukee.

Ahern, Patrick H. "John J. Keene." *New Catholic Encyclopedia*, vol. 8.

Ahlstrom, Sydney E. 1954. *A Religious History of the American People.* New Haven, Conn.

"Anniversary Waltz" (editorial, 15 July 1988), *Commonweal.*

Arciniegas, German. 1975. *America in Europe: A History of the New World in Reverse.* San Diego.

Barry, Colman J. 1953. *The Catholic Church and German-Americans.* Milwaukee.

Bates, Ernest S. 1929. "Orestes A. Brownson." *Dictionary of American Biography,* vol. 3. New York.

Bellah, Robert. 1967. "Civil Religion in America." *Daedalus* 96.

Benestad, J. Brian. 1982. *The Pursuit of a Just Social Order.* Washington, D.C.

Berns, Walter Fred. 1976. *The First Amendment and the Future of American Democracy.* New York.

Billington, Ray Allen. 1958. *The Protestant Crusade 1800–1860: A Study on the Origins of American Nativism.* New York.

Blanshard, Paul. 1958. *American Freedom and Catholic Power.* 2d ed. Boston.

Blantz, Thomas E. 1982. *A Priest in Public Service: Francis J. Haas and the New Deal.* Notre Dame, Ind.

Bleid, B. J. "Michael Heiss." *New Catholic Encyclopedia,* vol. 6.

——. "F. X. Katzer." *New Catholic Encyclopedia,* vol. 8.

Bloom, Harold. 1991. *The American Religion: The Emergence of the Post-Christian Nation.* Boston.

Boorstin, Daniel J. 1953. *The Genius of American Politics.* Chicago.

Braxton, Edward K. 1982. "American Bishops Meet." *America* (22 May).

——. 1987. "The National Black Catholic Congress." *America* (25 July).

Broderick, Francis L. 1963. *Right Reverend New Dealer John A. Ryan.* New York.

——. "John A. Ryan." In *New Catholic Encyclopedia,* vol. 12.

Brownson, Orestes A. [1852] 1972. *Essays and Reviews, Chiefly on Theology, Politics, and Socialism.* Reprint. New York.

Brown, Bernard E. 1983. *Great American Political Thinkers.* Vol. 1. New York.

Barnes, Timothy A. 1989. *Catholic Bishops in American Politics.* Princeton, N.J.

Burtchaell, James Tunstead. 1991. "The Decline and Fall of the Christian College." *First Things* (April–May).

Butler, John. 1991. *Awash in a Sea of Faith: Christianizing the American People.* Cambridge, Mass. and London.

Caplow, Theodore, *et al.* 1983. *All Faithful People: Change and Continuity in Middletown's Religion.* Minneapolis.

Caplow, Theodore. 1985. "Contrasting Trends in European and American Religion." *Sociological Analysis* 46.

Carey, Patrick W. 1987. *Priests and Prelates: Ecclesiastical Democracy and the Tensions of Trusteeism.* Notre Dame, Ind.

Cather, Willa. 1927. *Death Comes for the Archbishop.* New York.

Catholic Almanac 1991. Huntington, Ind.

1990 Census (U.S. Bureau of the Census): *Current Population Survey.* Washington, D.C.

Chaves, Mark, and David E. Cann. 1992. "Regulation, Pluralism, and Religious Market Structure." *Rationality and Society* 4, no. 3.

Christiano, Kevin J. 1992. "Contemporary Developments in American Religion." *The United States,* vol. 3. New York.

Clebsch, William B. 1973. *American Religious Thought.* Chicago.

Clements, Robert B. 1988. "Michael Williams and the founding of *Commonweal.*" In Kantowicz 1988a.

Cogley, John. 1986. *Catholic America.* 2d. ed. Kansas City, Mo.

Cohalan, F. D. "John J. Hughes." *New Catholic Encyclopedia,* vol. 7.

Coleman, James S., and Thomas Hoffer. 1987. *Public and Private High Schools: The Impact of Communities.* New York.

Colman, Barry. 1953. *The Catholic Church and German-Americans.* Milwaukee.

Conzen, Kathleen Neils. 1976. *Immigrant Milwaukee 1836–1860: Accommodation and Community in a Frontier City.* Cambridge, Mass.

Cooke, Bernard, ed. 1989. *The Papacy and the Church in the United States.* New York.

Coonen, L. P. "Martin J. Spalding." *New Catholic Encyclopedia,* vol. 13.

Cooney, John. 1984. *The American Pope: The Life and Times of Francis Cardinal Spellman.* New York.

Cox, Harvey. 1965. *The Secular City.* New York.

Cox, Harvery. 1984. *Religion in the Secular City: Toward a Postmodern Theology.* New York.

Cross, Robert D. 1968. *The Emergence of Liberal Catholicism in America.* Chicago.

Cross, Whitney R. 1950. *The Burned-Over District: The Social and Intellectual History of Enthusiastic Religion in Western New York 1800–1850.* Ithaca, N.Y.

Cuddihy, John Murray. 1974. *The Ordeal of Civility: Freud, Marx, Levi Strauss and the Jewish Struggle with Modernity.* New York.

———. 1979. *No Offense: Civil Religion and Protestant Taste.* New York.

Curran, Charles E. 1986. *Faithful Dissent.* New York.

———. 1987. "A Teaching Moment Continues." *America* (25 April).

Curran, Robert Emmett. 1978/1. *Michael Augustine Corrigan and the Shaping of Conservative Catholicism in America 1878–1902.* New York.

———. 1978. "Prelude to Americanism: The New York Academia and Clerical Radicalism in the Late Nineteenth Century." *Church History,* vol. 47, no. 2.

———. 1980. "The McGlynn Affair and the Shaping of the New Conservatism in American Catholicism 1886–1894." *Catholic Historical Review*, vol. 66.

D'Antonio, William V., et al. 1989. *American Catholic Laity in a Changing Church*. Kansas City, Mo.

Day, Dorothy. 1952. *The Long Loneliness*. New York.

Demerath, N.J., III. 1991. "Religious Capital and Capital Religions: Cross-Cultural and Non-Legal Factors in the Separation of Church and State." *Daedalus* 120.

Doerries, Reinhard R. 1986. *Iren und Deutsche in der Neuen Welt. Akkulturationsprozesse in der Amerikanischen Gesellschaft im spaten Neunzehnten Jahrhundert*. Stuttgart.

Dolan, Jay P. 1975. *The Immigrant Church: New York's Irish and German Catholics 1815–1865*. Baltimore.

———. 1985. *The American Catholic Experience: A Social History from Colonial Times to the Present*. Garden City, N.Y.

Dolan, Jay P., ed. 1988. *The American Catholic Parish: A History from 1850 to the Present*. 2 vols. New York.

Dougherty, Jude P. 1992. "Superior Education Needed for Priest to Fulfill Teaching Office; Reflections on Pastores Dabo Vobis." *Osservatore Romano* (English Edition), 35.

Dulles, Avery. 1986. "Sensus Fidelium." *America* (1 November).

———. 1987. *Models of the Church*. Garden City, N.Y.

———. 1988. *The Reshaping of Catholicism: Current Challenges in the Theology of Church*. New York.

Eagan, Robert J. 1992. "Who's Doing Catholic Theology? And Why, How and Where?" *Commonweal* (13 March).

Elliott, John H. 1970. *The Old World and the New, 1492–1650*. Cambridge.

Elliott, Walter. 1897. *The Life of Father Hecker*. New York 1891. Introduction by Mgr. Ireland. Preface by Abbot Felix Klein. Paris.

Ellis, John Tracy. 1946. *The Formative Years of the Catholic University of America*. Washington D.C.

———. 1952. *The Life of James Cardinal Gibbons*. 2 vols. Milwaukee.

———. 1956. *American Catholicism*. Vol. 1. Chicago.

———. 1956. *American Catholics and the Intellectual Life*. Vol. 2. Chicago.

———. 1961. *John Lancaster Spalding: First Bishop of Peoria, American Educator*. Milwaukee.

———. 1965. *Catholics in Colonial America*. Baltimore.

———. "James Gibbons." *New Catholic Encyclopedia*, vol. 6.

Ellis, John Tracy, ed. 1967. *Documents of American Catholic History*, Vol. 2. Chicago.

Fee, Joan L., et. al. 1981. *Young Catholics in the United States and Canada: A Report to the Knights of Columbus*. Los Angeles.

Feigelman, William, et. al. 1991. "The Social Characteristics of Black Catholics." *Sociology and Social Research* (SSR)," no. 3.

Fichter, Joseph. 1968. *Americas Forgotten Priests: What They Are Saying.* New York.

Fisher, James Terence. 1989. *The Catholic Counterculture in America, 1933–1962.* Chapel Hill.

Fitzpatrick, Joseph P. 1987. *One Church—Many Cultures: The Challenge of Diversity.* Kansas City.

Fogarty, Gerald P. 1989. "The Vatican and the American Church since World War II." In Cooke 1989.

Fox, H. "Peter E. Dietz." *New Catholic Encyclopedia,* vol. 4.

Gallup, George, Jr., and Jim Castelli. 1989. *The People's Religion: American Faith in the 90s.* New York, London.

Gann, Lewis H. and Peter J. Duignan. 1986. *The Hispanics in the United States: A History.* Boulder, Colo.

Gannon, Robert J. 1962. *The Cardinal Spellman Story.* Garden City, N.Y.

———. 1967. *Up to the Present: The Story of Fordham.* Garden City, N.Y.

Garraghan, Gilbert J. 1938. *The Jesuits of the Middle U.S.* 3 vols. New York.

Gaustad, Edwin Scott. 1957. *The Great Awakening in New England.* New York.

———. 1982. *A Documentary History of Religion in America.* 2 vols. Grand Rapids.

Geertz, Clifford. 1968. "Religion as a Cultural System." In Donald R. Cutler, ed., *The Religious Situation.* Boston.

Geoghegan, Thomas. 1988. "Confessions of a 'Practicing' Catholic." *America* (2 April).

Gerbi, Antonello. 1973. *The Dispute of the New World: The History of a Polemic.* New York. (Originally published as *La Disputa del Nuovo Mondo. Storia de una polemica 1750–1900.* Milan, 1955.)

Gilkey, Langdon. 1967. "Social and Intellectual Sources of Contemporary Protestant Theology in America." *Daedalus,* no. 4.

Gisler, Anton. 1912. *Der Modernismus.* Einsiedeln.

Glazer, Nathan, and Daniel P. Moynihan. 1963. *Beyond the Melting Pot.* Cambridge, Mass.

Gleason, A. "John Ireland." *New Catholic Encyclopedia,* vol. 7.

Gleason, Philip. 1968. *The Conservative Reformers: German-American Catholics and the Social Order.* Notre Dame, Ind.

———. 1979. "In Search of Unity: American Catholic Thought 1920–1960." *The Catholic Historical Review* 65, no. 2.

———. 1988. "Neo-Scholasticism as Preconciliar Ideology." *Annual Report 1988* (Catholic Commission on Intellectual and Cultural Affairs). Notre Dame, Ind.

Glock, Charles Y., and Rodney Stark. 1965. *Religion and Society in Tension.* Chicago.

Gower, Joseph F., and Richard M. Leliaert., eds. 1979. *The Brownson-Hecker Correspondence.* Notre Dame, Ind.

261

Bibliography

Grebler, Leo, *et al.* 1970. *The Mexican American People.* New York.

Greeley, Andrew M. 1972. *Priests in the United States.* Garden City, N.Y.

——. 1974. *Ethnicity in the United States: A Preliminary Reconnaissance.* New York.

——. 1979. "The Sociology of American Catholics." *Annual Review of Sociology* 5.

——. 1986. *Confessions of a Parish Priest: An Autobiography.* New York.

——. 1988. "Defection Among Hispanics." *America* (7 July).

——. 1989a. "Don't Sell Catholic Schools Short." *U.S. Catholic* (March).

——. 1989b. *Religious Change in America.* Cambridge, Mass.

Gremillion, Joseph, and David C. Leege. 1989. *Post–Vatican II Parish Life in the United States: Review and Preview.* Notre Dame Study of Catholic Parish Life, Report no. 15. Notre Dame, Ind.

Greven, Philip. 1977. *The Protestant Temperament: Patterns of Child-Rearing, Religious Experience and the Self in Early America.* Chicago.

Haley, Alex. 1976. *Roots.* New York.

Halsey, William M. 1980. *The Survival of American Innocence: Catholicism in an Era of Disillusionment 1920–1940.* Notre Dame, Ind.

Handlin, Oscar. 1959. *Al Smith and His America.* Boston.

——. 1959. *Boston's Immigrants, 1795–1865.* Cambridge, Mass.

Handy, Robert T. 1971. *A Christian America: Protestant Hopes and Historical Realities.* New York.

——. 1977. *A History of the Churches in the United States and Canada.* New York.

Hanna, Mary T. 1987. "Catholic Bishops as Political Leaders." Paper presented at the Annual Meeting of the American Political Science Association, Chicago.

Hatch, Nathan O. 1989. *The Democratization of American Christianity.* New Haven, Conn. and London.

Hebblethwaite, Peter. 1982. "The Popes and Politics: Shifting Patterns in Catholic Social Doctrine." In Mary Douglas and Steven Tipton, eds. *Religion in America,* Boston.

Heft, James L. 1989. "From the Pope to the Bishops: Episcopal Authority from Vatican I to Vatican II." In Cooke 1989.

Hegy, Pierre. 1993. "The End of American Catholicism? Another Look." *America* (1 May).

Hehir, J. Bryan. 1989. "From Church-State to Religion and Politics: The Case of the U.S. Catholic Bishops." In Kelly 1989.

Hellwig, Monika K. 1988. "Scholars and Bishops: Due Process on the Drawing Board." *Commonweal* (29 January).

Hemrick, Eugene F., and Dean R. Hoge. 1985. *Seminarians in Theology: A National Profile.* Washington, D.C.

——. 1987. *Seminary Life and Visions of the Priesthood: A National Survey of Seminarians.* Washington, D.C.

———. 1991. *A Survey of Priests Ordained Five to Nine Years.* Washington, D.C.

Hennesey, James J. 1981. *American Catholics: A History of the Roman Catholic Community in the United States.* New York.

———. 1989. "Rome and the Origins of the United States Hierarchy." In Cooke 1989.

Henni, John Martin. 1836. *Ein Blick ins Tal des Ohio.* Munich.

Herberg, Will. 1972. "The 'American Way of Life' as a Secular Faith." In Conrad Wright, *Religion in American Life,* Boston, 1972.

Hertling, Ludwig. 1954. *Geschichte der Katholischen Kirche in den Vereinigten Staaten.* Berlin.

Hofstadter, Richard. 1962. *Anti-Intellectualism in American Life.* New York.

Hoge, Dean R. 1976. *Division in the Protestant House: The Basic Reasons behind Intra-Church Conflicts.* Philadelphia.

———. "Vocations, Research on." *New Catholic Encyclopedia,* vol. 18.

———. 1987. *The Future of Catholic Leadership: Response to the Priest Shortage.* Kansas City, Mo.

Hoge, Dean R., Joseph J. Shields, and Mary Jeanne Verdieck. 1988. "Changing Age Distribution and Theological Attitudes of Catholic Priests 1970–1985." *Sociological Analysis* 49.

Hudson, Winthrop S. 1961. *American Protestantism.* Chicago.

———. 1981. *Religion in America.* 3d ed. New York.

Hughes, Thomas. 1907–1917. *History of the Society of Jesus in North America, Colonial and Federal.* 4 vols. London.

Hunter, James Davison. 1991. "American Protestantism: Sorting out the Present, Looking toward the Future." In Richard J. Neuhaus, ed., *The Believable Futures of American Protestantism.* Grand Rapids, Mich.

———. 1991. *Culture Wars: The Struggle to Define America.* New York.

Huntington, Samuel P. 1981. *American Politics: The Promise of Disharmony.* Cambridge, Mass.

Hurley, Francis T. 1988. "N.C.C.B./U.S.C.C./W.I.T.D.? What is the Difference?" *America* (19 March).

Hutchison, William F. 1976. *The Modernist Impulse in American Protestantism.* Cambridge, Mass.

Iannacone, Laurence R. 1991. "The Consequences of Religious Market Structure." *Rationality and Society* 3.

Jaffe, A. J., Ruth M. Cullen, and Thomas D. Boswell. 1980. *The Changing Demography of Spanish-Americans.* New York.

Johnson, Peter. 1959. *Crosier on the Frontier: The Life of John Martin Henni.* Madison, Wisc.

———. "John M. Henni." *New Catholic Encyclopedia,* vol. 6.

Kantowicz, Edward R. 1981. "Cardinal Mundelein of Chicago and the Shaping of Twentieth-Century American Catholicism." *Journal of American History* 68, no. 1.

———. 1983. *Corporation Sole: Cardinal Mundelein and Chicago Catholicism.* Notre Dame, Ind.

———, ed. 1988a. *Modern American Catholicism 1900–1965*. New York.

———. 1988b. "Schools and Sisters." In White 1988.

Keefe, Thomas M. 1988. "The Mundelein Affair: A Reappraisal." In Kantowicz 1988a.

Keller, Adolf. 1922. *Dynamis, Formen und Kräfte des amerikanischen Protestantismus*. Tübingen.

Keller, Charles. 1942. *The Second Great Awakening in Connecticut*. New Haven, Conn.

Kelley, Dean M. 1977. *Why Conservative Churches Are Growing: A Study in Sociology of Religion*. San Francisco.

Kelly, James R. 1989. "Data and Mystery: A Decade of Studies on Catholic Leadership." *America* (18 November).

Kelly, Joseph, ed. 1989. *American Catholics*. Wilmington, Del.

Kennedy, Eugene. 1985. *Re-Imagining American Catholicism: The American Bishops and Their Pastoral Letters*. New York.

———. 1988. *Tomorrow's Catholics/Yesterday's Church: The Two Cultures of American Catholicism*. New York.

Kennedy, Ruby J. R. 1944. "Single or Triple Melting Pot? Intermarriage Trends in New Haven 1810–1940." *American Journal of Sociology* 4.

Kinzer, Donald. 1964. *An Episode in Anti-Catholicism: The American Protective Association*. Seattle, Wash.

Koenig, H. C. "George W. Mundelein." *New Catholic Encyclopedia*, vol. 10.

Kress, Robert. 1986. *The People's Church, from Established Church to Voluntary Free Church*. (Cushwa Center: Working Paper Series). Notre Dame, Ind.

Kunkelman, Gary A. 1990. *A Religion of Ethnicity: Belief and Belonging in a Greek-American Community*. New York.

Lachman, Seymour P., and Barry A. Kosmin. 1991. "Black Catholics Get Ahead." *New York Times* (14 September).

Lamb, Matthew L. 1990. "Will There be a Catholic Theology in the United States?" *America* (26 May).

Larkin, Emmet. 1972. "The Devotional Revolution in Ireland 1850–1875." *American Historical Review* 77.

Lears, T. Jackson. 1981. *No Place of Grace: Antimodernism and the Transformation of American Culture 1880–1920*. New York.

Leege, David C. 1987. *Catholics and the Civic Order: Parish Participation, Politics, and Civic Participation*. Notre Dame Study of Catholic Parish Life, Report no. 11. Notre Dame, Ind.

———. 1993. "The Decomposition of the Religious Vote: A Comparison of White, Non-Hispanic Catholics with other Ethnoreligious Groups 1960–1992." (Ms. of a lecture.)

Leege, David C., and Joseph Gremillion. 1986. *The People, Their Pastors, and the Church: Viewpoints on Church Politics and Positions*. Notre Dame Study of Catholic Parish Life, Report no. 7. Notre Dame, Ind.

Leege, David C., and Thomas A. Trozzolo. 1985. *Religious Values and Parish Participation: The Paradox of Individual Needs in a Communitarian Church*. Notre Dame Study of Catholic Parish Life, Report no. 4. Notre Dame, Ind.

Lenski, Gerhard. 1961. *The Religious Factor: A Sociological Study of Religious Impact on Politics, Economics, and Family Life*. Garden City, N.Y.

Lipset, Seymour M. 1983. *Political Man: The Social Bases of Politics*. London.

Luckmann, Thomas. 1976. *The Invisible Religion*. New York.

Lynd, Robert S., and Helen Merrell Lynd. 1929. *Middletown: A Study in American Culture*. New York.

———. 1937. *Middletown in Transition: A Study of Cultural Conflicts*. New York.

Maier, Hans. 1975. *Revolution und Kirche. Zur Frühgeschichte der christlichen Demokratie*. 5th ed. Freiburg, Basel, and Vienna.

Marini, Stephen A. 1982. *Radical Sects of Revolutionary New England*. Cambridge, Mass. and London.

Marsden, George M. 1980. *Fundamentalism and American Culture: The Shaping of Twentieth-Century Evangelicalism 1870–1925*. New York.

Martin, David. 1990. *Tongues of Fire: The Explosion of Protestantism in Latin America*. Oxford.

———. 1991. "The Secularization Issue." *British Journal of Sociology* 42.

Marty, Martin E. 1970. *Righteous Empire: The Protestant Experience in America*. New York.

———. 1976. *A Nation of Behaviors*. Chicago and London.

———. 1979. *Religion in America: 1950 to the Present*. San Francisco.

———. 1984. *Pilgrims in Their Own Land: 500 Years of Religion in America*. New York.

———. 1991. *The Noise of Conflict*. Vol. 2 of *Modern American Religion*. Chicago.

Maurin, Peter. 1936. *Radical Christian Thought: Easy Essays*. New York.

Maynard, Theodore. 1949. *The Story of American Catholicsm*. 5th ed. New York.

McAvoy, Thomas T. 1957. *The Great Crisis in American Catholic History 1850–1900*. Notre Dame, Ind.

———. 1969. *A History of the Catholic Church in America*. Notre Dame, Ind.

McBrien, Richard P. 1988. "Academic Freedom in Catholic Universities: The Emergence of a Party Line." *America* (3 December).

———. 1989. "Catholicism. The American Experience." In Kelly 1989.

McCready, William C., and Andrew M. Greeley. 1972. "The End of American Catholicism." *America* (28 October).

McDermott, R. "Women Religious." *New Catholic Encyclopedia*, vol. 18.

McKeown, Elizabeth. 1980. "The National Bishops' Conference: An Analysis of its Origins." *Catholic Historical Review* 66.

McLaughlin, William G. 1978. *Revivals, Awakenings, and Reform.* Chicago.

McNamara, R. F. "Trusteeism." *New Catholic Encyclopedia,* vol. 14.

——. "Bernard J. McQuaid." *New Catholic Encyclopedia,* vol. 9.

McShane, Joseph M. 1987. *"Sufficiently Radical" Catholicism, Progressivism, and the Bishops' Program of 1919.* Washington, D.C.

McWilliams, Carey. 1990. *North from Mexico: The Spanish-Speaking People of the United States.* 2d ed. New York. (1st ed. Philadelphia 1949.)

Mead, Sidney E. 1975. *The Nation with the Soul of a Church.* New York.

Mexican-American Cultural Center. 1979. *Faith Expressions of the Mexican-American.* San Antonio.

Miller, Perry. 1953. *The New England Mind: From Colony to Province.* Cambridge, Mass.

——. 1956. *Errand into the Wilderness.* Cambridge, Mass.

Moltmann, Guenther, and Wolfgang Lindig. 1985. *USA-Ploetz.Geschichte der Vereinigten Staaten zum Nachschlagen.* Freiburg and Wurzburg.

Moore, Brian. 1985. *Black Robe.* London.

Moore, R. Lawrence. 1986. *Religious Outsiders and the Making of Americans.* New York.

Morgan, Edmund S. 1958. *The Puritan Dilemma: The Story of John Winthrop.* Boston and Toronto.

——. 1963. *Visible Saints: The History of a Puritan Idea.* New York.

Morrison, J. L. "John J. Spalding." *New Catholic Encyclopedia,* vol. 13.

Morse, Samuel F. B. [1835] 1969. *Imminent Dangers to the Free Institutions of the United States through Foreign Immigration.* Reprint. New York.

Moynihan, James. 1953. *The Life of Archbishop John Ireland.* New York.

Muldoon, James. 1979. *Lawyers and Infidels.* Philadelphia.

Murray, John Courtney. 1960. *We Hold These Truths.* New York.

Myrdal, Gunnar. 1975. *An American Dilemma: The Negro Problem and Modern Democracy.* New York.

National Conference of Catholic Bishops. 1983a. *The Hispanic Presence: Challenge and Commitment.* Washington, D.C.

National Conference of Catholic Bishops. 1983b. *The Challenge of Peace, God's Promise and Our Response: A Pastoral Letter on War and Peace.* Washington, D.C.

National Conference of Catholic Bishops, 1987. *Economic Justice for All: Pastoral Letter on Catholic Social Teaching and the U.S. Economy.* Washington, D.C.

National Opinion Research Center. 1971. *American Priests.* Chicago.

Neuhaus, Richard John. 1984. *The Naked Public Square.* Grand Rapids, Mich.

———. 1987. *The Catholic Moment: The Paradox of the Church in the Post-Modern World.* San Francisco.

New Catholic Encyclopedia. 1967. 17 vols. Washington, D.C. (Vols. 18, 19, 1989.)

Niebuhr, H. Richard. [1919] 1968. *The Social Sources of Denominationalism.* 2d ed. Cleveland, Ohio.

Novak, Michael. 1971. *The Rise of the Unmeltable Ethnics.* New York.

———. 1985. *Moral Clarity in the Nuclear Age.* Washington, D.C.

———. 1989. *Will It Liberate?* Mahwah, N.J.

———. 1990. *Morality, Capitalism, and Democracy.* Washington, D.C.

Nygren, David, and Miriam Ukeritis. 1992. "The Future of Religious Orders in the United States." *Origins* 15.

O'Brien, David J. 1968. *American Catholics and Social Reform: The New Deal Years.* New York.

O'Brien Steinfels, Margaret. 1992. "The Unholy Alliance between the Right and the Left in the Catholic Church." *America* (2 May).

O'Connell, Marvin R. 1989. "John Ireland, the Vatican, and the French Connection." In Cooke 1989.

O'Dea, Thomas F. 1970. *Sociology and the Study of Religion.* New York.

Ochs, Stephen J. 1988. "The Ordeal of Black Priests." In White 1988.

Pattison, Robert. 1991. *The Great Dissent: John Henry Newman and the Liberal Heresy.* New York.

Perko, Michael F., ed. 1988. *Enlightening the Next Generation: Catholics and Their Schools 1830–1980.* New York.

Pfeffer, Leo. 1953. *Church, State, and Fredom.* Boston.

Pietschmann, Horst. 1980. *Staat und staatliche Entwicklung am Beginn der spanischen Kolonisation Amerikas.* Munster.

———. 1992. *500 Jahre Entdeckung Amerikas. Die spanische Eroberung und Kolonisation (1492 bis ca. 1580).* (Vol. 192 in the series, "Kirche und Gesellschaft" published by the Katholische Sozialwissentschaftlichen Zentralstelle.) Mönchengladbach.

Polsby, Nelson W. 1960. "Towards an Explanation of McCarthyism." *Political Studies* 8.

Portier, William L. 1989. "Church Unity and National Traditions: The Challenge to the Modern Papacy 1682–1870." In Cooke 1989.

Potvin, Raymond H., and Antanas Suziedelis. 1969. *Seminarians of the Sixties: A National Survey.* Washington, D.C.

Potvin, Raymond H., and Felipe L. Muncada. 1990. *Seminary Outcomes: Perseverance and Withdrawal.* Washington, D.C.

Rauschenbusch, Walter. 1912. *Christianizing the Social Order.* New York.

Reese, Thomas J. 1989a. *Archbishop: Inside the Power Structure of the American Catholic Church.* New York.

———. 1989b. "Bishops and Theologians." *America* (8 July).

———. 1989c. "Bishops on Bishops." *America* (4 November).

Reher, Margaret Mary. 1980. "Americanism and Modernism—Continuity or Discontinuity?" *U.S. Catholic Historian* 1.

Reichley, A. James. 1985. *Religion in American Public Life*. Washington, D.C.

Reilly, Daniel F. 1943. *The School Controversy, 1891-1893*. Washington, D.C.

Rieff, Philip. 1966. *The Triumph of the Therapeutic: Uses of Faith after Freud*. New York.

Roemer, Theodore. 1950. *The Catholic Church in the United States*. St. Louis, Mo.

Rouse, Irving. 1992. *The Tainos: Rise and Decline of the People Who Greeted Columbus*. New Haven, Conn.

Rousseau, Jean-Jacques. 1947. *The Social Contract*. New York.

Rovere, Richard. 1959. *Senator Joe McCarthy*. New York.

Royal, Robert. 1992. *Columbus on Trial: 1492-1992*. Herndon, Va.

Russell, Jeffrey Burton. 1991. *Inventing the Flat Earth: Columbus and Modern Historians*. New York.

Sale, Kirkpatrick. 1990. *The Conquest of Paradise*. New York.

Sanchez, Jose. 1972. *Anticlericalism: A Brief History*. Notre Dame, Ind.

Sandoval, Moises. 1983. *Fronteras: A History of the Latin American Church in the USA since 1513*. San Antonio, Tex.

Santayana, George. 1920. *Character and Opinion in the United States*. New York.

Schatz, Ronald W. 1988. "American Labor and the Catholic Church 1919–1950." In Kantowicz 1988a.

Schleck, C. A. "Vocation, Religious and Clerical." *New Catholic Encyclopedia*, vol. 14.

Schlereth, Thomas J. 1976. *The University of Notre Dame: A Portrait of Its History and Campus*. Notre Dame, Ind.

Schlesinger, Arthur M. 1963. *Orestes A. Brownson*. New York.

———. 1992. *The Disuniting of America*. New York.

Schoenherr, R. A. and A. Sorenson. 1982. "Social Change in Religious Organizations: Consequences of Clergy Decline in the United States." *Sociological Analysis* 43.

Segers, Mary C. 1988. "Equality and Christian Anarchism: The Political and Social Ideas of the Catholic Worker Movement." In Kantowicz 1988a.

Shanabruch, Charles. 1981. *Chicago's Catholics: The Evolution of an American Identity*. Notre Dame, Ind.

Shapiro, Edward S. 1988. "Catholic Agrarian Thought and the New Deal." In Kantowicz 1988a.

Shaughnessy, Gerald. 1925. *Has the Immigrant Kept the Faith?* New York.

Shaw, Stephen J. *The Catholic Parish as a Way Station of Ethnicity and Americanization: Chicago's Germans and Italians, 1903-1939*. New York.

Shepard, Robert S. 1987. *God's People in the Ivory Tower: Religion in the Early American University.* New York.

Shils, Edward. 1981. *Tradition.* Chicago.

Siegfried, André. 1927. *America Comes of Age.* New York.

Silberman, Charles E. 1985. *A Certain People: American Jews and Their Lives Today.* New York.

Simpson, Alan. 1955. *Puritanism in Old and New England.* Chicago.

Smith, Timothy L. 1980. *Revivalism and Social Reform: American Protestantism on the Eve of the Civil War.* Baltimore and London.

Stark, Rodney. 1992. "Do Catholic Societies Really Exist?" *Rationality and Society* 4, no. 3.

Stark, Rodney, and William Sims Bainbridge. 1985. *Secularization, Revival, and Cult Formation.* Berkeley, Calif.

Stark, Rodney, and Charles Y. Glock. 1974. *American Piety: The Nature of Religious Commitment.* Berkeley, Calif.

Stoll, David. 1990. *Is Latin America Turning Protestant?* Berkeley, Calif.

Sweet, William Warren. 1944. *Revivalism in America.* New York.

Thwaites, Reuben Gold, ed. 1896–1901. *Jesuit Relations and Allied Documents.* 73 vols. Cleveland, Ohio.

Trisco, Robert F. 1988. *Bishops and Their Priests in the United States 1789–1918.* New York.

Troeltsch, Ernst. 1906. "Die Bedeutung des Protestantismus für die Entstehung der modernen Welt." *Historisches Zeitschrift* 97.

Troy, Thomas F. 1991. "Jesuit Colleges without Jesuits?" *Commonweal* (18 May).

Tull, Charles J. 1965. *Father Coughlin and the New Deal.* Syracuse, N.Y.

Tyack, David B. 1988. "The Perils of Pluralism: The Background of the Pierce Case." In Kantowicz 1988a.

U.S. Catholic. 1989. "Why Catholic Schools Outperform All Others." Interview with James S. Coleman. *U.S. Catholic* (July).

Uthmann, Jörg von. 1992. "Mein Name is Morse, ich weiß von nichts." Frankfurter Allgemeine Zeitung (2 May).

Valaik, J. David. 1988. "American Catholic Dissenters and the Spanish Civil War." In Kantowicz 1988a.

Varacalli, Joseph A. 1983. *Toward the Establishment of Liberal Catholicism in America.* Lanham, N.Y., and London.

Walch, Timothy, ed. 1988. *Early American Catholicism 1634–1820: Selected Historical Essays.* New York.

Walzer, Michael. 1965. *The Revolution of the Saints: A Study in the Origins of Radical Politics.* Cambridge, Mass. and London.

Ward, Nathaniel. 1983. "The Simple Cobbler." In Brown 1983.

Warner, R. Stephen. 1991. "Starting Over: Reflections on American Religion." *Christian Century* (4–11 September).

Weakland, Rembert G. 1985. "Explaining Myself to Rome." *America* (21 September).

Weber, Donald. 1988. *Rhetoric and History in Revolutionary New England*. New York.

Webster's Guide to American History. 1971. Springfield, Mass.

Weigel, George. 1987. *Tranquillitas Ordinis*. New York.

———. 1989. *Catholicism and the Renewal of American Democracy*. New York.

Wentz, Richard E. 1990. *Religion in the New World: The Shaping of Religious Traditions in the United States*. Minneapolis, Minn.

White, Joseph M., ed. 1988. *The American Catholic Religious Life: Selected Historical Essays*. New York.

———. 1989. *The Diocesan Seminary in the United States: A History form the 1780s to the Present*. Notre Dame, Ind.

Will, Allen S. 1931. "James Gibbons." *Dictionary of American Biography*, vol. 7.

Wilson, John F., and Donald L. Drakeman. 1987. *Church and State in American History*. 2d ed. Boston.

Winthrop, John. 1983. "A Model of Christian Charity." In Brown 1983.

Wohl, Robert. 1979. *The Generation of 1914*. Cambridge, Mass.

Woodward, C. Vann. 1991. *The Old World's New World*. New York and Oxford.

Wuthnow, Robert. 1988. *The Restructuring of American Religion: Society and Faith since World War II*. Princeton, N.J.

Zöller, Michael. 1985. "Die neue Mehrheit und das Ende des New-Deal-Liberalismus." *Zeitschrift für Politik* 32, no. 4.

———. 1991. "Individualismus und Populismus. Religion und Politik in Amerika." In Ehrhard Fordran, ed. 1991. *Religion und Politik in einer säkularisierten Welt*. Baden Baden.

———. 1992. "Gibt es den amerikanischen Charakter? Politische Kultur und politische Soziologie der Vereinigten Staaten." In Adams 1992.

Zwierlein, Frederick J. 1927. *The Life and Letters of Bishop McQuaid*. 3 vols. Rochester NY.

———. ed. 1946. *Letters of Archbishop Corrigan to Bishop McQuaid and Allied Documents*. Rochester, N.Y.

NAME INDEX

Abbelen memorandum, 105, 118
Abbelen, Peter M., 118
Abenaki Indians, 12, 15
Acadia, 11, 15, 17
Acadians, 33
Act Concerning Religion, 30
Actae Sanctae Sedis, 147
Ad Hoc Committee on Catholic Social
  Teaching and the U.S. Economy, 204
Ad Hoc Committee on War and Peace
  in the Nuclear Age, 204
Adams, John, 38
Ahern, Patrick H., 96
Alexander VI, 3, 10
Allen, John, 37, 38
Althom, John, 30
America, 160, 206
American Bible Society, 65
American Civil Liberties Union, 142
American College, 74, 100, 101, 105,
  106, 129, 150, 151
American Federation of Labor (AFL),
  159
American Jewish Committee, 197
American Party (Know-Nothing
  Party), 61, 80–81, 83
American Protective Association
  (APA), 83, 139
American Republican Party, 80–82
American Society to Promote the Prin-
  ciples of the Protestant Reforma-
  tion, 79
American Sunday School Union, 65
American Tract Society, 65
Americanists (Americanist Party, Irish
  Party), 95, 97, 100, 102–3, 104, 105,
  106, 110, 120, 123, 129, 130, 146,
  148, 169, 197, 234
Anglican church, 54
Anglicans, 18, 27, 28–29, 39, 40, 165
Antonelli, Lorenzo, 46

Association for Rights of Catholics in
  the Church (ARCC), 196
Augustine, 22
Aztecs, 3

Backus, Isaac, 27, 28, 38
Baird, Pierre, 14
Bancroft, 88
Baptists, 18, 20, 27, 28, 38, 39, 40, 58,
  63, 64, 65, 84, 165, 219, 222
Barnabo, Alessandro, 90
Barry, Colman, 96
Bayley, James Roosevelt, 94, 99, 106,
  107
Becker, Thomas, 109
Bedini, Gaetano, 77, 78
Beecher, Henry Ward, 140–41
Beecher, Lyman, 65, 66, 80
Benedict XV, 145, 147
Benedictines, 73, 158
Bernardin, Joseph L., 202, 204, 239
Bill of Establishing Religious Free-
  dom, 44
Bill of Rights, 34, 169
Billington, Ray Allen, 78
Blanshard, Paul, 167
Boff, Leonardo, 228
Bohemia Manor, 33
Book of Martyrs, The, 31
Borgia, Franciscus, 7
Boston College, 13, 168, 231, 233
Boston Quarterly Review, 88
Bouquillon, Thomas, 122
Brandi, Salvatore, 124, 126
Brebéuf, Jean de, 14
Briand, Joseph Olivier, 45
Brook Farm, 88, 89
Brownson, Orestes, 67, 88–89, 90, 93,
  130, 131, 148
Brownson's Quarterly Review, 88
Bryan, William Jennings, 142

271